Tel.: Day—South Shore 41317. Night—South Shore 41392.

Squires Gate Aerodrome,
South Shore, BLACKPOOL.

Daily Service - - Sundays included
LIVERPOOL, BLACKPOOL, ISLE OF MAN

Booking Offices: LIVERPOOL—H. G. Crosthwaite & Co., 11, Rumford Street, Liverpool. Tel.: Bank 1094.
Grams: Punjaub, Liverpool. And at Speke Air Port. Tel.: Garston 1020.
BLACKPOOL CO.'S OFFICE—Squires Gate. Grams: Aeros, Blackpool.
DOUGLAS—W. H. Chapman, 63, Athol Street, Douglas. Tel.: Douglas 816. Grams: Value, Douglas.

FARES—Liverpool to Blackpool—Single 10/-; Return 15/-.
Liverpool to I.O.M.—Single 30/-; Return 50/-. Blackpool to I.O.M.—Single 25/-; Return 40/-.
20lbs. baggage allowed free per passenger.

EXCESS RATES—Liverpool to I.O.M.—2½d. per lb. Blackpool to I.O.M.—2d. per lb.
CHILDREN—Up to 3 years of age—10% full fare. Over 3 and up to 7—50% full fare. Over 7—full fare.

AIR TAXIS AT ANY TIME.

● **Make movies of your travels**

USE A MOTOCAMERA

Real motion pictures of your journeys can be made easily with this small amateur cine outfit costing **£6 6 0** and no more to use than an ordinary camera. Everyone can use a Motocamera.

Only 4/7d. for each complete film ! That is the all-in cost of a permanent movie record that is sure to delight everyone, especially those at home. Films cost 2/7d. with developing 2/-

PATHÉSCOPE, LTD

5, LISLE STREET, LONDON, W.C.2.

Published in Great Britain in 2013 by Old House books & maps
Midland House, West Way, Botley, Oxford OX2 0PH, United Kingdom.
44-02 23rd Street, Suite 219, Long Island City, NY 11101, USA.

Website: www.oldhousebooks.co.uk

© 2013 Old House

All rights reserved. Apart from any fair dealing for the purpose of private
study, research, criticism or review, as permitted under the Copyright,
Designs and Patents Act, 1988, no part of this publication may be reproduced,
stored in a retrieval system, or transmitted in any form or by any means,
electronic, electrical, chemical, mechanical, optical, photocopying, recording
or otherwise, without the prior written permission of the copyright owner.
Enquiries should be addressed to the Publishers.

Every attempt has been made by the Publishers to secure the appropriate
permissions for materials reproduced in this book. If there has been any
oversight we will be happy to rectify the situation and a written submission
should be made to the Publishers.

A CIP catalogue record for this book is available from the British Library.

ISBN-13: 978 1 90840 257 8

Originally published in 1934 by Henry Blacklock & Co. Ltd.

Printed in China through Worldprint Ltd.

13 14 15 16 17   10 9 8 7 6 5 4 3 2 1

No. 1] NOVEMBER, 1934 [PRICE, 1/- NET

BRADSHAW'S
INTERNATIONAL
AIR GUIDE

ISSUED MONTHLY

ISSUED MONTHLY

The Tables in this book are compiled with as much care as circumstances will permit; but it must be distinctly understood that the Proprietors do not hold themselves in any way responsible for inaccuracies. It will be esteemed a favour if early intimation be given of any error that may be found in the Guide.

PROPRIETORS AND PUBLISHERS: HENRY BLACKLOCK & Co., LTD., BRADSHAW HOUSE, SURREY STREET, STRAND, LONDON, W.C.2. 'Phone: Temple Bar, 2676. Telegrams: "Bradshaw, London." AND ALBERT SQUARE, MANCHESTER.
ADVERTISEMENT AND EDITORIAL OFFICES: BRADSHAW HOUSE, SURREY STREET, LONDON, W.C.2.

CONTENTS

VICTORIA COACH STATION - - HESTON - - RYDE

London-Isle of Wight in 1½ hrs.

19/6 Single

WEEK-END SERVICE
DURING WINTER MONTHS
For Time Table, see Table No. 14

38/6 Return

Reservations and full Information from :—
THE BRITISH AIR NAVIGATION CO., HESTON AIRPORT.
Telephone : Hounslow, 3244.

PORTSMOUTH, SOUTHSEA, & ISLE OF WIGHT AVIATION, LTD.

B11

2

INDEX
The numbers in the index refer to Table numbers

S.A.B.E.N.A.
BELGIAN AIR LINES
**ENGLAND – BELGIUM – GERMANY – HOLLAND –
DENMARK – SWEDEN – NORWAY**   See Tables 36, 37, 41, 70, 77, 82.

FROM DOOR TO DOOR
IN PERFECT COMFORT

The New De-Luxe Service

Travel by the route which gives you private saloon car service at either end of your flight, as comfortable and convenient as the planes themselves.

Write or telephone for full details of our DAILY SERVICE to and from London and the South-west Coast, also for our special charter booklet.

SPECIAL CHARTER

When time is money—save it—travel by air! Our fleet of fast comfortable private planes, seating from two to eight, it is at your service at any time of the day or night, to take you where you will, at home or abroad.

| Tel. No: |
| Fairfield |
| 4117. |

PROVINCIAL
AIRWAYS
Croydon Aerodrome

LONDON — SOUTHAMPTON — TORQUAY — PLYMOUTH — PORTSMOUTH
BOURNEMOUTH — WEYMOUTH AND LAND'S END On Request

TRAVEL JERSEY AIRWAYS

| DAILY SERVICES |

PORTSMOUTH
City Airport.
Phone: **PORTSMOUTH 6592.**

| SINGLE | RETURN |
| **32/6** | **55/-** |

PARIS, LE BOURGET
Twice Weekly.

| SINGLE | RETURN |
| **75/-** | **125/-** |

LONDON
11, Elizabeth St., S.W.1.
Phone: **SLOANE 5184.**

| SINGLE | RETURN |
| **59/6** | **99/6** |

SOUTHAMPTON
Eastleigh Aerodrome.
Phone: **EASTLEIGH 123.**

| SINGLE | RETURN |
| **35/-** | **60/-** |

JERSEY
1, Mulcaster Street, St. Helier.
Phone: **JERSEY 1221.**

BEXHILL.   **GRANVILLE HOTEL**

Most centrally situated.   Own Garage.

Every modern convenience.   Moderate inclusive terms.

Phone—BEXHILL 1437.   *'Grams*—" GRANVILLE, BEXHILL."

THE
HONYWOOD HOTELS
"The Hotels that are different"

LONDON

HOTEL WASHINGTON, Curzon Street, Mayfair, W. 1
Telegrams: "Comfortful, Audley."   *Telephone: Gros. 3101, London.*

BATT'S HOTEL, Dover Street, London, W. 1
Telegrams: "Batt's Hotel, London."   *Telephone: Reg. 1622.*

COUNTRY

Balmer Lawn Hotel, Brockenhurst.   Queen's Hotel, Cheltenham.
Gloucester Hotel, Weymouth.   Angel Hotel, Cardiff.
County Hotel, Malvern.   Raven Hotel, Shrewsbury.
Pump House Hotel, Llandrindod Wells.

LADY HONYWOOD, Managing Director.

London Offices: 15 Albemarle Street, W. 1.   *Tel.:* REGent 2485.

● **Make movies of your travels**

USE A MOTOCAMERA

Real motion pictures of your journeys can be made easily with this small amateur cine outfit costing £6 6 0 and no more to use than an ordinary camera. Everyone can use a Motocamera.

Only 4/7d. for each complete film! That is the all-in cost of a permanent movie record that is sure to delight everyone, especially those at home. Films cost 2/7d. with developing 2/-

PATHÉSCOPE, LTD

5, LISLE STREET, LONDON, W.C.2.

BRIGHTON.   ROYAL CRESCENT HOTEL

Situated on King's Cliff, facing Sea.   Own Garage.
Every modern convenience.   Moderate inclusive terms.
Phone—BRIGHTON 4171.   *Grams*—CRESCENT HOTEL, BRIGHTON.

Blackpool and West Coast Air Services, Ltd.,
Squires Gate Aerodrome,
South Shore, **BLACKPOOL.**

Tel.: Day—South Shore 41347.   Night—South Shore 41392.

Daily Service - - Sundays included
LIVERPOOL, BLACKPOOL, ISLE OF MAN

Booking Offices: LIVERPOOL—H. G. Crosthwaite & Co., 11, Rumford Street, Liverpool. Tel.: Bank 1094.
Grams: Punjaub, Liverpool. And at Speke Air Port. Tel.: Garston 1020.
BLACKPOOL CO.'S OFFICE—Squires Gate. Grams: Aeros, Blackpool.
DOUGLAS—W. H. Chapman, 63, Athol Street, Douglas. Tel.: Douglas 816. Grams: Value, Douglas.
FARES—Liverpool to Blackpool—Single 10/-; Return 15/-.
Liverpool to I.O.M.—Single 30/-; Return 50/-.   Blackpool to I.O.M.—Single 25/-; Return 40/-.
20lbs. baggage allowed free per passenger.
EXCESS RATES—Liverpool to I.O.M.—2½d. per lb.   Blackpool to I.O.M.—2d. per lb.
CHILDREN—Up to 3 years of age—10% full fare.   Over 3 and up to 7—50% full fare.   Over 7—full fare.
AIR TAXIS AT ANY TIME.

W. H. CHAPMAN, SHIPPING AND TOURIST AGENT,
63, ATHOL STREET, DOUGLAS.
Telegrams: - "Value, Douglas."   *Telephones:* – 816 and 647 (night residence) Douglas.

Travel Agent for all Air Lines,
including
**BLACKPOOL, LIVERPOOL,
ISLE OF MAN SERVICE.**

Shipping Agent for all Lines.
——TOURS——
**OF THE ISLAND
ARRANGED ON NOTIFICATION.**

ROYAL HIBERNIAN HOTEL,
DUBLIN'S MOST FASHIONABLE AND CENTRAL HOTEL.
Renowned for its Wines and Cuisine.————————First Class French Restaurant.
ORCHESTRA DAILY.   **TERMS MODERATE.**   **GARAGE**
Tels.: HIBERNIA, DUBLIN.   Phone: 2205 & 708.   P. G. BESSON, Managing Director.

HENRY BLACKLOCK & CO. LTD.

(Proprietors of Bradshaw's Guides)

General Printers, Lithographers, Bookbinders, and Account-Book Manufacturers

Bookwork, Invoices, Statements, Memo Forms,
Letter Headings, Note Headings, Bill Forms, Cheques,

SHOW CARDS, POSTERS, PAMPHLETS, BROCHURES, AND TIME TABLES FOR AIR SERVICES SPECIALLY DESIGNED AND PRINTED ESTIMATES FREE

BRADSHAW HOUSE, SURREY ST., STRAND, LONDON, W.C. 2 Telephone : TEMPLE BAR, 2676 Telegrams : BRADSHAW, LONDON	**AND**	**ALBERT SQUARE, MANCHESTER** Telephone : BLACKFRIARS 4218 (2 lines) Telegrams : GUIDE, MANCHESTER

BRADSHAW'S
FOREIGN PHRASE BOOKS

WILL FIT THE WAISTCOAT POCKET

ENGLISH—FRENCH.

ENGLISH—GERMAN.

ENGLISH—SPANISH.

ENGLISH—ITALIAN.

A Correspondent writes: "They are quite the best I have ever seen."

Bound in Red Cloth, 1/6 each.

Bradshaw's Guide Offices :—

LONDON : BRADSHAW HOUSE, SURREY STREET, STRAND, W.C.2.

MANCHESTER : Albert Square.   Henry Blacklock & Co. Ltd., Proprietors and Publishers.

CONSULT
DEAN AND **DAWSON** LTD
SEE MAP

HASTINGS.   QUEEN'S   HOTEL
Centrally situated on Sea Front. Every modern convenience.
Own Garage.   Orchestra and Dance Bands.
INCLUSIVE TERMS from 15/- DAILY.   Phone—HASTINGS 201.

The "*Buff Book*" (LONDON TRADES DIRECTORY)
—— *Ask for it.* ——

LONDON   DE VERE HOTEL
(KENSINGTON).   Overlooking Palace Gardens. Adjacent to Shopland and Theatres.
Own Garage.   Riding Stables.   Every modern convenience.
Phone—WESTERN 0051.   Moderate Inclusive Terms.   'Grams—"IMPROVISOR, LONDON."

BATH. **GRAND PUMP ROOM HOTEL**
Intercommunication with World-famed Baths. Own Garage.
Every modern convenience. Moderate inclusive terms.
Phone—BATH **3266**. 'Grams—" PUMPOTEL, BATH.

DAY AND NIGHT TAXIS
from 9d. per mile

FULL FLYING INSTRUCTION
New and Second Hand Aircraft

AIRCRAFT EX

7, PARK LANE

ANGE & MART LTD.

Phone : GROsvenor 3071 (3 lines)

HANWORTH AIR PARK

Tel.: **Day**—FELTHAM 236
    Night— ,, 273

Th numbers in the index refer to Table numbers.

BRADSHAW'S FOREIGN PHRASE BOOKS.

ENGLISH—FRENCH.   ENGLISH—GERMAN.   ENGLISH—ITALIAN.   ENGLISH—SPANISH.

Bound in Red Cloth, 1/6 each.   Will fit the waistcoat pocket.

A Correspondent writes : " They are quite the best I have ever seen."

BRADSHAW'S GUIDE OFFICES—LONDON : BRADSHAW HOUSE, SURREY STREET, STRAND, W.C.2.
MANCHESTER: ALBERT SQUARE.   HENRY BLACKLOCK & CO. LTD., PROPRIETORS AND PUBLISHERS.

INDEX TO ADVERTISERS ANNOUNCEMENTS

INDEX TO HOTEL PAGES

INFORMATION FOR TRAVELLERS.

THE 24 HOUR SYSTEM IS USED THROUGHOUT THE GUIDE.

GENERAL CONDITIONS OF CARRIAGE OF PASSENGERS AND BAGGAGE (see pages 158 to 163)

Extracts from the conditions under which the different Companies operate are printed on every air ticket.

FARES.

In most instances fares are payable in the currency of the country of embarkation and are subject to alteration without notice.

TICKET REGULATIONS.

Reservations

Seats should be reserved in advance at the offices of the different Companies or at the principal booking offices (see pages 26 to 29). The cost of any telegrams or trunk telephone calls in connection with reservations will be charged to the passenger.

Provisional reservations in most instances are accepted only on payment of a deposit (up to 25% of the full fare).

Cancellation of Tickets

In the event of the passenger wishing to cancel (or transfer) a reservation giving less than 24 hours' notice (in some cases 48 hours' or even two weeks according to the service), the full fare may be forfeited or a transfer fee charged. The regulations covering a cancellation of a Ticket on long distance bookings are indicated in the Time Tables of the Company concerned.

Return Tickets

Return Tickets are issued at reduced rates, but the holder of such ticket does not receive any preferential claim to accommodation. Reservation for the return journey must be effected in the same way as for the outward journey.

Validity of return tickets varies. As a rule such tickets are valid for 60 or 15 days on the Continent and for one month on the English services. The validity of return tickets on the Empire and long-distance services is extended to one year.

Transport between Airport and Town Terminus (see information at the foot of each table)

In most towns, transport is provided by the Air Company inclusive in the fare unless otherwise indicated in the tables. Passengers should be at Town Terminus or Airport in good time (15 minutes at least before scheduled time) to allow of completion of the necessary ticket and baggage formalities.

BAGGAGE INFORMATION.

(See General Conditions for the Carriage of Baggage, pages 158 to 163)

Free Baggage Allowance

On most services each passenger is entitled to a free baggage allowance of 33 lbs. or 15 kilogrammes. (Any deviation from this rule is indicated in the time tables.) Excess baggage can accompany passengers, but is charged for at the rates shown in the tables. Passengers' baggage must contain personal effects only. Other articles must be declared as merchandise and carried as freight. Arrangements are made by all Companies to send heavy baggage in advance at cheap rates. No free baggage allowance is granted to children.

Registration of Baggage

Passengers should see that their luggage is distinctly labelled. It will be registered and a receipt issued before departure. Passengers must present this receipt when claiming their baggage.

INSURANCE

Most Assurance Companies will include air travel on a life policy without extra charge. Personal and baggage insurance may be arranged at a low premium when booking or at station of departure.

PASSPORTS

Passengers are reminded that passports endorsed for all countries through which they intend to travel, and containing visas where necessary, should be carried on the person.

MEALS

Many air-liners are provided with a fully-equipped restaurant and bar or buffet. On services where such facilities are not obtainable, refreshment baskets will be provided if ordered at time of booking. On long-distance services meals as well as hotel accommodation and tips are included in the fare.

Smoking as a general rule is not allowed.

PRIVATE RADIO TELEGRAMS

Passengers may send or receive telegrams during flight on many Continental and on the long-distance services. Enquiries should be made at Companies' offices.

PERSONAL HINTS

The cabins of the air-liners are enclosed and heated, therefore no special clothing is required, similar clothing to that worn for rail or boat travel being sufficient. Prospective passengers on the Empire and other long-distance services can obtain all necessary information when booking.

COMPARATIVE INTERNATIONAL TIMES

ALL TIMES GIVEN IN THE TABLES ARE LOCAL TIMES

Simultaneous Time

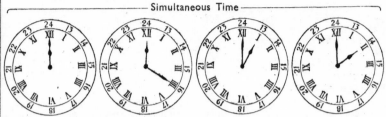

| West Europe Time (Greenwich Mean Time) | Amsterdam Time (used in Holland) Twenty minutes in advance of Greenwich Mean Time | Central Europe Time One hour in advance of Greenwich Mean Time | East Europe Time Two hours in advance of Greenwich Mean Time |

WEST EUROPE TIME is applicable to Great Britain, Belgium, France, Algeria, Spain and Portugal.

CENTRAL EUROPE TIME is applicable to Germany, Austria, Hungary, Switzerland, Italy, Czechoslovakia, Yugoslavia, Lithuania, Poland, Denmark, Norway, Sweden, Tunis and Morocco.

EAST EUROPE TIME is applicable to Bulgaria, Estonia, Finland, Greece, Latvia, Rumania, Russia and Turkey.

DIFFERENCES IN LOCAL TIME AND LONDON (i.e., GREENWICH)

Fast on Greenwich Time

New Zealand	$11\frac{1}{2}$ hours
Victoria, New South Wales, Queensland	10 ,,
South Australia	$9\frac{1}{2}$,,
Sarawak	$7\frac{1}{2}$,,
French Indo-China, Siam, Malaya	7 ,,
Burma	$6\frac{1}{2}$,,
India (except Calcutta)	$5\frac{1}{2}$,,
Iraq, Tanganyika, Kenya	3 ,,
Uganda	$2\frac{1}{2}$,,
Sudan, Rhodesia, South Africa	2 ,,

Slow on Greenwich Time

Madeira, Canary Islands	1 hour
Azores, Cape Verde Islands	2 hours
Eastern Brazil	3 ,,
Uruguay	$3\frac{1}{2}$,,
Central Brazil, Argentina	4 ,,

ALMANAC (Greenwich Time)

MOON'S CHANGES.—NOVEMBER—New Moon, 7th, 4-43 mrn.; First Quarter, 14th, 2-39 mrn.; Full Moon, 21st, 4-26 mrn.; Last Quarter, 29th, 5-39 mrn.

NOVEMBER, 1934					DECEMBER, 1934				
Day	Sun Rises mrn	Sun Sets aft	Moon Rises mrn	Moon Sets aft	Day	Sun Rises mrn	Sun Sets aft	Moon Rises mrn	Moon Sets aft
	h.m.	h.m.	h.m.	h.m.		h.m.	h.m.	h.m.	h.m.
1 Thursday	6 54	4 33	0 16	2 15	1 Saturday	7 44	3 53	1 29	12 57
2 Friday............	6 56	4 31	1 26	2 21	2 SUNDAY	7 46	3 52	2 42	1 12
3 Saturday	6 58	4 29	2 37	2 39	3 Monday	7 47	3 52	3 58	1 29
4 SUNDAY	6 59	4 27	3 50	2 53	4 Tuesday	7 49	3 51	5 18	1 51
5 Monday	7 1	4 26	5 4	3 8	5 Wednesday ...	7 50	3 51	6 40	2 23
6 Tuesday	7 3	4 24	6 23	3 27	6 Thursday	7 51	3 50	7 59	3 7
7 Wednesday ...	7 5	4 22	7 44	3 53	7 Friday............	7 52	3 50	9 8	4 8
8 Thursday	7 6	4 20	9 5	4 29	8 Saturday	7 54	3 50	10 1	5 27
9 Friday............	7 8	4 19	10 20	5 19	9 SUNDAY	7 55	3 49	10 39	6 53
10 Saturday	7 10	4 17	11 20	6 25	10 Monday	7 56	3 49	11 6	8 22
11 SUNDAY	7 12	4 16	12 5	7 46	11 Tuesday	7 57	3 49	11 26	9 49
12 Monday	7 13	4 14	12 38	9 11	12 Wednesday ...	7 58	3 49	11 43	11 13
13 Tuesday	7 15	4 13	1 2	10 38	13 Thursday	7 59	3 49	11 58	0 35
14 Wednesday ...	7 17	4 11	1 21	0 2	14 Friday............	8 0	3 49	12 13	1 56
15 Thursday	7 19	4 10	1 36	1 24	15 Saturday	8 1	3 49	12 29	3 16
16 Friday............	7 20	4 8	1 51	2 46	16 SUNDAY	8 2	3 49	12 48	4 36
17 Saturday	7 22	4 7	2 6	4 8	17 Monday	8 3	3 49	1 11	5 52
18 SUNDAY	7 24	4 6	2 23	5 29	18 Tuesday	8 3	3 50	1 41	7 2
19 Monday	7 26	4 5	2 44	6 50	19 Wednesday ...	8 4	3 50	2 22	8 2
20 Tuesday	7 27	4 3	3 10	8 7	20 Thursday	8 5	3 50	3 14	8 49
21 Wednesday ...	7 29	4 2	3 44	9 14	21 Friday............	8 5	3 51	4 16	9 24
22 Thursday	7 31	4 1	4 29	10 10	22 Saturday	8 6	3 51	5 25	9 50
23 Friday............	7 32	4 0	5 25	10 53	23 SUNDAY	8 6	3 52	6 35	10 10
24 Saturday	7 34	3 59	6 29	11 24	24 Monday	8 7	3 52	7 45	10 25
25 SUNDAY	7 35	3 58	7 39	11 47	25 Tuesday	8 7	3 53	8 56	10 39
26 Monday	7 37	3 57	8 50	12 5	26 Wednesday ...	8 7	3 54	10 4	10 51
27 Tuesday	7 38	3 56	10 0	12 20	27 Thursday	8 8	3 54	11 13	11 3
28 Wednesday ...	7 40	3 55	11 10	12 33	28 Friday............	8 8	3 55	...	...
29 Thursday	7 41	3 54	...	...	29 Saturday	8 8	3 56	0 23	11 16
30 Friday............	7 43	3 54	0 19	12 45	30 SUNDAY	8 8	3 57	1 36	11 32
					31 Monday	8 8	3 58	2 51	11 51

FOREIGN CURRENCIES

Approximate exchange value of the £ sterling.

(Supplied from the records of Westminster Bank Limited, Foreign Branch Office,
41, Lothbury, London, E.C. 2.)

Country	Town	Currency	Value per £ 12-10-1934
ALBANIA	Tirana	Gold Franc	15·00
AUSTRIA	Vienna	Schilling (Sch.)	26·00
BELGIUM	Brussels	Belga=5 Bel. Francs ...(Bgas)	20·86
BULGARIA	Sofia	Lev	415·00
CANADA	Montreal	Dollar ($)	4·82
CZECHOSLOVAKIA ..	Prague	Koruna (Kc.)	116·75
DENMARK	Copenhagen ...	Krone (Kr.)	22·40
EGYPT	Alexandria ...	Piastre	97·50
ESTONIA	Tallinn	E. Kroon (E. Kr.) ...	18·25
FINLAND	Helsingfors ...	F. Mark	226·50
FRANCE	Paris	Franc (Fr.)	74·00
GERMANY	Berlin	Reichsmark (RM.) ...	12·11
GREECE	Athens	Drachma (Drach.) ...	514·00
HOLLAND	Amsterdam ...	Guilder or Florin (Fl.)	7·19
HUNGARY	Budapest	Pengoe (Pen.)	24·50
ITALY	Milan	Lira	56·87
LATVIA	Riga	Lat.	15·00
LITHUANIA	Kaunas	Litas.	29·00
NORWAY	Oslo	Krone (Kr.)	19·90
POLAND	Warsaw	Zloty (Zl.)	25·80
PORTUGAL...	Lisbon	Escudo	110·10
RUMANIA	Bucharest ...	Leu	490·00
SPAIN	Madrid	Peseta (Pta.)	35·62
SWEDEN	Stockholm ...	Krona (Kr.)	19·39
SWITZERLAND ...	Berne	Franc (S. Fr.)	14·95
TURKEY	Istanbul	Piastre	610·00
U.S.A.	New York ...	Dollar ($)	4·92
U.S.S.R.	Moscow	Rouble	5·65
YUGOSLAVIA	Belgrade	Dinar	213·00

THE METRIC SYSTEM OF WEIGHTS AND MEASURES, WITH ENGLISH EQUIVALENTS

LINEAR MEASURE
- 1 Centimètre (10 millimètres) = 0·3937 inch.
- 1 MÈTRE (100 centimètres) = 39·3701 inch = 3·28 feet = 1·093 yard.
- 1 Kilomètre (1,000 mètres) = 1093·6 yards = 0·62137 mile.

To convert mètres into yards, add $\frac{1}{10}$th; to convert yards into mètres, subtract $\frac{1}{11}$th.

One kilomètre = $\frac{5}{8}$ths. of a British mile; 5 miles = 8 kilomètres (nearly), or 10 miles = 16 kilomètres.

WEIGHT
- 1 Milligramme = 0·015 grains troy.
- 1 GRAMME = 15·43 ,,
- 1 Kilogramme = 2·205 lb. avoirdupois.
- 1 Quintal mètrique = 100 kilogrammes = 220·5 ,, ,,
- 1 Tonneau = 1000 ,, = 2205 ,, ,,

MEASURE OF CAPACITY ... 1 LITRE = 1·76 pint.

Comparative Tables

Table of Kilomètres and English Miles					Table of Mètres, Yards, and Feet				
Kilomètres	Miles		Miles	Kilomètres	Mètres		Yards		Feet
1 =	0·621		1 =	1·609	1	=	1·09	=	3·281
2 =	1·243		2 =	3·219	2	=	2·18	=	6·562
3 =	1·864		3 =	4·828	3	=	3·27	=	9·843
4 =	2·485		4 =	6·437	4	=	4·36	=	13·123
5 =	3·107		5 =	8·047	5	=	5·45	=	16·404
6 =	3·728		6 =	9·656	6	=	6·54	=	19·685
7 =	4·349		7 =	11·27	7	=	7·63	=	22·966
8 =	4·971		8 =	12·87	8	=	8·72	=	26·247
9 =	5·592		9 =	14·48	9	=	9·81	=	29·527
10 =	6·214		10 =	16·09	10	=	10·936	=	32·809
11 =	6·835		11 =	17·7	11	=	12·03	=	36·09
12 =	7·456		12 =	19·31	12	=	13·12	=	39·37
13 =	8·078		13 =	20·92	13	=	14·22	=	42·65
14 =	8·699		14 =	22·53	14	=	15·31	=	45·93
15 =	9·321		15 =	24·14	15	=	16·4	=	49·21
16 =	9·942		16 =	25·76	16	=	17·5	=	52·49
17 =	10·563		17 =	27·36	17	=	18·59	=	55·76
18 =	11·185		18 =	28·97	18	=	19·68	=	59·06
19 =	11·806		19 =	30·58	19	=	20·78	=	62·34
20 =	12·427		20 =	32·18	20	=	21·87	=	65·618
30 =	18·64		30 =	48·28	30	=	32·81	=	98·427
40 =	24·85		40 =	64·37	40	=	43·74	=	131·236
50 =	31·07		50 =	80·47	50	=	54·68	=	164·045
60 =	37·28		60 =	96·56	60	=	65·616	=	196·84
70 =	43·49		70 =	112·65	70	=	76·58	=	229·66
80 =	49·71		80 =	128·74	80	=	87·49	=	262·47
90 =	55·92		90 =	144·84	90	=	98·42	=	295·28
100 =	62·14		100 =	160·93	100	=	109·36	=	328·09
200 =	124·28		200 =	321·86	200	=	218·72	=	656·18
300 =	186·41		300 =	482·79	300	=	328·08	=	984·27
400 =	248·55		400 =	643·72	400	=	437·44	=	1312·36
500 =	310·69		500 =	804·65	500	=	546·8	=	1640·45
600 =	372·83		600 =	965·59	600	=	656·16	=	1968·54
700 =	434·97		700 =	1126·52	700	=	765·52	=	2296·63
800 =	497·10		800 =	1287·45	800	=	874·88	=	2624·72
900 =	559·24		900 =	1448·38	900	=	984·24	=	2952·81
1000 =	621·38		1000 =	1609·31	1000	=	1093·63	=	3280·9
					8000	=	5 miles, nearly		

BOOKING OFFICES
Tickets may be obtained through all the principal Tourist Agencies

AACHEN—See Aix-la-Chapelle.
ABBAZIA—A.L.S.A., Seaplane Station, Nel Porticciolo.
ABERDEEN
    Highland Airways, Messrs. T. C. Smith & Co Ltd., Garage, Bon-Accord Street.
    Highland Airways, Mackay Bros. & Co. Ltd., 35a, Union Street.
    Aberdeen Airways, Dyce Airport or Caledonian Hotel, Union Terrace.
ABO—Aero O/Y., Turun Toimisto.
AGRINION—S.H.C.A., Place Centrale.
AIX-LA CHAPELLE—D.L.H., Airport.
AJACCIO—Air France, Seaplane Station.
AKYAB—Air France, C. V. Price, Point Road.
ALCUDIA—Air France, Seaplane Station.
ALEXANDRIA—Imperial Airways, Marine Airport, Ras-el-Tin. P.O. Box 1705.
ALGIERS—Air France, 4 Bvd. Carnot.
ALICANTE—Air France, Paséo de Los Martires 26.
ALLAHABAD
    Air France, Steele & Co., 14, Albert Road.
    K.N.I.L.M., Steele & Co., 14, Albert Road.
    Imperial Airways, Indian National Airways, 12, Hastings Road.
ALOR STAR—K.N.I.L.M., Guan Hin Co., No. 78, Pekan, China.
AMSTERDAM—K.L.M., Leidscheplein.
ANCONA—A.L.S.A., " Sanzio Andreoli," Seaplane Station.
ANTWERP—Sabena, Gare Centrale.
ATHENS
    Air France, 4 Rue du Stade, 3rd Floor, No. 3.
    A.E.I., 3 Rue Université.
    S.H.C.A., Place de la Constitution (Mitropoléos 5).
    I.A.L., Phaleron Bay, Old Phaleron, 8.
BADEN-BADEN—D.L.H., Airport.
BAGHDAD
    Imperial Airways, Baghdad Airport
    Air France, Lumsden & Greene.
    K.L.M., Baghdad Airport.
BANDOENG—K.N.I.L.M., Kon Ned-Ind Luchtuaart Mij.
BANGKOK
    Imperial Airways, c/o The Aerial Transport Co. of Siam Ltd.
    Air France, Aerial Transport Co. of Siam Ltd., Airway House
    K.N.I.L.M., Handelsufrein, Holland, Siam P.O. Box 77.
BARCELONA
    Air France, 19 Paseo de Gracia.
    L.A.P.E., Diputacion, 260 (Iunto al P.O. de Gracia).
BARI—A.L.S.A., Via Piccini 94.
BASLE—Swissair, Airport, Basel-Birsfelden.
BASRA—Imperial Airways, Shaibah, Airport.
BATAVIA—K.N.I.L.M., Kon Ned-Ind Luchtuaart Mij.
BELFAST—Railway Air Services, York Road Station.
    Railway Air Services, Smithfield Omnibus Station, 11, Donegal Place.
    Hillman's Airways, M. McLeod, 18, Royal Avenue.

BELGRADE
    Air France, 36 Rue Kralja Petra.
    Aeropout, 36 Rue Kralja Petra.
    D.L.H., Deutsches Verkchrsbüro, Knezey, Spomenik 5.
BEMBRIDGE
    Spartan Air Line, Bambridge Airport.
    P.S. and I. of W., H. W. Bartlett and Son, Foreland Road.
BENGASI—N.A.A.S.A., Agenzie Della Cassa di Risparmio Della Cirenaica.
BERLIN—D.L.H., Lindenstrasse 35, Berlin, S.W. 68.
BERNE—Alpar-Bern, Bern-Belpmoos, Airport.
BEYROUTH—Air France, Rue Foch.
BIARRITZ
    Air Service, Agence Havas, Place de la Liberté.
    Air Service, Casino de Biarritz.
BIRMINGHAM
    Railway Air Services, Snow Hill Station.
    Railway Air Services, New Street Station.
    Messrs. Dean & Dawson, Ltd. 3, Ethel Street.
BLACKPOOL—Blackpool and West Coast Air Services, Squires Gate Airport.
BORDEAUX—Air Service, Agence Havas, Place de la Comédie.
BORKUM—D.L.H., Airport.
BOUCHIR—Air France, H.S.M.R. Kazerooni & Sons.
BOURNEMOUTH—Norman Edgar (Western Airways), Shamrock & Rambler Coaches. 77, Holdenhurst Road.
BRATISLAVA—C.S.A., Hotel Carlton (Cedok).
BREMEN—D.L.H., Airport.
BREMERHAVEN—D.L.H., Airport.
BRESLAU—D.L.H., Airport.
BRIGHTON—P. S.and I. of W., 25 Marine Parade.
BRINDISI
    Imperial Airways, Casella Postale 59.
BRIONI—A.L.S.A., Compagnia Adriatica di Navigazione.
BRISTOL
    Railway Air Services, Temple Gate Enquiry Office, Temple Meads Station.
    Norman Edgar (Western Airways), Maple Leaf Coaches, Tramways Centre.
BRNO
    " Lot," Cernowlce, Airport.
    C.S.A., 4, Nam Svobody (Cedok).
BROKEN HILL—Imperial Airways, Broken Hill, Airport.
BRUSSELS
    Imperial Airways, 19 Rue St. Michel.
    Sabena, Haren, Airport.
BUCHAREST
    Air France, 2 Rue Clémenceau.
    " Lot," Str. Clémenceau 2.
    C.S.A., Arpa Fundatia Carol I.
BUDAPEST
    Air France, Vorosmarty Ter 2.
    Malert, Vaci Ucca 1, Budapest IV.
BULAWAYO—Imperial Airways, Albany House, Main Street.
BUSHIRE
    K.N.I.L.M., Junkers Luftuerkehr Persien Vertreter.
    Kazerooni & Sons.

CAGLIARI—A.L.S.A., Via Roma 53.
CAIRO
  Imperial Airways, Heliopolis, Airport.
  K.L.M., Gerrit, Vogel 5 Bis, Rue Maghraby.
CALCUTTA
  Imperial Airways, Indian National Airways, 24 Parganas, Dum-Dum.
  20, Park Street, Calcutta.
  Air France, Messageries Maritimes, Stephen House, 8, Dalhousie Square.
CANNES—Air France, 4 Rue Bivouac Napoleon.
CAPE TOWN—Imperial Airways, Wingfield, Airport.
CARDIFF
  Railway Air Services, Cardiff General Station.
  Messrs. Dean & Dawson Ltd., Borough Chambers, Wharton Chambers.
  Norman Edgar (Western Airways), Red and White Services, Ltd. 1a, Wood Street.
CASABLANCA—Air France, 13, Rue Nolly.
CASTELROSSO—Air France.
CAWNPORE—Imperial Airways, Indian National Airways, The Mall.
CERNAUTI—"Lot," Czachor, Airport.
CHEMNITZ—D.L.H., Airport.
CHERBOURG—Air France, Agence le Jeune, Rue Alfred Rossel.
CIRENE—N.A.A.S.A., Apply to Agency at Bengasi or Tobruch.
CLUJ—C.S.A., Piata Unirei, 23.
COLOGNE—D.L.H., Domhotel.
CONSTANCE—D.L.H., Airport.
COPENHAGEN—D.D.L., Passage-Bureau, Vesterport, Meldahlsgade 5.
CORFU—Air France, Aéroport de Phaiakon.
CORITZA—A.L.S.A., Agenzia Adria Aerolloyd
COWES
  Railway Air Services, Cowes Station.
  Spartan Air Lines, Fountain Garage Ltd.
  P.S. and I. of W., B. Groves, 5 & 6, Arcade.
CRACOW—"Lot," Ul. Szpitalna 32.
CREFELD—D.L.H., Airport.

DAMASCUS—Air France, 30, Rue Salhyé.
DANZIG—Deruluft, Danzig-Langfuhr, Deutsche Lufthansa, A.G.
DARMSTADT—D.L.H., Airport.
DEAUVILLE—Banco, Airways Terminus (situated in Casino).
DELHI—Imperial Airways, Indian National Airways, 10, Alipore Road.
DERNA—N.A.A.S.A., Apply to Agency at Bengasi or Tobruch.
DJASK—Air France, Sayed Mohamed Saleh & Sons.
DODOMA—Imperial Airways, Dodoma.
DORTMUND—D.L.H., Airport.
DRESDEN—D.L.H., Airport.
DURAZZO—C.I.T. Office, Boulevard Zog, N. 1.
DÜSSELDORF—D.L.H., Airport.

EINDHOVEN—K.L.M., Hotel du Commerce.
ERFURT—D.L.H., Airport.
ESSEN/MÜLHEIM—D.L.H., Airport.

FIUME—C.I.T. Office, Riva Emanuele Filiberto 8.
FLENSBURG—D.L.H., Airport.
FLORENCE—A.L.S.A., Via Cerretani.
FRANKFORT—D.L.H., Airport.
FREIBURG—D.L.H., Airport.

FRIEDRICHSHAFEN
  D.L.H., Airport.
  Hamburg-Amerika-Line, 11-13, Goldschmiedstrasse.
GAZA
  Imperial Airways, Gaza, Airport.
  K.N.I.L.M., Gaza, Airport.
GDYNIA—"Lot," Airport, Langfuhr.
GENEVA
  Swissair, Aérodrome Genève-Cointrin.
  Hotel des Bergues.
GENOA—C.I.T. Office, Via XX Settembre 237r.
GERA—D.L.H., Airport.
GLASGOW
  Railway Air Services, Central Station.
  Aberdeen Airways, Kenilworth Hotel, Queen Street.
GLEIWITZ—D.L.H., Airport.
GÖRLITZ—D.L.H., Airport.
GOTHENBURG—A.B.A., Torslanda Airport.
GRAZ—Austraflug, Airport.
GRONINGEN—K.L.M., Groote Markt.
HAAMSTEDE—K.L.M., Agency Zierikzee, Kraanplein.
HAGUE, THE—K.L.M., Head Office, 9-11, Hofweg.
HALDON—Provincial Airways, Haldon Airport.
HALLE/LEIPZIG—D.L.H., Airport.
HAMBURG—D.L.H., Airport.
HANOVER—D.L.H., Airport.
HELSINGFORS—Aero O/Y., Alexandergatan 7.
HIDDENSEE/KLOSTER—D.L.H., Airport.
HIRSCHBERG—See Riesengebirge/H.
HULL—K.L.M., Paragon Station (L.N.E.R.).

INNSBRUCK—Austraflug, Airport.
INVERNESS—Highland Airways, Messrs. Macrae and Dick Ltd., 36, Academy Street.
ISLE OF MAN
  Blackpool and West Coast Air Services, W. H. Chapman, 63, Athol Street, Douglas
  Hillman's Airways, Ronaldsway, Airport.
ISTANBUL—
  Air France, Airport.
  A.E.I., Rue Voivoda, Union Han, Galata.
  A.E.I., Lloyd Triestino.
JANNINA—S.H.C.A., Rue Souliou 4.
JASK—K.N.I.L.M., Syed Mohamed Saleh and Sons.
JERSEY—Jersey Airways, 1 Mulcaster Street, St. Helier.
JODHPUR
  Air France, Sanghi Brothers, Minto Road.
  K.N.I.L.M., Sanghi Brothers, Minto Road.
  Imperial Airways, Indian National Airways.
JOHANNESBURG—Imperial Airways, The Airport of Johannesburg (Germiston).
JUBA—Imperial Airways, Juba.
KAPOSVÁR—Malert, Fö Ucca 12.
KARACHI
  Imperial Airways, Mohatta Buildings, McLeod Road.
  Air France, Ghizri Road, Cantonment.
  K.N.I.L.M. Compagnie, Agent Air France.
KARLSBAD
  C.L.S., Air Travel Office, Theaterplatz.
  C.S.A., Divadelni Namesti.
KARLSRUHE—D.L.H., Airport.
KATOWICE—"Lot" Muchawiec, Airport.
KAUNAS—Deruluft, Aerodromas Linksmaduaris Aerostotis.

KHARTOUM—Imperial Airways, Khartoum Aerodrome.
KIEL—D.L.H., Airport.
KIMBERLEY
  Imperial Airways, Kimberley, Airport.
  11, Stockdale Street.
KIRKWALL—Highland Airways, The "Orcadian" News Office.
KLAGENFURT—Austraflug, Airport.
KNOCKE-LE ZOUTE—Sabena, Aerodrome du Zoute.
KÖNIGSBERG/Pr.
  Deruluft, Deuau, Airport.
  D.L.H., Airport.
KOSICE—C.S.A., Hotel Salkhaz.
KUKUŠ—Agenzia Adria, Aerolloyd.
LA CHAUX DE FONDS—Alpar-Bern, J. Vernon, Grauer et Cie, Place de la Gare.
LAGOSTA—Cia Adriatica di Nav., Via Armando Diaz.
LANGEOOG—D.L.H., Airport.
LAUSANNE
  Air France, Aérodrome de la Blécherette.
  Swissair, Aérodrome de la Blécherette.
LEEDS—L.S. & P.A., Messrs. R. Barr (Leeds) Ltd., Wallace Arnold Tours, The Corn Exchange.
LEMBERG—"Lot," Plac Marjacki 5.
LENINGRAD—Deruluft, Uliza Gerzena 28.
LE TOUQUET
  Imperial Airways, Airway Terminus, Casino Ground.
  Banco, Airways Terminus (situated in Casino).
LIVERPOOL
  Railway Air Services, 11, James Street.
  Railway Air Services, Lime Street Station.
  Blackpool and West Coast Air Services, H. G. Crosthwaite & Co., 11, Rumford Street.
  Hillman's Airways, H. G. Crosthwaite & Co., Speke Aerodrome.
  K.L.M., Wm. H. Müller & Co. (London) Ltd., Cunard Building.
LJUBLJANA—Aéropout, Rue Tirsova.
LONDON
  Railway Air Services, Airway Terminus, Victoria Station, S.W. 1.
  Imperial Airways, Airway Terminus, Victoria Station, S.W. 1.
  D.L.H., Airway Terminus, Victoria Station, S.W. 1.
  Spartan Air Lines, 53, Parliament Street, S.W.1 .
  P.S. and I. of W., 164, Buckingham Palace Road, S.W. 1.
  Banco, Victoria Coach Station, 164, Buckingham Palace Road, S.W. 1.
  Jersey Airways, Victoria Coach Station, 11, Elisabeth Street, S.W. 1.
  L.S. & P.A., Heston, Airport.
  Air France, 52, Haymarket, S.W. 1.
  Air Service, 52, Haymarket, S.W. 1.
  K.L.M., Wm. H. Müller & Co. (London) Ltd., Greener House, 66-68, Haymarket, S.W. 1.
  Sabena, Croydon Aerodrome and Airway Terminus, Victoria Station, S.W. 1.
LUCERNE—Swissair, Verhehrsbüro, Löwenstrasse.
LUSSINO—Agenzia A. Niccoli, Riva IV Novembre.
LWOW—See Lemberg.
LYONS—Air France, Airport.

MADRID
  Air France, Edificio Carrion Avenida Edouardo Dato.
  L.A.P.E.—4, Antonio Maura.
MALMÖ
  A.B.A., Bulltofta, Airport.
  D.D.L., Central Station.
MALTA
  Air France, Ed. T. Agius & Co. Ltd., 27, Strada Mezzodi.
  C.I.T. Office, Strada Mezzodi, n. 14.
MANCHESTER—Railway Air Services, 47 Piccadilly.
MANNHEIM—D.L H., Airport.
MARIENBAD
  C.L.S., Air Travel Office "Sanssouci" House C.S.A., "Sanssouci."
MARIEHAMN—Aero O/Y., Er k Nylund.
MARIENBURG—D.L.H., Airport.
MARSEILLES—Air France, 1, Rue Papère.
MEDAN—K N.I.L.M., Kon Ned-Ind, Luchtvaart, Mij.
MERZA MATRUH—K.L.M., Hiller & Co., Hillier Hotel.
MILAN—A.L.I., Via S. Margherita 16.
MOSCOW—Deruluft, Leningradskoe Chaussee
MUNICH—D.L.H., Airport
NAIROBI—Imperial Airways, Rhodes House, 6th Avenue.
NAPLES
  Air France, 265, Via Roma.
  C.I.T. Office, Piazza Municipio 732.
NORDERNEY—D.L.H., Airport.
NOTTINGHAM—L.S. & P.A., Richardson's Car Park, 9, Derby Road.
NÜRNBERG—D.L.N., Airport.

OSLO—D.L.H., Norske, Luftruter A. S. Skippergaten.
OSNABRÜCK—D.L.H., Airport.
OSTEND—Sabena, Boulevard Adolphe, Max 32, 34.

PALEMBANG—K N.I.L.M., Kon Paketvaart, Maatschappij.
PALERMO—A.L.S.A., Via Roma 318.
PARIS
  Imperial Airways, Airways House 38 Avenue de l'Opera.
  Air France, 9 Rue Auber.
  Hillman's Airways, Air Express, 25 Rue Royale.
  Air Service, 9 Rue Auber.
  L.S. & P.A., Mon. Maurice Finat Le Bourget Aerodrome.
PÉCS—Malert Kiraly Ucca 22.
PESKOPEJA—Agenzia, Adria Aerolloyd.
PLAUEN—D.L.H., Airport
PLYMOUTH
  Railway Air Services, Plymouth North Road Station.
  Provincial Airways, Crownhill Airport.
PORTSMOUTH
  Jersey Airways, 87e, Commercial Road
  P.S. and I. o W City Airport.
POSEN—"Lot" Law ca, Airport.
PRAGUE
  Air France, 6, Narodn Trida
  C.L.S., Czechosl, Air Transport Co., Air Travel Office, 11., Vodičkova 38.
  C.S.A., Vodičkova Ul. 20, Praha

RABAT—Air France, Agence Prima, Cours Lyautey.
RANGOON
    Imperial Airways c/o The Irrawaddy Flotilla
    Co. Ltd., Phayre Street.
    Air France, Du Bern, 4-5, Sooly Pagoda Road.
    K.N.I.L.M. Massink & Co. Ltd , P.O. Box 119.
RECIFE/PERNAMBUCO—Synd Condor, Hermann,
    Stolz & Co., 35 Avenida Marquez de Olinda.
RHODES—A.E.I. Seaplane Station.
RIESENGEBIRGE/HIRSCHBERG—D.L.H., Airport.
RIGA
    Deruluft, Kaufstr 5.
    " Lot," Spilve, Aerodrome.
RIO DE JANEIRO—S. Condor Ltda, 5-3 Rua da
    Alfandega.
ROME
    Air France, 75, Largo Tritone.
    A.L.I., C.I.T. Piazza Colonna
    Servizi Aerei, Piazza Esedra 64/6.
    C.I.T. (Air Station), Piazza Esedra.
ROTTERDAM—K.L.M., 115 Coolsingel.
RUTBAH—K.N.I.L.M., Rutbah, Airport.
RYDE—P.S. and I. of W., 61, Union Street.

SAARBRÜCKEN—D.L H., Airport.
SAIGON—Air France, 4 Rue Catinat.
SALISBURY, S. RHODESIA—Imperial Airways
    Salisbury, Airport.
SALONICA—S.H.C.A., Angle Rues Comninon et
    Mitropoleos.
SALZBURG—Austraflug, Airport.
SCUTARI—Agenzia, Adria, Aerolloyd.
SEAVIEW—P.S. and I. of W., the Double H.
SEMARANG—K.N.I.L.M., Simongan Airport.
SELLIN—D.L.H., Airport.
SEVILLE—L.A.P.E. Avenida de a Libertad, 1
SHANKLIN—P.S. and I. of W. Office, Regal
    Theatre or Summer Arcade.
SINGAPORE
    Imperial Airways, c/o Mansfield & Co. Ltd.,
    Ocean Building
    K.N.I.L.M. Agent K.N.I.L.M., Scotts Road, 31.
SIRTE—N.A.A.S.A., Apply to Agency at Bengasi
    or Tripoli.
SKOPLJE—Aéropout, Café Marguère.
SOFIA
    Air France, 5, Bd. Dondoukoff.
    " Lot," Chambre de Commerce Polono-
    Bulgare UI Benkovski.
    D.L.H , 1 UI. Lewski (Grand Hotel Bulgaria).
SOURABAYA—K.N.I.L.M., Darmo, Airport.
SOUTHAMPTON
    Railway Air Services, Southampton (Terminus
    Station).
    Railway Air Services, Southampton (West
    Station).
    Messrs. Dean & Dawson Ltd., Bank Chambers,
    Canute Road.
    Jersey Airways, Eastleigh, Airport.
    Provincial Airways Atlantic Park, Eastleigh,
    Airport.
SOUTHEND—Southend Flying Services, Rochford,
STETTIN—D.L.H., Hotel Preussenhof 10-12 Luisen-
    strasse.
ST. GALLEN—Swissair, Altenrhein, Airport.
STOCKHOLM
    A.B.A., Flygplats Lindarängen.
    Deruluft, Flygpauiljongen, Nybroplan.

STRASBOURG—Air France, Airport.
STOLP—D.L.H., Airport.
STRALSUND—D.L.H. Airport.
STUTTGART
    D.L.H., Airport.
    Luftverkehr Württemberg A.G., 1, Fürsten-
    strasse.
SUSAK—Aéropout, Masarikovo Šetalište 9.
SWINEMÜNDE—D.L.H., Airport.
SYRACUSE—C.I.T. Office, Via Savola 80.

TALLINN
    Aero O/Y., Ülemiste Järv, Airport.
    Deruluft, Vana Viru 11.
    " Lot," Hotel Kuld Lovi.
TANIGER—Air France, Wagon-Lits Cook.
THURSO—Highlands Airway. The Royal Hotel.
TILSIT—Deruluft, Airport.
TIRANA—Agenzia C.I.T., Via Abdi Bey Toptani.
TOBRUK—N.A.A.S.A., Aeroport, Campo Militare.
TOULOUSE—Air France Office des Voyages de la
    Dépéche, 42 Bis Rue Alsace Lorraine.
TRIESTE—C.I.T. Office, Piazza Unita 5.
TRIPOLI
    N.A.A.S.A., Luciano Abrial Corso Vittorio
    Emanuele 67-71.
    C.I.T. Office, 18 Galleria de Bono.
TUNIS
    Air France, 46, Avenue Jules-Ferry.
    A.L.S.A., Avenue Jules Ferry 19.
TURIN—A.L.I., C.I.T. Via XX Settembre 3.
TWENTE—K.L.M., Enschede: Van. Loenshof.

UZHOROD—C.S.A., Hotel Koruna.

VALENCIA—L.A.P.E., Manises, Airport.
VALONA—Agenzia, Adria Aerolloyd.
VENICE—A.L S.A., Piazza S. Marco 49-50.
VENTNOR—P.S. and I. of W., Nash's Garage
    1 Pier Street.
VIENNA
    Air France, Kärntnerring 7.
    Austraflug, Vienna, 1 Kärntnerring, Nr. 5
    (Hotel Bristol).
    D.L.H., Vienna, 1 Kärntnerring, Nr. 5 (Hotel
    Bristol).

WANGEROOGE—D.L.H., Airport.
WARSAW
    Air France, Place Napoleon.
    " Lot," 35, UI. Jerozolimskie.
WELIKIJE LUKI—Deruluft, Airport Welikije Luki.
WESTERLAND—D.L.H., Airport.
WICK—Highland Airways, Messrs. Alex Robertson
    and Sons, Bridge Street.
WILNO—" Lot," Porubanek, Airport.
WYK—D.L.H., Airport.

ZAGREB
    Aeropout, Jelaicicev Trg. 9.
    C.S.A., Jelacicev Trg. 6, Putnik.
ZARA—A.L.S.A., Ufficio Viaggi Fratelli Tolja, Calle
    Larga, 2.
ZÜRICH
    Swissair, Flugplatz, Zurich, Dubendorf.
    Hotel Schweizerhof.
ZWICKAU—D.L.H., Airport.

AIR COMPANIES' ADDRESSES WITH TELEGRAPHIC ADDRESSES AND TELEPHONE NUMBERS.

(For Booking Offices, see pages 26-29)

Air Company	Office Address	Telegraphic Address	Telephone Number
A.B.A.—AB Aerotransport	Travel Bureau, Flygpaviljongen, Nybro-plan, Stockholm, Sweden	Airticket, Stockholm	10 38 15; 10 38 17
ABERDEEN AIRWAYS LTD.	Aberdeen Airport, Dyce, Aberdeen		Dyce 32
AEROESPRESSO—Soc. Anon. Aero Espresso Italiana	A.L.S.A. Office, Aeroporto del Littorio, Rome, Italy		
AERO O. Y. (Finnish Air Lines)	Helsinki (Helsingfors), Finland	Aero, Helsinki	27912; 23860
AEROPOUT—Soc. de Nav. Aerienne Yougo-slave	Rue Briand 3, Beograd (Belgrade), Yugo-slavia	Aeroput, Beograd	25-312; 23-096; 20-406
AERO ST. GALLEN—Ostschweiz Aeroge-sellschaft	Altenrhein Airport, St. Gallen, Switzer-land	Aero St. Gallen	Altenrhein 2141
AIR FRANCE	{52, Haymarket, London, S.W. 1, England	Airfrans Lesquare, London	Whitehall 9671-2-3-4
	9, Rue Auber, Paris, France	Airfransas, Paris	Opera 41-00
AIR SERVICE	Air France Office, 9 Rue Auber, Paris, France	Airfransag, Paris	Opera 41-00
ALPAR-BERN	Flugplatz Bern-Belpmoos, Berne, Switzer-land	Alpar-Bern, Berne	Bern 44,044; Belp 101
A.L.I.—Avio Linee Itallane, S.A.	Via Victor Hugo 4, Milano, Italy	Aviolinee-Milano	17-022
A.L.S.A.—Ala Littoria Societa Anonima	Aeroporto del Littorio, Rome, Italy	Alerea, Roma	864-151 to 154
AUSTROFLUG—Österreichische Luftver-kehrs, A.G.	Kärntnerring 5 (Hotel Bristol), Wien I. (Vienna), Austria	Austroflug, Wien	R 28-1-21; R 28-1-96
AVIOSLAVA—See C.L.S.			
BANCO—British Air Navigation Co. Ltd.	Heston Airport, Middlesex, England	Bancoair, London	Hounslow 3244,
BLACKPOOL AND WEST COAST AIR SERVICES LTD.	Squire's Gate Aerodrome, Blackpool, Eng.	Aeros, Blackpool	South Shore 41347
C.L.S.—Ceskoslovenská Letecká Spoleřnost.	Vodičkova ul. 38, Praha (Prague), Czecho-slovakia	Avioslava, Praha	41392 (night) 295-44
C.S.A.—Ceskoslovenske Ststni Aerolinie	Vodičkova ul. 20, Praha (Prague), Czecho-slovakia	Statoaero, Praha	355-08
CONDOR—Syndicato Condor Ltda	Rua da Alfandega 5, Rio de Janeiro, South America		
D.D.L.—Det Danske Luffartselskab A.S.	Vesterport, Kobenhavn V. (Copenhagen), Denmark	Luffart, Kobenhavn	Central 8800
DERULUFT—Deutsch-Russische Luftver-kehrs, Ges	Lindenstrasse 35, Berlin, S.W. 68, Germany	Deruluft, Berlin	Dönhoff (A7) 8630-39
D.L.H.—Deutsche Lufthansa A.G.	{Lindenstrasse 35, Berlin, S.W. 68, Germany	Lufthansa, Berlin	Dönhoff (A7) 8630
	Airway Terminus, Victoria Station, London, S.W. 1, England	Impairlim, London	Victoria 2211
HIGHLAND AIRWAYS LTD. HILLMAN'S AIRWAYS LTD.	36, Academy Street, Inverness, Scotland Stapleford Airport, near Abridge, Essex England	Dick, Inverness	7, 8 and 19 Stapleford 291
IMPERIAL AIRWAYS LTD.	Airway Terminus, Victoria Station, London, S.W. 1, England	Impairlim, London	Victoria 2211 (10 lines)

AIR COMPANIES' ADDRESSES WITH TELEGRAPHIC ADDRESSES AND TELEPHONE NUMBERS—Continued.

(For Booking Offices, see pages 26-29)

Air Company	Office Address	Telegraphic Address	Telephone Number
JERSEY AIRWAYS LTD.	1, Mulcaster Street, St. Helier, Jersey, Channel Islands		1221
	Victoria Coach Station, 11, Elizabeth St., London, S.W. I, England		Sloane 5184
K.L.M.—Koninklijke Luchtvaart Mij	9-11, Hofweg, The Hague, Holland	Transaera, The Hague	117600 and 180070
	Leidscheplein, Amsterdam, Holland	Transaera, Amsterdam	33480 and 35982
	Wm. H. Muller & Co., 66 Haymarket, London, S.W. I, England		
K.N.I.L.M.—Kon. Ned. Ind. Luchtvaart Mij.	Sluisburg, Batavia, Dutch East Indies	Bataviline, London	Whitehall 7331
L.A.P.E.—Lineas Aéreas Postales Espanolas.	Plaza de La Lealtad 2, Madrid, Spain	Lapa, Madrid	1173
L.S. and P.A.—London, Scottish & Provincial Airways Ltd.	Heston Airport, Middlesex, England		18230-18238
			Hounslow 2345
L.O.T.—Polskie Linje Lotnicze	Plac Napoleona 9, Warszawa (Warsaw), Poland	Lot, Warszawa	563-60
LUFTSCHIFFBAU ZEPPELIN GMBH	11, Goldschmidtstrasse 11, Friedrichshafen, Germany	Hapag, Friedrichshafen	325
MALERT—Magyar Légiforgalmi R.T.	Hamburg American Line, 66-68, Haymarket, London, S.W. I, England	Bataviline, London	Whitehall 7331
	Vaci Utca I, Budapest IV, Hungary	Malert, Budapest	80-8-80; 80-8-88
N.A.A.S.A.—Nord Africa Aviazione S.A.	Bengasi, Cirenaica, North Africa		
NORMAN EDGAR (WESTERN AIRWAYS) LTD.	The Airport, Bristol, England		41133
NORSKE LUFTRUTER A.S.	Skippergaten 21, Oslo, Norway	Norskluftruter, Flugleitung	21089
P.S. & I.o.W.—Portsmouth, Southsea and Isle of Wight Aviation Ltd.	Portsmouth City Airport, Portsmouth, England	Balmurlux, Portsmouth	6689
PROVINCIAL AIRWAYS LTD.	Croydon Airport, Surrey, England	Provairway, Phone, London	Fairfield 4117 and 4118
RAILWAY AIR SERVICES LTD.	Airway Terminus, Victoria Station, London, S.W. I, England	Impairlim, London	Victoria 2211
SABENA—Soc. Anon. Belge d'Exploitation de la Nav. Aerienne	32-34, Boulevard Adolphe Max, Brussels, Belgium	Airsabena, Brussels	17 10 06
	Airway Terminus, Victoria Station, London, S.W. I, England	Impairlim, London	Victoria 2211
S.H.C.A.—Soc. Hellénique des Communications Aeriennes S.A.	8 Rue Sophocles, Athens, Greece	Aerellenic, Athens	21-991 and 21-992
SOUTHEND FLYING SERVICES LTD.	Rochford Aerodrome, Essex, England	Aerodrome, Rochford	561101
SPARTAN AIR LINES LTD.	53, Parliament Street, London, S.W. I, England	Sparline, Parl, London	Whitehall 7271
	Airway Terminus, Victoria Station, London, S.W. I, England	Impairlim, London	Victoria 2211
SWISSAIR—Swiss Air Traffic Co. Ltd.	Zürich—Flugplatz, Zürich, Switzerland	Swissair, Zürich	934. 201
	Flugplatz Birsfelden, Basel, Switzerland	Swissair, Basel	43. 880

PITMAN'S

WELL-KNOWN BOOKS ON AVIATION.

THE AIR ANNUAL OF THE BRITISH EMPIRE, 1934-35

Edited by C. G. Burge, O.B.E. An exhaustive record of Imperial Aviation, both military and civil. during the past year. 862 pages, 21/- net.

THE AIRMAN'S YEAR BOOK

Edited by C. G. Burge, O.B.E. Published under the authority of the Royal Aero Club, this is one of the most informative handbooks obtainable. 156 pages, 3/6 net.

FLYING AS A CAREER

By Major Oliver Stewart, M.C., A.F.C. For all contemplating the profession, this book gives all the information they need about remuneration, duties, prospects, etc. Second Edition. 94 pages, 3/6 net.

LEARNING TO FLY

By Frank A. Swoffer, M.B.E. This is the recognised instruction manual for everyone taking up flying. Third Edition. 156 pages, 7/6 net.

AIRSENSE

By W. O. Manning, F.R.Ae.S. Gives a well-written and simply expressed account of the theory of flight. 94 pages, 3/6 net.

AIR LICENCES

By T. Stanhope Sprigg. Contains full information on the civil flying licences and shows how they are obtained and how to apply for them. 130 pages, 3/6 net.

PILOT'S "A" LICENCE

By John F. Leeming. This popular handbook describes in detail the conditions governing the issue of flying certificates and shows exactly how to qualify. Completely up-to-date with the latest regulations. Sixth Edition. 92 pages, 3/6 net.

THE AUTOGIRO AND HOW TO FLY IT

By Reginald Brie. Includes very latest models, together with accounts of recent experiments. It gives the fascinating story of Autogiro development from its origin. Second Edition, 128 pages, 5/- net.

A SELECTION OF PITMAN'S TECHNICAL AVIATION BOOKS

METAL AIRCRAFT CONSTRUCTION

By M. Langley, A.M.I.N.A., A.M.I.Ae.E. 344 pages. Second Edition. 15/- net.

HANDBOOK OF AERONAUTICS

Published under the authority of the Royal Aeronautical Society. 2 Volumes. Vol. 1.—740 pages, 25/- net. Vol. 11.—420 pages, 15/- net. Second Edition.

MARINE AIRCRAFT DESIGN

By William Munro, A.M.I.Ae.E. 236 pages, 20/- net.

MATERIALS OF AIRCRAFT CONSTRUCTION

By F. T. Hill, F.R.Ae.S. Second Edition. 384 pages, 20/- net.

GROUND ENGINEERS' TEXT BOOKS

A series of five books covering the requirements of the A, B, C, D, or X licences.

Aero Engines, 3/6 net. Rigging, Maintenance and Inspection of Aircraft, 5/- net. Inspection of Aircraft after Overhaul, 3/6 net. Instruments, 5/- net. Electrical and Wireless Equipment, 6/- net.

SIR ISAAC PITMAN & SONS, LTD., PARKER ST., KINGSWAY, W.C.2

All times given in the Tables are local times, see page 22

Passengers should be at the Town Terminus or Airport at least 15 minutes before scheduled time

Conveyance between an Airport and the Town Terminus is free unless otherwise indicated in the Table

The full names and addresses, etc., of the Companies will be found on pages 30 and 31
The Tables have been numbered with an allowance for the addition of new Services

The Air routes on the Continent are known by certain official numbers; these are printed in the respective Tables, thus:—Route 454

LONDON—LIVERPOOL—BELFAST
(Weekdays only)
RAILWAY AIR SERVICES

Miles	Airports of			Airports of		
0	LONDON ... ... dep	10 15		GLASGOW ... ...dep	...	
	BIRMINGHAM ... ... arr	...		BELFAST ... ... arr	...	
	,, ... dep	...		,, ...dep	9 45	
	MANCHESTER... ... arr	...		LIVERPOOL ... ... arr	11 10	
	,, ... dep	...		,, ...dep	11 30	
180	LIVERPOOL ... ... arr	11 45		MANCHESTER ... arr	...	
	,, ... dep	12 5		,, ...dep	...	
344	BELFAST ... ... arr	13 30		BIRMINGHAM ... arr	...	
	,, ...dep	...		,, ...dep	...	
	GLASGOW... ... ... arr	...		LONDON ... ... arr	13 0	

Distance and Time allowance for conveyance between Airport and Town Terminus

TOWN	AIRPORT	TOWN TERMINUS	Miles	Minutes
LONDON	Croydon	Airway Terminus, Victoria Station, S.W.1	12	45
BIRMINGHAM	Castle Bromwich {	Snow Hill Station	5	30
		New Street Station	5	35
MANCHESTER	Barton ....{	Midland Hotel..	6	50
		L.M.S. Office, Piccadilly	6	55
LIVERPOOL............	Speke	Lime Street Station or Adelphi Hotel...........	6	30
BELFAST	Aldergrove ......{	Smithfield Omnibus Station	17	40
GLASGOW	Renfrew	York Road Station	17	50
		Central Station	5	25

FARES

FROM LONDON	Single	Return	Excess Baggage per lb.
	s. d.	s. d.	s. d.
To LIVERPOOL	60 0	90 0	0 5
BELFAST	110 0	185 0	0 9
FROM LIVERPOOL			
To BELFAST	55 0	100 0	0 5

Children under 3 years not occupying a separate seat carried free; half fare if occupying a seat. From 3 to 7 years, half fare.
Free baggage allowance—35 lbs. (no free baggage for children travelling at half fare or free).
Cancellation of reservations—At least 24 hours' notice should be given.

2   LONDON—ISLE OF WIGHT
(Service suspended during Winter)
RAILWAY AIR SERVICES AND SPARTAN AIR LINES

Miles	Airports of						
0	**LONDON** ... ...dep						
	RYDE § ... ... arr						
66	**BEMBRIDGE** ... ... arr						
76	**COWES** ... ... arr						

	Airports of						
	COWES ... ...dep						
	BEMBRIDGE ... ...dep						
	RYDE § ... ...dep						
	LONDON ... ... arr						

§ Lands at Ryde on request if circumstances permit

Distance and Time allowance for conveyance between Airport and Town Terminus

TOWN	AIRPORT	TOWN TERMINUS	Miles	Minutes
LONDON	Croydon	Airway Terminus, Victoria Station, S.W. 1	12	40
RYDE	Ryde	Pickford's Office (on the Front)	—	—
BEMBRIDGE	Bembridge	Central Garage	½	—
COWES	Somerton	West Pier	1½	—

FARES

FROM LONDON TO	Single	Return	Excess Baggage per lb.
	£ s. d.	£ s. d.	s. d.
RYDE			
BEMBRIDGE			
COWES			

3   BIRMINGHAM—BRISTOL—SOUTHAMPTON—COWES
(Service suspended during Winter)
RAILWAY AIR SERVICES

Miles	Airports of			Airports of			
0	**BIRMINGHAM** ...dep			**COWES** ... ...dep			
84	**BRISTOL** ... ... arr			**SOUTHAMPTON** .. arr			
	" ... ...dep			" ... ...dep			
146	**SOUTHAMPTON** ... arr			**BRISTOL** ... ... arr			
	" ... ...dep			" ... ...dep			
161	**COWES** ... ... arr			**BIRMINGHAM** ... arr			

Distance and Time allowance for conveyance between Airport and Town Terminus

TOWN	AIRPORT	TOWN TERMINUS	Miles	Minutes
BIRMINGHAM	Castle Bromwich {	Snow Hill Station	5	25
		New Street Station	5	20
BRISTOL	Whitchurch ..... {	Temple Meads Station	4	15
		Terminus Station	4	20
SOUTHAMPTON ...	Southampton ... {	West Station	4	15
COWES	Somerton	Cowes (S.R.) Station	1½	5

FARES

FROM BIRMINGHAM TO	Single	Return	Excess Baggage per lb.
	£ s. d.	£ s. d.	s. d.
BRISTOL			
SOUTHAMPTON			
COWES			

4

PLYMOUTH—TEIGNMOUTH—CARDIFF—BIRMINGHAM—LIVERPOOL
(Service suspended during Winter)
RAILWAY AIR SERVICES

Miles	Airports of				Airports of	
0	**PLYMOUTH** ...	... dep			**LIVERPOOL** ...	... dep
28	**HALDON**	{ arr			**BIRMINGHAM**	... arr
	(Teignmouth)	{ dep			,,	... dep
93	**CARDIFF**	... arr			**CARDIFF**	... dep
	,, ...	... dep			,, ...	... dep
185	**BIRMINGHAM**	... arr			**HALDON**... ...	... arr
	,,	... dep			,, ...	... dep
258	**LIVERPOOL**	... arr			**PLYMOUTH** ...	... arr

Distance and Time allowance for conveyance between Airport and Town Terminus

TOWN	AIRPORT	TOWN TERMINUS	Miles	Minutes
PLYMOUTH	Roborough, Crownhill	North Road Station	4	20
TEIGNMOUTH	Haldon	Enquiry Bureau, The Den, Teignmouth...........	2	10
CARDIFF	Cardiff	General Station	2	10
		Snow Hill Station	5	25
BIRMINGHAM	Castle Bromwich {	New Street Station	5	20
		Lime Street Station or Adelphi Hotel...........	6	15
LIVERPOOL............	Speke............... {	11, James Street	6	20

FARES

FROM PLYMOUTH TO	Single	Return	Excess Baggage per lb.
	£ s. d.	£ s. d.	s. d.
TEIGNMOUTH			
CARDIFF			
BIRMINGHAM			
LIVERPOOL			

5 LONDON—SOUTHAMPTON—HALDON—PLYMOUTH—HAYLE
(Daily)
PROVINCIAL AIRWAYS

Mls	4ls	Airports of			Airports of	
0		**LONDON** ... ...dep	14 0		**HAYLE** ... ...dep	...
0		**SOUTHAMPTON**			**NEWQUAY** ... ...dep	...
		or **PORTSM'TH** ...dep	14 40		**PLYMOUTH** ... ...dep	9 0
		BOURNEM'TH §...dep	14 55		**HALDON**† § ... ...dep	9 15
		DORCHESTER§ or			**DORCHESTER**§ or	
		WEYMOUTH†§...dep	15 10		**WEYMOUTH**§...dep	10 0
		HALDON† §... ...dep	15 55		**BOURNEMOUTH**§ dep	10 15
127	‡187	**PLYMOUTH** ... arr	16 10		**SOUTHAMPTON**	
167	227	**NEWQUAY** ... arr	...		or **PORTSM'TH**... dep	10 30
187	247	**HAYLE** ... ... arr	...		**LONDON** ... ... arr	11 10

† Haldon Airport serves:—Exeter, Teignmouth, Dawlish, Paignton, Newton Abbot and Torquay.
‡ 193 miles via Southampton. § Machines call on request only

Distance between Airport and Town

TOWN	AIRPORT	TOWN TERMINUS	Miles
LONDON	Croydon	Company's car from residence to Airport § ...	12
SOUTHAMPTON	Atlantic Park, Eastleigh	Company's car from residence to Airport	—
PORTSMOUTH	Municipal Airport	Company's car from residence to Airport	2
BOURNEMOUTH	Christchurch	Company's car from residence to Airport	3
DORCHESTER	Dorchester	Company's car from residence to Airport	1
WEYMOUTH	Dorchester	Company's car from residence to Airport	½
HALDON	Haldon	Company's car from residence to Airport	—
PLYMOUTH	Roborough, Crownhill	Company's car from residence to Airport	—
NEWQUAY	St. Columb, Major Road	Company's car from residence to Airport	2½
HAYLE	Near Redruth Rd.	Company's car from residence to Airport	3

§ For London a charge is made which is deducted from Air transport fare

FARES—WITH ROAD TRANSPORT

		SOUTH-AMPTON	PORTS-MOUTH	BOURNE-MOUTH	DORCHESTER or WEYMOUTH	HALDON ***	PLYMOUTH	NEWQUAY	HAYLE
		s. d.	s. d.	s. d.	s. d.	s. d.	s. d.	s. d.	s. d.
LONDON	Single ...	25 0	25 0	37 6	50 0	60 0	62 6	...	...
	Return ...	47 6	47 6	71 0	95 0	114 0	119 0	...	...
SOUTHAMPTON ...	Single ...		10 0	15 0	25 0	40 0	45 0	...	...
	Return ...		19 0	28 6	47 6	76 0	85 6	...	...
PORTSMOUTH	Single ...	10 0		20 0	30 0	47 6	50 0	...	...
	Return ...	19 0		38 0	57 0	90 0	95 0	...	...
BOURNEMOUTH ...	Single ...	15 0	20 0		...	35 0	37 6	...	...
	Return ...	28 6	38 0		...	66 0	71 0	...	...
DORCHESTER or WEYMOUTH	Single ...	25 0	30 0	...		20 0	22 6	...	...
	Return ...	47 6	57 0	...		38 0	43 0	...	...
HALDON ***	Single ...	40 0	47 6	35 0	20 0		12 6	...	...
	Return ...	76 0	90 0	66 0	38 0		24 0	...	...
PLYMOUTH...	Single ...	45 0	50 0	37 6	22 6	12 6		...	...
	Return ...	85 6	95 0	71 0	43 0	24 0		...	...

*** The fares for the Towns served by Haldon are the same as for Haldon (except to or from Plymouth§).

§ Plymouth—Teignmouth, Dawlish or Paignton, 15/- Single; 28/6 Return.
Plymouth—Exeter, 17/6 Single; 33/6 Return.
Plymouth—Torquay or Newton Abbot, 16/6 Single; 31/6 Return.
Free baggage allowance 30 lbs.—excess baggage 3d. per lb.

All times given in the Tables are local times, see page 22
Conveyance between an Airport and the Town Terminus is free unless otherwise indicated in the Table
The full names and addresses, etc., of the Companies will be found on pages 30 and 31

6

LEEDS—NOTTINGHAM—LONDON—PARIS
(Daily)
L. S. and P.A.

Miles	Airports of		§			Airports of			§
0	**LEEDS** ... ...dep	11 20	13 40		**PARIS** ... ...dep	...	9 30
65	**NOTTINGHAM** ... arr	11 50	14 10		**HESTON** ... ... arr	...	11 25
	,, ...dep	12 0	14 20		,, ...dep	9 30	11 45
175	**HESTON** ... ... arr	12 55	15 15		**NOTTINGHAM** ... arr	10 25	12 40
	,, ...dep	13 25	...		,, ...dep	10 35	12 50
435	**PARIS** ... ... arr	15 20	...		**LEEDS** ... ... arr	11 5	13 20

§ Lands at Berck (for Le Touquet) by special arrangement

Distance and Time allowance for conveyance between Airport and Town Terminus

TOWN	AIRPORT	TOWN TERMINUS	Miles	Minutes
LEEDS	Sherburn in Elmet	Corn Exchange	12	40
NOTTINGHAM	Tollerton	Black Boy Hotel...	2½	30
LONDON	Heston	Langham Hotel, Portland Place, W. 1.	14	45
PARIS	Le Bourget	France—Tourisme, 4-6 Rue de Sèze	—	45

FARES

	NOTTINGHAM			LONDON			LE TOUQUET			PARIS		
	Single	Ret.	Ex. Bg.	Single	Ret.	Ex. Bg.	Single	Ret.	Ex. Bg.	Single	Ret.	Ex. Bg.
	s. d.	s. d.	s. d.	s. d.	s. d.	s. d.	s. d.	s. d.	s. d.	s. d.	s. d.	s. d.
LEEDS	18 0	30 0	0 3	42 0	70 0	0 6	84 0	147 0	0 6	105 0	189 0	0 6
NOTTINGH'M	...	...	...	25 0	45 0	0 6	70 0	130 0	0 6	90 0	170 0	0 6

Ex. Bag.—Excess Baggage per lb.

7

BOURNEMOUTH—BRISTOL—CARDIFF
(Service on demand)
NORMAN EDGAR (WESTERN AIRWAYS)

Miles	Airports of			Airports of		
0	**BOURNEMOUTH**... dep	...	...	**CARDIFF** ... ...dep	11 15	15 15
62	**BRISTOL** ... ... arr	...	...	**BRISTOL** ... ... arr	11 40	15 40
	,, ...dep	10 45	14 45	,, ...dep	...	...
88	**CARDIFF** ... ... arr	11 10	15 10	**BOURNEMOUTH**.. arr	...	...

Distance and Time allowance for conveyance between Airport and Town

TOWN	AIRPORT	TOWN TERMINUS	Miles	Minutes
BOURNEMOUTH ...	Christchurch	Free Road Service	5	—
BRISTOL	Whitchurch	Tramways Centre or Travel Bureau, Prince St....	4½	25
CARDIFF	Cardiff	Small charge for Taxi	3	—

FARES

FROM BRISTOL TO	Single	Return
	s. d.	s. d.
CARDIFF	9 6	17 6

* LONDON—JERSEY
JERSEY AIRWAYS

NOVEMBER

Miles	Airports of		1st	2nd	3rd	4th	5th	6th
0	HESTON	...dep	8 30	9 15	10 15	10 30	‡	‡
200	JERSEY	... ...arr	10 30	11 15	12 15	12 30		
	JERSEY	... ...dep	11 15	12 15	13 15	13 30	‡	‡
	HESTON	... ...arr	13 15	14 15	15 15	15 30		

Airports of			7th	8th	9th	10th	11th	12th
HESTON	... ...	...dep	‡	‡	‡	‡	‡	‡
JERSEY	... ...	...arr	‡	‡	‡	‡	‡	‡
JERSEY	... ...	...dep	‡	‡	‡	‡	‡	‡
HESTON	... ...	...arr	‡	‡	‡	‡	‡	‡

Airports of			13th	14th	15th	16th	17th	18th
HESTON	... ...	...dep	11 15	12 25	...	9 0	9 45	10 30
JERSEY	... ...	...arr	13 15	14 25	...	11 0	11 45	12 30
JERSEY	... ...	...dep	14 15	...	10 30	11 45	12 40	13 30
HESTON	... ...	...arr	16 15	...	12 30	13 45	14 40	15 30

Airports of			19th	20th	21st	22nd	23rd	24th
HESTON	... ...	...dep	§	§	§	§	§	§
JERSEY	... ...	...arr	§	§	§	§	§	§
JERSEY	... ...	...dep	§	§	§	§	§	§
HESTON	... ...	...arr	§	§	§	§	§	§

Airports of	25th	26th	27th	28th	29th	30th	
HESTON dep	§	§	§	11 15	12 0		
JERSEY ...arr	§	§	§	13 15	14 0	...	
						...	
JERSEY ...dep	§	§	§	14 0	...	10 0	
HESTON arr	§	§	§	16 0	...	12 0	

‡ This service is the same as for November 4th. § This service is the same as for November 18th.

Distance and Time allowance for conveyance between Airport and Town Terminus

TOWN	AIRPORT	TOWN TERMINUS	Miles	Minutes
LONDON	Heston	Coach Station, 11, Elizabeth Street, S.W. 1......	12	70
ST. HELIER	St. Helier	Landing on the Beach. No Special Conveyance	—	—

FARES FROM LONDON TO	Single	Return	Excess Baggage per lb.	Baggage Allowance
	£ s. d.	£ s. d.	d.	
JERSEY	2 19 6	4 19 6	4	25lbs.

Children under 3 years 20% of above Fares, from 3 to 7 years 50%.

* SMOKING ON THIS ROUTE IS PERMITTED.

*SOUTHAMPTON—PORTSMOUTH—JERSEY
JERSEY AIRWAYS

NOVEMBER

Mls.	Airports of	1st	2nd	3rd	4th	5th	6th	7th	8th
0	SOUTHAMPTON dep	8 45	9 30	10 30	10 45	‡	‡	‡	‡
	PORTSMOUTH dep	9 15	10 0	11 15	11 15				
120	JERSEY arr	10 30	11 15	12 15	12 30				
	JERSEY dep	11 15	12 15	13 15	13 30	‡	‡	‡	‡
	PORTSMOUTH arr	12 30	13 30	14 30	14 45				
	SOUTHAMPTON arr	13 0	14 0	15 0	15 15				

Airports of	9th	10th	11th	12th	13th	14th	15th	16th
SOUTHAMPTON dep	†	10 45	†	†	11 30	12 40	8 30	9 15
PORTSMOUTH dep		11 15			12 0	13 10	9 45	9 45
JERSEY arr		12 15			13 15	14 25	11 45	11 0
JERSEY dep	†		†	†	14 15	15 0	10 30	11 45
PORTSMOUTH arr		14 45			15 30	16 15	11 45	13 0
SOUTHAMPTON arr		15 15			16 0		12 15	13 30

Airports of	17th	18th	19th	20th	21st	22nd	23rd	24th
SOUTHAMPTON dep	10 0	10 45	§	§	§	§	§	§
PORTSMOUTH dep	10 30	11 15						
JERSEY arr	11 45	12 30						
JERSEY dep	12 40	13 30	§	§	§	§	§	§
PORTSMOUTH arr	13 55	14 45						
SOUTHAMPTON arr	14 25	15 15						

Airports of	25th	26th	27th	28th	29th	30th
SOUTHAMPTON dep	§	§	§	11 30	12 15	....
PORTSMOUTH dep				12 0	12 45	8 0
JERSEY arr				13 15	14 0	9 15
JERSEY dep	§	§	§	14 0	14 45	
PORTSMOUTH arr				15 15	16 0	11 15
SOUTHAMPTON arr				15 45		11 45

‡ This service is the same as for November 4th.
† This service is the same as for November 4th.
§ This service is the same as for November 18th.

Distance and Time allowance for conveyance between Airport and Town Terminus

AIRPORT	Miles	Minutes
Eastleigh	3¾	—
Portsmouth	2½	30
St. Helier		

TOWN TERMINUS

TOWN TERMINUS	
SOUTHAMPTON	No Special Conveyance
PORTSMOUTH	87e, Commercial Road (Fare 1/6)
ST. HELIER	Landing on the Beach. No Special Conveyance

FARES

FROM	Single	Return	Excess Baggage per lb.	Baggage Allowance
	£ s. d.	£ s. d.	d.	
SOUTHAMPTON TO JERSEY	1 15 0	3 0 0	2	25lbs.
PORTSMOUTH TO JERSEY	1 12 6	2 15 0	2	

Children under 3 years, 20% of above fares, from 3 to 7 years 50%

✱ SMOKING ON THIS ROUTE IS PERMITTED.

12   JERSEY—PARIS
(Service temporarily suspended)
JERSEY AIRWAYS

13   LIVERPOOL—BLACKPOOL—ISLE OF MAN
(Daily)
BLACKPOOL AND WEST COAST AIR SERVICES

Miles	Airports of				Airports of		
0	LIVERPOOL ... ...dep	9 30			ISLE OF MAN ...dep	14 15	
35	BLACKPOOL ... arr	9 50			BLACKPOOL ... arr	14 55	
"	... ...dep	10 0			" ... ...dep	15 5	
100	ISLE OF MAN ... arr	10 40			LIVERPOOL .... arr	15 25	

Distance and Time allowance for conveyance between Airport and Town Terminus

TOWN	AIRPORT	TOWN TERMINUS	Miles	Minutes
LIVERPOOL............	Speke	Adelphi Hotel	6	25
BLACKPOOL	Squires Gate§ ...	No Special Conveyance	3	—
CASTLETOWN	Ronaldsway ‡	No Special Conveyance	1½	—

‡ 6 miles from Douglas.   § 3 minutes' walk from Squires Gate Station.

FARES

FROM LIVERPOOL	Single	Return	Free Baggage
	s. d.	s. d.	lbs.
To BLACKPOOL	10 0	15 0	20
ISLE OF MAN *	30 0	50 0	
FROM BLACKPOOL	s. d.	s. d.	
To ISLE OF MAN	25 0	40 0	

Heavy baggage is forwarded at reasonable rates.
* Fare from Hooton (by arrangement) to Isle of Man—Single 32/6; Return 52/6.

14   LONDON—RYDE—SHANKLIN (Isle of Wight)
PORTSMOUTH, SOUTHSEA, & ISLE OF WIGHT AVIATION

Miles	Airports of	M	M	S	F		
0	HESTON ... ...dep	9 20	11 20	13 20	15 20		
60	RYDE ... ... arr	10 0	12 0	14 0	16 0		
68	SHANKLIN ... ... arr	...	...	...	...		

Miles	Airports of	M	M	S	F		
0	SHANKLIN ... ...dep	...	...	...	...		
8	RYDE ... ...dep	8 30	10 30	12 30	14 30		
68	HESTON ... ... arr	9 10	11 10	13 10	15 10		

M—On Monday only   S—On Saturday only   F—On Friday and Saturday only

Distance and Time allowance for conveyance between Airport and Town Terminus

TOWN	AIRPORT	TOWN TERMINUS	Miles	Minutes
LONDON	Heston	Coach Station, 164, Buckingham Palace Road, S.W.	13	50
RYDE	Ryde	No Special Conveyance	1	—
SHANKLIN	Apse	No Special Conveyance	1	—

FARES

FROM LONDON TO	Single	Return	Excess Baggage per lb.	Baggage Allowance
	£ s. d.	£ s. d.	s. d.	lbs.
RYDE	0 19 6	1 18 6	0 3	30
SHANKLIN	...	...	...	

All times given in the Tables are local times, see page 22
Conveyance between an Airport and the Town Terminus is free unless otherwise indicated in the Table
The full names and addresses, etc., of the Companies will be found on pages 30 and 31
40

15

PORTSMOUTH—RYDE
(Daily)
PORTSMOUTH, SOUTHSEA, and ISLE OF WIGHT AVIATION

Miles	Airports of								
0	**PORTSMOUTH** ... ...dep	9 10	10 10	12 40	14 10	15 40		
10	**RYDE** ... ... arr	9 20	10 20	12 50	14 20	15 50		

	Airports of								
	RYDE ... ...dep	9 22	10 22	12 52	14 22	15 52		
	PORTSMOUTH ... ... arr	9 30	10 30	13 0	14 30	16 0		

Distance and Time allowance for conveyance between Airport and Town Terminus

TOWN	AIRPORT	TOWN TERMINUS	Miles	Minutes
PORTSMOUTH	Hilsea	Clarence Pier	5	20
		South Parade Pier	4	15
RYDE	Ryde	No Special Conveyance	1¼	—

FARES
Inclusive of Car Conveyance between Hilsea Airport (Portsmouth) and Southsea

FROM PORTSMOUTH TO	Single	Return	Day Return
	s. d.	s. d.	s. d.
RYDE	4 6	8 6	6 6§

§ Available up to the 10 10 service from Portsmouth and the 10 22 from Ryde.
Children under 12 years—Single 3/-; Return 5/-.
Freight of a suitable nature carried at the rate of 2d. per lb. (Minimum 1/-).

21

ABERDEEN—WICK—KIRKWALL
(Daily)
HIGHLAND AIRWAYS

Miles	Airports of				Airports of			
0	**ABERDEEN** ... ...dep	...		**KIRKWALL** ... ...dep	8 0	
*100	**WICK** ... ... arr	...		**WICK** ... ... arr	8 25	
	,, ...dep	13 10		,, ...dep	...	
135	**KIRKWALL**... ... ... arr	13 30		**ABERDEEN** ... ... arr	...	

* In bad weather the route is via Lossiemouth. Distance 132 miles.

Distance and Time allowance for conveyance between Airport and Town Terminus

TOWN	AIRPORT	TOWN TERMINUS	Miles	Minutes
ABERDEEN	Seaton	No Special Conveyance	2	—
WICK	Hillhead	No Special Conveyance	¾	—
KIRKWALL	Wideford	Company's Car—Apply "Orcadian" News Office	2	—

FARES

FROM WICK TO	Single	Return	Excess Baggage per lb.
	£ s. d.	£ s. d.	d.
KIRKWALL	1 0 0	1 15 0	2

Baggage Allowance 25 lbs.

41

22 INVERNESS—WICK—KIRKWALL
(Daily)
HIGHLAND AIRWAYS

Miles	Airports of				Airports of			
0	**INVERNESS** ...	...dep	...		**KIRKWALL** ...	...dep	8	0
83	**WICK**	...arr	...		**WICK**	...arr	8	25
	,, ...	...dep	13 10		,, ...	...dep	...	
118	**KIRKWALL** ...	...arr	13 30		**INVERNESS** ...	...arr	...	

Distance and Time allowance for conveyance between Airport and Town Terminus

TOWN	AIRPORT	TOWN TERMINUS	Miles	Minutes
INVERNESS	Longman	Macrae and Dick's Garage—Adjoining Station	1	—
WICK	Hillhead	No Special Conveyance	¾	—
KIRKWALL	Wideford	Company's Car—Apply "Orcadian" News Office	2	—

FARES

FROM WICK TO	Single	Return	Excess Baggage per lb.
	£ s. d.	£ s. d.	d.
KIRKWALL	1 0 0	1 15 0	2

Baggage Allowance 25 lbs.

24 ABERDEEN—GLASGOW
ABERDEEN AIRWAYS

Miles	Airports of		**W**		Airports of		**W**
0	**ABERDEEN** ...	...dep	9 15		**GLASGOW** ...	...dep	14 30
127	**GLASGOW**	...arr	10 40		**ABERDEEN** ...	...arr	15 45

W—On Wednesday and Friday

Distance and Time allowance for conveyance between Airport and Town Terminus

TOWN	AIRPORT	TOWN TERMINUS	Miles	Minutes
ABERDEEN	Dyce	Caledonian Hotel	—	15
GLASGOW	Renfrew	Kenilworth Hotel, Queen Street	—	30

FARES

FROM ABERDEEN TO	Single	Return 14 Days	Free Baggage	Excess Baggage per lb.
	£ s. d.	£ s. d.	lbs.	d.
GLASGOW	3 5 0	5 5 0	20	5

Children under 7 years are charged two-thirds of above rates (no free baggage)
Cancellation of tickets cannot be accepted

25 LONDON—LIVERPOOL—ISLE OF MAN—BELFAST
(Service suspended during Winter)
HILLMAN'S AIRWAYS

Miles	Airports of				Airports of		
0	**ESSEX**				**BELFAST** ... ...dep		
	(Stapleford†) ... ...dep				**ISLE OF MAN** ... ...dep		
180	**LIVERPOOL** ... ...dep				**LIVERPOOL** ... ...dep		
260	**ISLE OF MAN** ... ...dep				**ESSEX**		
325	**BELFAST** ... ...arr				(Stapleford†)... ...arr		

†—Near Abridge

Distance and Time allowance for conveyance between Airport and Town Terminus

TOWN	AIRPORT	TOWN TERMINUS	Miles	Minutes
LONDON	Essex.....,..........	Coaching Station, King's Cross, N..................	25	60
LIVERPOOL............	Speke	No Special Conveyance	6	—
CASTLETOWN	Ronaldsway	No Special Conveyance (Frequent Bus Services)	1½	—
BELFAST	Aldergrove	Grand Central Hotel	—	—

FARES

FROM LONDON TO	Single	Return	Excess Baggage per lb.
	£ s. d.	£ s. d.	s. d.
LIVERPOOL			
ISLE OF MAN			
BELFAST			

26 SOUTHEND—ROCHESTER
(Daily)
SOUTHEND FLYING SERVICES

Miles	Airports of								
0	**SOUTHEND** ... ...dep	10 0	11 0	14 30	15 30				
18	**ROCHESTER** ... ...arr	10 15	11 15	14 45	15 45				

Miles	Airports of								
0	**ROCHESTER** ... ...dep	10 0	11 0	14 30	15 30				
18	**SOUTHEND** ... ...arr	10 15	11 15	14 45	15 45				

Distance and Time allowance for conveyance between Airport and Town Terminus

TOWN	AIRPORT	TOWN TERMINUS	Miles	Minutes
SOUTHEND	Rochford	Frequent Bus Services. No Special Conveyance	3½	—
ROCHESTER	Rochester	Frequent Bus Services. No Special Conveyance	2¾	—

FARES

FROM SOUTHEND TO	Single	Return
	s. d.	s. d.
ROCHESTER	8 0	12 0

Light Baggage is carried free, Excess Baggage by arrangement

Overlooking the Green Park, with its frontage along Piccadilly, the "Ritz" is situate in the most fashionable part of London. The Hotel embodies all those character-istics of taste and distinction for which the Ritz-Carlton Hotels are world-famous

Ritz

HOTEL LONDON

Standing at the corner of Pall Mall and the Haymarket, the "Carlton" occupies a unique position in the West End of London. With its per-fect equipment, comfort and cuisine, it is the favourite Hotel of visitors from the Continent and America

Carlton

HOTEL LONDON

Situated in the historic Place Vendome in the heart of Paris, the Ritz Hotel has over 200 delightful rooms, a large number of which overlook extensive private gardens where absolute quietness is assured. Its Restaurant, Grill Room and Bar are famous as the rendezvous of International Society

Ritz

HOTEL PARIS

THE RITZ CARLTON GROUP OF HOTELS

CONTINENTAL SERVICES

All times given in the Tables are local times, see page 22

Passengers should be at the Town Terminus or Airport at least 15 minutes before scheduled time

Conveyance between an Airport and the Town Terminus is free unless otherwise indicated in the Table

The Air routes on the Continent are known by certain official numbers; these are printed in the respective Tables, thus:—Route 454

The full names and addresses, etc., of the Companies will be found on pages 30, 31

The Tables have been numbered with an allowance for the addition of new Services

---

27   LONDON—PARIS
(Daily unless otherwise stated)
IMPERIAL AIRWAYS

Route 454

Miles	Airports of					**S**	**W**		
0	**LONDON** ... ...dep				9 30	12 30	18 30		
224	**PARIS** ... ... arr				11 45	14 45	20 45		

	Airports of				**W**	**S**			
	PARIS ... ...dep				9 30	12 30	18 30		
	LONDON ... ... arr				11 45	14 45	20 45		

S—Silver Wing.   **W—Not on Sunday.**

Distance and Time allowance for conveyance between Airport and Town Terminus

TOWN	AIRPORT	TOWN TERMINUS	Miles	Minutes
LONDON	Croydon	Airway Terminus, Victoria Station, S.W. 1	12	45
PARIS	Le Bourget	Airway Terminus, Rue de Italiens.................	8	45

FARES

FROM LONDON	Single	Return 15 Days	Return 60 Days	Excess Baggage per Kg (2·2 lbs.)
	£ s. d.	£ s. d.	£ s. d.	d.
To PARIS	4 15 0	7 12 0	8 1 6	6
FROM PARIS	Frs.	Frs.	Frs.	Frs.
To LONDON	405	650	690	2·50

BROWN'S HOTEL, **LONDON, W.I.,** **DOVER STREET AND ALBEMARLE STREET.**
First Class in Every Way.   The Hotel of Traditions, where the height of modern comfort is combined with Old English hospitality.
Telephone—**Regent 6020**   *Telegrams*—**Brownotel, London.**

30

LONDON—PARIS
(Daily unless otherwise stated)
AIR FRANCE

Route 476

Miles	Airports of		W					
0	LONDON ... ...dep		9 0	13 30				
224	PARIS ... ... arr		10 30	15 0				

	Airports of		W					
	PARIS ... ...dep		10 30	13 30				
	LONDON ... ... arr		12 0	15 0				

W—On Weekdays only

Distance and Time allowance for conveyance between Airport and Town Terminus

TOWN	AIRPORT	TOWN TERMINUS	Miles	Minutes
LONDON	Croydon	Air France, 52, Haymarket, S.W.1................	13	50
PARIS	Le Bourget	Air France, Place Lafayette	6¾	35

FARES

FROM LONDON	Single £ s. d.	Week-end £ s. d.	Return 15 Days £ s. d.	Return 60 Days £ s. d.	Excess Baggage per Kg (2·2 lbs) d.
To PARIS	4 15 0	6 15 0	7 12 0	8 1 6	6
FROM PARIS	Frs.	Frs.	Frs.	Frs.	Frs.
To LONDON	405	540	650	690	2·50

31

LONDON—PARIS
(Daily)
HILLMAN'S AIRWAYS

Miles	Airports of							
0	ESSEX (Stapleford †) ... ...dep		10 0	13 45				
225	PARIS ... ... arr		12 0	15 45				

	Airports of							
	PARIS ... ...dep		10 0	13 45				
	ESSEX (Stapleford †) ... ... arr		12 0	15 45				

†—Near Abridge.

Distance and Time allowance for conveyance between Airport and Town Terminus

TOWN	AIRPORT	TOWN TERMINUS	Miles	Minutes
LONDON	Essex	Coaching Station, King's Cross, N.1...............	25	60
PARIS	Le Bourget	25 Rue Royale	8	45

FARES

FROM LONDON	Single	Return	Week-end	Day Return	Excess Baggage per lb.
	£ s. d.	£ s. d.	£ s. d.	£ s. d.	d.
To PARIS	3 10 0	5 10 0	4 15 0	4 5 0	3
FROM PARIS	Frs.	Frs.	Frs.	Frs.	Frs.
To LONDON	300	475	400	375	...

AIR FRANCE
Apply B.G. AIR FRANCE, 52, Haymarket, London, S.W.1. Phone: Whitehall 9671. Or all Travel Agents.

Fastest to **87** cities in **29** countries, **4** continents.

32

LONDON—LE TOUQUET
(Service suspended during Winter)
IMPERIAL AIRWAYS

Routes 454a, 454b

Miles	Airports of				Airports of		
0	**LONDON** ... ...dep				**LE TOUQUET** ...dep		
110	**LE TOUQUET** ... arr				**LONDON** ... ... arr		

Distance and Time allowance for conveyance between Airport and Town Terminus

TOWN	AIRPORT	TOWN TERMINUS	Miles	Minutes
LONDON	Croydon	Airway Terminus, Victoria Station, S.W.I.	12	45
LE TOUQUET	Berck	Airway Terminus, Casino Grounds	8	45

FARES

FROM LONDON TO	Single	Return 18 Days	Sunday Excursion	Excess Baggage per Kg (2·2 lbs.)
	£ s. d.	£ s. d.	£ s. d.	s. d.
LE TOUQUET				

33

LONDON—LE TOUQUET—DIEPPE
(Service suspended during Winter)
BANCO

Miles	Airports of				Airports of		
0	**HESTON** ... ...dep				**DIEPPE** ... ...dep		
115	**LE TOUQUET** ... arr				**LE TOUQUET** ...dep		
140	**DIEPPE** § ... ... arr				**HESTON** ... ... arr		

§ For Pourville

Distance and Time allowance for conveyance between Airport and Town Terminus

TOWN	AIRPORT	TOWN TERMINUS	Miles	Minutes
LONDON	Heston	Coach Station, 164, Buckingham Palace Rd., S.W.	13	60 § / 45 ‡
LE TOUQUET	Berck	Le Touquet Casino	8	45 § / 30 ‡
DIEPPE	Dieppe		2½	

§—From Terminus to Airport   ‡—From Airport to Terminus

FARES

FROM LONDON TO	Single	Return	Free Baggage Allowance	Excess Baggage per lb.
	£ s. d.	£ s. d.		s. d.
LE TOUQUET				
DIEPPE				

All times given in the Tables are local times, see page 22
Conveyance between an Airport and the Town Terminus is free unless otherwise indicated
in the Table
The full names and addresses, etc., of the Companies will be found on pages 30 and 31

34

LONDON—PARIS—BASLE—ZÜRICH
(Service suspended during Winter)
IMPERIAL AIRWAYS

Route 451

Miles	Airports of				Airports of		
0	**LONDON** ... ...dep				**ZÜRICH** ... ...dep		
224	**PARIS** ... ... arr				**BASLE** ... ... arr		
	,, ... dep				,, ... dep		
480	**BASLE** ... ... arr				**PARIS** ... ... arr		
	,, ... dep				,, ... dep		
501	**ZÜRICH** ... ... arr				**LONDON** ... ... arr		

Distance and Time allowance for conveyance between Airport and Town Terminus

TOWN	AIRPORT	TOWN TERMINUS	Miles	Minutes
LONDON	Croydon	Airway Terminus, Victoria Station, S.W. 1......	12	45
PARIS	Le Bourget	Airway Terminus, Rue des Italiens	8	45
BASLE	Birsfelden	Luftreisebüro Swissair, Centralbahnplatz (Central Station Square)	2½	30
ZÜRICH	Dübendorf	Hotel Schweizerhof, Bahnhofplatz (Station Square)	7½	40

FARES

FROM LONDON TO	Single	Return 15 Days	Return 60 Days	Excess Baggage per Kg (2·2 lbs.)
	£ s. d.	£ s. d.	£ s. d.	s. d.
BASLE				
ZÜRICH				

35

LONDON—DEAUVILLE
(Service suspended during Winter)
BANCO

Miles	Airports of				Airports of		
0	**HESTON** ... ...dep				**DEAUVILLE** ... ...dep		
150	**DEAUVILLE** ... ... arr				**HESTON** ... ... arr		

Distance and Time allowance for conveyance between Airport and Town Terminus

TOWN	AIRPORT	TOWN TERMINUS	Miles	Minutes
LONDON	Heston	Coach Station, 164, Buckingham Palace Rd., S.W.	13	60§ / 45‡
DEAUVILLE	St. Gatien	Deauville Casino	5	45§ / 30‡

§—From Terminus to Airport   ‡—From Airport to Terminus

FARES

FROM LONDON TO	Single	Return	Excess Baggage per lb.
	£ s. d.	£ s. d.	s. d.
DEAUVILLE			

36 LONDON—BRUSSELS—COLOGNE
(Weekdays only)
IMPERIAL AIRWAYS; SABENA
Routes, 501, 452

Miles	Airports of		*	S		Airports of		S	‡
0	**LONDON**	...dep	8 45	12 45		**COLOGNE**	...dep	...	14 50
199	**BRUSSELS**	... arr	10 45	14 45		**BRUSSELS**	... arr	...	15 5
	,,	...dep	11 0	...		,,	...dep	9 20	15§20
312½	**COLOGNE**	... arr	13 0	...		**LONDON**	... arr	11 30	17 30

*—Operated by Imperial Airways on Mon., Wed., and Fri., and by Sabena on Tues., Thurs., and Sat.
‡—Leave Brussels at 15 15 for Antwerp—see Table 37   S—Operated by Sabena   ‡ Operated by
Sabena on Mon., Wed., and Fri., and by Imperial Airways on Tues., Thurs., and Sat.

Distance and Time allowance for conveyance between Airport and Town Terminus

TOWN	AIRPORT	TOWN TERMINUS	Miles	Minutes
LONDON	Croydon	Airway Terminus, Victoria Station, S.W. 1......	12	45
BRUSSELS	Haren	Sabena, Boulevard Adolphe Max 32/34............	3¾	45
COLOGNE	Butzweiler Hof ...	Domhotel, Domhof	4¼	30

FARES.

FROM LONDON	Single	Return 15 Days	Return 60 Days	Excess Baggage per Kg (2·2 lbs.)
	£ s. d.	£ s. d.	£ s. d.	s. d.
To BRUSSELS	4 0 0	6 8 0	6 16 0	0 9
COLOGNE	5 10 0	8 16 0	9 7 0	1 1
FROM COLOGNE	RM.	RM.	RM.	RM.
To BRUSSELS	25	40	42·50	0·25
LONDON ... ..., ...	75	120	127·50	0·75

37 LONDON—BRUSSELS—ANTWERP
(Weekdays only)
IMPERIAL AIRWAYS; SABENA
Route 505

Miles	Airports of		‡	S	S		Airports of		S	S	
0	**LONDON**	...dep	8 45	...	12 45		**ANTWERP**	...dep	8 45	14 45	...
202	**BRUSSELS**	... arr	10 45	\...	14 45		**BRUSSELS**	... arr	9 5	15 5	...
	,,	...dep	...	10 55	15 15		,,	...dep	9 20	...	15‡20
227	**ANTWERP**	... arr	...	11 15	15 35		**LONDON**	... arr	11 30	...	17 30

S—Operated by Sabena.   ‡—See Table 36 for service to and from Cologne

Distance and Time allowance for conveyance between Airport and Town Terminus

TOWN	AIRPORT	TOWN TERMINUS	Miles	Minutes
LONDON	Croydon	Airway Terminus, Victoria Station, S.W. 1......	12	45
BRUSSELS	Haren	Sabena, Boulevard Adolphe Max 32/34............	3¾	45
ANTWERP	Deurne	Sabena Office, Zentralbahnhof (Central Station)	2½	30

FARES

FROM LONDON	Single	Return 15 Days	Return 60 Days	Excess Baggage per Kg (2·2 lbs.)
	£ s. d.	£ s. d.	£ s. d.	s. d.
To BRUSSELS or ANTWERP	4 0 0	6 8 0	6 16 0	0 9
FROM ANTWERP	B. Frs.	B. Frs.	B. Frs.	B. Frs.
To BRUSSELS	60	96	...	1·0
LONDON §	480	768	816	4·80

§ The fares to London apply from Antwerp or Brussels.

40

LONDON—(Paris)—BRUSSELS—HAMBURG—COPENHAGEN—
(Gothenburg—Oslo)—MALMÖ
(Service suspended during Winter)
SABENA

Miles	Airports of				Airports of	
0	**LONDON** ... ...dep				**MALMÖ** ... ...dep	
202	**BRUSSELS** ... ...arr				**COPENHAGEN** ...arr	
	Paris (Table 70) ...dep				Oslo (Table 106) ...dep	
202	**BRUSSELS** ... ...dep				Gothenburg	
500	**HAMBURG** ... ...arr				(Table 106) ... ...dep	
	,, ...dep				**COPENHAGEN** ...dep	
680	**COPENHAGEN** ...arr				**HAMBURG** ... ...arr	
	Gothenburg				,, ...dep	
821	(Table 106) ... ...arr				**BRUSSELS** ... ...arr	
980	Oslo (Table 106) ...arr				Paris (Table 70) ...arr	
680	**COPENHAGEN** ...dep				**BRUSSELS** ... ...arr	
697	**MALMÖ** ... ...arr				**LONDON** ... ...arr	

Distance and Time allowance for conveyance between Airport and Town Terminus

TOWN	AIRPORT	TOWN TERMINUS	Miles	Minutes
LONDON	Croydon	Airway Terminus, Victoria Station, S.W. 1......	12	45
BRUSSELS	Haren	Sabena, Boulevard Adolphe Max 32/34	3¾	45
HAMBURG	Fuhlsbüttel	Hauptbahnhof (Central Station), Hapag Reise-		
		büro	7½	40
COPENHAGEN	Kastrup..............	Passagebüro der D.D.L. Meldahlsgade 5	6¼	45
MALMÖ	Bultofta...............	Zentralbahnhof (Central Station)	2	30

FARES

FROM LONDON TO	Single	Return 15 Days	Return 60 Days	Excess Baggage per Kg (2·2 lbs.)
	£ s. d.	£ s. d.	£ s. d.	s. d.
BRUSSELS				
HAMBURG				
COPENHAGEN				
GOTHENBURG				
OSLO				
MALMÖ				

41 LONDON—BRUSSELS—(Düsseldorf—Essen—Dortmund—Berlin)
(Weekdays only)
SABENA
Routes 505, 510

Miles	Airports of				Airports of			
0	**LONDON** ... ...dep	12 45			**Berlin** (*Table 82*) ...dep	11 30		
202	**BRUSSELS** ... ...arr	14 45			**Dortmund** (*Tble 82*) dep	14 15		
307½	**Düsseldorf** (*Table 82*) arr				**Essen** (*Table 82*) ...dep	14 40		
326	**Essen** (*Table 82*) ... arr		B		**Düsseldorf** (*Tble 82*) dep	15 5		
347	**Dortmund** (*Table 82*) arr				**BRUSSELS** ... ...dep	15 20		
608	**Berlin** (*Table 82*) ... arr				**LONDON** ... ... arr	17 30		

B—These connections from London are suspended during Winter

Distance and Time allowance for conveyance between Airport and Town Terminus

TOWN	AIRPORT	TOWN TERMINUS	Miles	Minutes
LONDON	Croydon	Airway Terminus, Victoria Station, S.W. 1	12	45
BRUSSELS	Haren	Sabena, Boulevard Adolphe Max 32/34............	3¾	45

FARES

FROM LONDON	Single	Return 15 Days	Return 60 Days	Excess Baggage per Kg (2·2 lbs.)
	£ s. d.	£ s. d.	£ s. d.	s. d.
To BRUSSELS ... .., ...	4 0 0	6 8 0	6 16 0	0 9
DÜSSELDORF	...	...	...	...
ESSEN	...	...	...	...
DORTMUND	...	...	...	...
BERLIN	...	...	...	...
FROM BERLIN	RM.	RM.	RM.	RM.
To DORTMUND	50	...	85	0·50
ESSEN	55	...	93·50	0·55
DÜSSELDORF	60	...	102	0·60
BRUSSELS	85	...	144·50	0·85
LONDON	140	...	238	1·40

42 LONDON—OSTEND—KNOCKE-LE ZOUTE
(Service suspended during Winter)
SABENA
Route 504

Miles	Airports of				Airports of			
0	**LONDON** ...dep				**KNOCKE—**			
143	**OSTEND** ... arr				**LE ZOUTE**... dep			
	,, ...dep				**OSTEND**... ... arr			
	KNOCKE—				,, ...dep			
166	**LE ZOUTE**... arr				**LONDON** ... arr			

Distance and Time allowance for conveyance between Airport and Town Terminus

TOWN	AIRPORT	TOWN TERMINUS	Miles	Minutes
LONDON	Croydon	Airway Terminus, Victoria Station, S.W. 1	12	45
OSTEND	Steene	Place Marie José (Tramway Waiting Room)......	3	30
KNOCKE	Zoute	Place Albert	2½	30

FARES

FROM LONDON TO	Single	Return 15 Days	Return 60 Days	Excess Baggage per Kg (2·2 lbs.)
	£ s. d.	£ s. d.	£ s. d.	s. d.
OSTEND				
KNOCKE-LE ZOUTE ...				

All times given in the Tables are local times, see page 22
Conveyance between an Airport and the Town Terminus is free unless otherwise indicated in the Table
The full names and addresses, etc., of the Companies will be found on pages 30 and 31

43 LONDON—AMSTERDAM—HANOVER—BERLIN
(Daily unless otherwise stated)
D.L.H.
Route

Miles	Airports of			**W**		Airports of			**W**	
0	**LONDON**	...dep	10 0	...		**BERLIN**	...dep	8 30	...	
252	**AMSTERDAM** ...	...arr	12 15	...		**HANOVER** ...	...arr	9 45	...	
	,, ...	...dep	...	12 30		,, ...	...dep	10 0	...	
461¼	**HANOVER** ...	...arr	...	14 50		**AMSTERDAM** ...	...arr	11 0	...	
	,, ...	...dep	...	15 5		,, ...	...dep	...	11 15	
619¼	**BERLIN**	...arr	...	16 20		**LONDON** ...	...arr	...	12 50	

W—Not on Sundays

Distance and Time allowance for conveyance between Airport and Town Terminus

TOWN	AIRPORT	TOWN TERMINUS	Miles	Minutes
LONDON	Croydon	Airway Terminus, Victoria Station, S.W. 1	12	45
AMSTERDAM	Schiphol	K.L.M. Office, Leidscheplein............................	8	40
HANOVER	Stader Chaussee...	Central Stn., Ernst August Platz—On application	4⅛	25
BERLIN.................	Tempelhof	Linden/Friedrichstrasse—No Special Conveyance	3	—

FARES

FROM LONDON	Single	Return 15 Days	Return 60 Days	Excess Baggage per Kg (2·2 lbs.)
	£ s. d.	£ s. d.	£ s. d.	s. d.
To AMSTERDAM...	5 10 0	...	9 7 0	1 1
HANOVER	8 7 6	...	14 4 9	1 8
BERLIN	10 10 0	...	17 17 0	2 1
FROM BERLIN	RM.	RM.	RM.	RM.
To HANOVER	30	...	51	0·30
AMSTERDAM...	70	...	119	0·70
LONDON	140	...	238	1·40

44 LONDON—AMSTERDAM—BERLIN
(Weekdays only)
K.L.M.
Route 515

Miles	Airports of				Airports of			
0	**LONDON**	...dep	...		**BERLIN**	...dep	14 0	
265	**AMSTERDAM** ...	...arr	...		**AMSTERDAM** ...	...arr	16 15	
	,, ...	...dep	8 0		,, ...	...dep	...	
627	**BERLIN**	...arr	11 20		**LONDON** ...	...arr	...	

Distance and Time allowance for conveyance between Airport and Town Terminus

TOWN	AIRPORT	TOWN TERMINUS	Miles	Minutes
LONDON	Croydon	Hotel Victoria, Northumberland Avenue, W.C. 2	13	50
AMSTERDAM	Schiphol	K.L.M. Office, Leidscheplein............................	8	40
BERLIN.................	Tempelhof	Linden/Friedrichstrasse—No Special Conveyance	3	—

FARES

FROM AMSTERDAM	Single	Return 15 Days	Return 60 Days	Excess Baggage per Kg (2·2 lbs.)
	Fl.	Fl.	Fl.	Fl.
To BERLIN	42	...	71·40	0·40
FROM BERLIN	RM.	RM.	RM.	RM.
To AMSTERDAM...	70	...	119	0·70
LONDON	140	...	238	1·40

45

LONDON—AMSTERDAM—(Hamburg—Copenhagen—Malmö)
(Daily)
K.L.M.; A.B.A.

Routes 516, 511, 517

Miles	Airports of				Airports of		
0	**LONDON** ... ...dep	8 30			**Malmö** (Table 91)...dep	8 30	
265	**AMSTERDAM** ... ... arr	11 5			**Copenhagen**		
507	**Hamburg** (Table 91) arr	14 5			(Table 86) ... ...dep	9 0	
687	**Copenhagen** (Table86)arr	15 35			**Hamburg** (Table 91) dep	10 10	
706	**Malmö** (Table 91) ... arr	15 50			**AMSTERDAM** ... dep	12‡10	
					LONDON ... ... arr	14 15	

‡—See Table 46 for times at Rotterdam

Distance and Time allowance for conveyance between Airport and Town Terminus

TOWN	AIRPORT	TOWN TERMINUS	Miles	Minutes
LONDON	Croydon	Hotel Victoria, Northumberland Avenue, W.C. 2	13	50
AMSTERDAM	Schiphol	K.L.M. Office, Leidscheplein	8	40

FARES

FROM LONDON	Single	Return 15 Days	Return 60 Days	Excess Baggage per Kg (2·2 lbs.)
	£ s. d.	£ s. d.	£ s. d.	s. d.
To AMSTERDAM...	5 10 0	...	9 7 0	1 1
HAMBURG	8 15 0	...	14 17 6	1 2
COPENHAGEN	12 10 0	...	21 5 0	1 7
MALMÖ	13 0 0	...	22 2 0	1 7
FROM MALMÖ	S. Kr.	S. Kr.	S. Kr.	S. Kr.
To LONDON	225	...	382·50	1

46

LONDON—ROTTERDAM—AMSTERDAM
(Daily unless otherwise stated)
K.L.M.

Routes 512, 516

Miles	Airports of		**W**		Airports of		**W**	
0	**LONDON** ... ...dep	8 30	13 15		**AMSTERDAM** ...dep	8 30	12 10	
229	**ROTTERDAM** ... ... arr	10 30	15 15		**ROTTERDAM** ... arr	8 55	12 35	
	,, ...dep	10 40	15 25		,, ...dep	9 5	12 45	
265	**AMSTERDAM** ... ... arr	11 5	15 50		**LONDON** ... ... arr	10 35	14 15	

W—Not on Sunday

Distance and Time allowance for conveyance between Airport and Town Terminus

TOWN	AIRPORT	TOWN TERMINUS	Miles	Minutes
LONDON	Croydon	Hotel Victoria, Northumberland Avenue, W.C. 2	13	50
ROTTERDAM	Waalhaven	K.L.M Office, Coolsingel 115	4¼	40
AMSTERDAM	Schiphol	K.L.M. Office, Leidscheplein	8	40

FARES

FROM LONDON	Single	Return 15 Days	Return 60 Days	Excess Baggage per Kg (2·2 lbs.)
	£ s. d.	£ s. d.	£ s. d.	s. d.
To ROTTERDAM	5 10 0	...	9 7 0	1 1
AMSTERDAM...	5 10 0	...	9 7 0	1 1
FROM AMSTERDAM	Fl.	Fl.	Fl.	Fl.
To LONDON	42	...	71·40	0·40

47

LIVERPOOL—HULL—AMSTERDAM
(Service suspended during Winter)
K.L.M.

Miles	Airports of				Airports of		
0	**LIVERPOOL** ... ...dep				**AMSTERDAM** ...dep		
114	**HULL** ... ... arr				**HULL**... ... ... arr		
	,, ...dep				,, ...dep		
350	**AMSTERDAM** ... ... arr				**LIVERPOOL** ... ... arr		

Distance and Time allowance for conveyance between Airport and Town Terminus

TOWN	AIRPORT	TOWN TERMINUS	Miles	Minutes
LIVERPOOL............	Speke	Adelphi Hotel	6½	25
HULL	Hedon	Royal Station Hotel	5	20
AMSTERDAM	Schiphol	K.L.M., Office, Leidscheplein	8	40

FARES

FROM LIVERPOOL TO	Single	Return 15 Days	Return 60 Days	Excess Baggage Per Kg (2·2 lbs.)
	£ s. d.	£ s. d.	£ s. d.	s. d.
HULL				
AMSTERDAM				

50 LONDON—GERMANY—AUSTRIA, Etc.—ISTANBUL
(See Tables 36 and 121)
(See local Tables for names of Airports, etc.)

Miles	Airports of	1M	D
0	LONDON ... ...dep	8 45	
199	BRUSSELS ... ...arr	10 45	
	" ...dep	11 0	
312	COLOGNE ... ...arr	13 0	
612	Berlin (Table 63) ... arr	15 35	
312	COLOGNE ... ...dep	...	13 10
543	HALLE/LEIPZIG ...arr	...	16 5
592	Chemnitz (Table 156) arr	...	...
634	Karlsbad (Table 156) arr	...	...
653	Marienbad (Table156) arr	...	...
543	HALLE/LEIPZIG ...dep	...	...
613	DRESDEN ... ...arr	...	...
757	Breslau (Table) ... arr		
613	DRESDEN ... ...dep		
688	PRAGUE ... ...arr		
809	Brno (Table 203) ... arr		
	Paris (Table 60) ...dep		
688	PRAGUE ... ...dep		
862	VIENNA ... ...arr		
	" ... ...dep		
1003	BUDAPEST ... ...arr		
	" ... ...dep		
1207	BELGRADE ... ...arr		
1413	Sofia (Table 60) ... arr		
1616	Salonica (Table 107) arr		
1846	Athens (Table 232) ... arr		
1207	BELGRADE ... ...dep		
1500	BUCHAREST ... ...arr		
	" ... ...dep		
	ISTANBUL ... ...arr		

Airports of		
ISTANBUL ... ...dep		
BUCHAREST ... ...arr		
" ... ...dep		
BELGRADE ... ...arr		
Athens (Table 232) dep		
Salonica (Table 107) dep		
Sofia (Table 60) ...dep		
BELGRADE ... ...dep		
BUDAPEST ... ...arr		
" ... ...dep		
VIENNA ... ...arr		
" ... ...dep		
PRAGUE ... ...arr		
Paris (Table 60) ... dep		
Brno (Table 203) ...dep		
PRAGUE ... ...dep		
DRESDEN ... ...arr		
Breslau (Table)... dep		
DRESDEN ... ...dep		
HALLE/LEIPZIG ... arr	D	
Marienbad (Tble156)dep		
Karlsbad (Table156) dep		
Chemnitz (Tble 156) dep		
HALLE/LEIPZIG ... dep	11 20	
COLOGNE ... ... arr	14 15	
Berlin (Table 63) ...dep	...	11 35
COLOGNE ... ... dep	...	14S50
BRUSSELS ... ... arr	...	15 5
" ... ...dep	...	15 20
LONDON ... ...arr	...	17 30

D Operated by D.L.H. on weekdays only. **1M** Operated by 'Imperial Airways' on Mon., Wed. and Fri., and by 'Sabena' on Tues., Thurs. and Sat. **S** Operated by 'Sabena' on Mon., Wed. and Fri., and by 'Imperial Airways' on Tues., Thurs. and Sat.

¶ FARES
¶ These Fares are subject to modification according to the fluctuation in Exchange Rates.

FROM LONDON TO	Single	Return 15 Days	Return 60 Days
	£ s. d.	£ s. d.	£ s. d.
BRUSSELS	4 0 0	6 8 0	6 16 0
COLOGNE	5 10 0	8 16 0	9 7 0
BERLIN	10 10 0	...	17 17 0
HALLE/LEIPZIG	9 2 11	14 19 11	15 10 11
CHEMNITZ			
KARLSBAD	...	...	...
MARIENBAD...	...	...	...
DRESDEN	...	...	...
BRESLAU	...	...	...
PRAGUE	...	...	...
BRNO	...	...	...
VIENNA	...	...	...
BUDAPEST	...	...	...
BELGRADE	...	...	...
SOFIA	...	...	...
SALONICA	...	...	...
ATHENS...	...	...	...
BUCHAREST	...	...	...
ISTANBUL	...	...	...

51

LONDON—BRUSSELS—GERMANY—ITALY.
(See Tables 36, 138, 130, and 103)
(See local Tables for names of Airports, etc.)

Miles	Airports of		IM	D	A	Airports of		A	D	
0	LONDON ... ...dep		8 45			ROME ... ...dep		8 0		
199	BRUSSELS ... ... arr		10 45			VENICE ... ... arr		10 15		
	,, ...dep		11 0			Pola (Table 183) ...dep		8 45		
313	COLOGNE ... ... arr		13 0			Trieste (Table 182) dep		8 55		
	,, ...dep		...	10 55		VENICE ... ...dep		10 45		
406	FRANKFORT-o-M. ... arr		...	11 55		MUNICH ... ... arr		12 45		
507	Stuttgart (Table 132).. arr		...	...		,, ...dep		...	10 15	
406	FRANKFORT-o-M. ...dep			12 10		NÜRNBERG ... ... arr		...	11 20	
535	NÜRNBERG ... ... arr			13 35		,, ...dep		...	11 35	
	,, ...dep			13 50		FRANKFORT-o-M. arr		...	13 0	
628	MUNICH ... ... arr			14 55		Stuttgart (Table 132) dp		...	...	
	,, ...dep			...	11 20	FRANKFORT-o-M. dep			13 15	
903	VENICE ... ... arr			...	13 20	COLOGNE ... ... arr			14 15	S
	Trieste (Table 182) ... arr				15 0	,, ...dep			...	14 50
	Pola (Table 183) ... arr				15 20	BRUSSELS ... ... arr			...	15 5
903	VENICE ... ...dep			...	13 50	,, ...dep			...	15 20
1159	ROME ... ... arr			...	16 5	LONDON ... ... arr			...	17 30

A Operated by D.L.H. and A.L.S.A. on weekdays only.   **D** Operated by D.L.H. on weekdays only.

IM Operated by 'Imperial Airways' on Mon., Wed. and Fri., and by 'Sabena' on Tues., Thurs. and Sat.

S Operated by 'Sabena' on Mon., Wed. and Fri., and by 'Imperial Airways' on Tues., Thurs. and Sat.

FARES

FROM LONDON TO	Single	Return 15 Days	Return 60 Days
	£ s. d.	£ s. d.	£ s. d.
BRUSSELS	4 0 0	6 8 0	6 16 0
COLOGNE	5 10 0	8 16 0	9 7 0
FRANKFORT.o.M.	7 9 0	12 2 4	12 13 4
STUTTGART	9 4 7	15 2 10	15 13 10
NÜRNBERG	9 8 0	15 8 8	15 19 8
MUNICH	11 3 7	18 9 2	19 0 2
VENICE	15 16 10	26 7 8	26 18 8
TRIESTE	17 3 11	28 13 8	29 4 8
BRIONI	17 9 3	29 2 9	29 13 9
ROME	18 16 2	31 8 7	31 19 7

All times given in the Tables are local times, see page 22
Conveyance between an Airport and the Town Terminus is free unless otherwise indicated in the Table
The full names and addresses, etc., of the Companies will be found on pages 30 and 31
56

53

LONDON—BRUSSELS—GERMANY

(See Tables 36, 138, and 142)

(See local Tables for names of Airports, etc.)

Miles	Airports of		IM	D		Airports of		D	
0	LONDON ... ...dep		8 45	...		CONSTANCE ...dep		...	...
199	BRUSSELS ... ... arr		10 45	...		FREIBURG ... ... arr		...	...
	,, ...dep		11 0	...		,, ...dep		...	...
300	COLOGNE ... ... arr		13 0	...		BADEN-BADEN ... arr		...	...
	,, ...dep		...	10 55		,, ...dep		...	...
392	FRANKFORT.o.M. ... arr		...	11 55		KARLSRUHE ... ... arr		...	...
493	Stuttgart (Table 132) arr		...	...		,, ...dep		11 50	...
392	FRANKFORT.o.M. ...dep		...	12 10		MANNHEIM ... ... arr		12 15	...
436	MANNHEIM ... ... arr		...	12 45		,, ...dep		12 25	...
	,, ...dep		...	12 55		FRANKFORT.o.M. arr		13 0	...
470	KARLSRUHE ... ... arr		...	13 20		Stuttgart (Table 132)dep		...	...
	,, ...dep		...	...		FRANKFORT.o.M. dep		13 15	...
489	BADEN-BADEN ... arr		...	...		COLOGNE ... ... arr		14 15	S
	,, ...dep		...	...		,, ...dep		...	14 50
544	FREIBURG ... ... arr		...	...		BRUSSELS ... ... arr		...	15 5
	,, ...dep		...	...		,, ...dep		...	15 20
609	CONSTANCE ... arr		...	...		LONDON ... ... ar		...	17 30

D Operated by D.L.H. on weekdays only.   **IM** Operated by 'Imperial Airways' on Mon., Wed. and Fri., and by 'Sabena' on Tues., Thurs. and Sat.   **S** Operated by 'Sabena' on Mon., Wed. and Fri. and by 'Imperial Airways' on Tues., Thurs. and Sat.

¶ FARES

¶ **These Fares are subject to modification according to the fluctuation in Exchange Rates**

FROM LONDON TO	Single	Return 15 Days	Return 60 Days
	£ s. d.	£ s. d.	£ s. d.
BRUSSELS	4 0 0	6 8 0	6 16 0
COLOGNE	5 10 0	8 16 0	9 7 0
FRANKFORT.o.M.	7 9 0	12 2 4	12 13 4
STUTTGART	...	...	...
MANNHEIM	8 4 3	13 8 3	13 19 3
KARLSRUHE	9 1 3	14 17 0	15 8 0
BADEN-BADEN	...	...	...
FREIBURG	...	...	...
CONSTANCE	...	...	...

54

LONDON—FRANCE—(Switzerland—Rome)—SPAIN
(See Tables 30; 61; 72; 73; 214; 212 and 215)
Weekdays only unless otherwise stated.
(See local Tables for names of Airports, etc.)

Miles	Airports of	A	A	L
0	LONDON ... ...dep	9 0		
224	PARIS ... ... arr	10 30		
514	Lausanne (Table 62).. arr	...		
224	PARIS ... ...dep	11 0		
500	LYONS ... ... arr	13 10		
571	Geneva (Table 61) ... arr	15 10		
500	LYONS ... ... dep	13 25		
677	MARSEILLES ... ... arr	14 45		
772	Cannes (Table 72) ... arr	15 45		
	Rome (Table 215) ... arr	...		
677	MARSEILLES ... ...dep		5*0	
1002	BARCELONA ... ... arr		8*0	
	„ ... ... dep			9 30
1313	MADRID ... ... arr			12 45
1574	Seville (Table 212) ... arr			16 50

Airports of	S	A	L
Seville (Table 212) dep			7 0
MADRID ... ...dep			10 0
BARCELONA ... arr	§		13 0
„ ... ...dep	7 0		
MARSEILLES ... arr	8 50		
Rome (Table 215) ...dep			
Cannes (Table 72)... dep		8 15	
MARSEILLES ... ...dep		9 15	
LYONS ... ... arr		10 45	
Geneva (Table 61)... dep		10 50	
LYONS ... ...dep		11 0	
PARIS ... ... arr		13 10	
Lausanne (Table 62) dep			...
PARIS ... ...dep		13*30	
LONDON ... ... arr		15*0	

A Operated by 'Air France.'   L Operated by 'L.A.P.E.'   S Operated by 'A.L.S.A.'
* Daily.   § On Monday, Wednesday and Friday.

¶ FARES.

¶ These Fares are subject to modification according to the fluctuation in Exchange Rates.

FROM LONDON TO	Single	Return 15 Days	Return 60 Days
	£ s. d.	£ s. d.	£ s. d.
PARIS	See Table 30	...	...
GENEVA	See Table 61	· ...	...
LAUSANNE	...	...	...
LYONS	8 13 0	13 17 0	14 14 0
CANNES	See Table 61	...	...
MARSEILLES	12 10 0	20 0 0	21 5 0
ROME	20 17 7	32 11 5	35 9 10
BARCELONA	16 3 4	25 5 0	26 10 0
MADRID	20 9 1	32 10 9	33 15 9
SEVILLE	24 0 6	38 12 2	39 17 2

55
LONDON—PARIS—SWITZERLAND—ITALY—MALTA (Tripoli)
(Through Connection beyond Paris suspended during Winter.)
(See local Tables for names of Airports, etc.)

Miles	Airports of			Airports of		
0	**LONDON** ... ...dep			**Tripoli** (Table 175) dep		
224	**PARIS** ... ... arr			**MALTA** ... ...dep		
	,, ...dep			**SYRACUSE** ... ... arr		
480	**BASLE** ... ... arr			,, ...dep		
530	**Berne** (Table 163) ... arr			**NAPLES** ... ... arr		
480	**BASLE** ... ...dep			**Palermo** (Table 177) dep		
502	**ZÜRICH** ... ... arr			**NAPLES** ... ...dep		
	Lucerne (Table)... arr			**ROME** ... ... arr		
	ZÜRICH ... ...dep			,, ...dep		
	MILAN ... ... arr			**MILAN** ... ... arr		
	Turin (Table 174) ... arr			**Turin** (Table 174)...dep		
	MILAN ... ...dep			**MILAN** ... ...dep		
	ROME ... ... arr			**ZÜRICH** ... ... arr		
	,, ...dep			**Lucerne** (Table)..dep		
	NAPLES ... ... arr			**ZÜRICH** ... ...dep		
	Palermo (Table 177) arr			**BASLE** ... ... arr		
	NAPLES ... ...dep			**Berne** (Table 163)...dep		
	SYRACUSE... ... ... arr			**BASLE** ... ...dep		
	,, ...dep			**PARIS** ... ... arr		
	MALTA ... ... arr			,, ...dep		
	Tripoli (Table 175)... arr			**LONDON** ... ... arr		

FARES

FROM LONDON TO	Single	Return 15 days	Return 60 Days
	£ s. d.	£ s. d.	£ s. d.
PARIS	See Tables 27, 30	...	...
BASLE	...	...	...
BERNE	...	...	...
ZÜRICH	...	...	...
LUCERNE	...	...	...
MILAN	...	...	...
TURIN	...	...	...
ROME	...	...	...
NAPLES	...	...	...
PALERMO	...	...	...
SYRACUSE	...	...	...
MALTA	...	...	...
TRIPOLI	...	...	...

56

LONDON—(Hull)—AMSTERDAM—GERMANY—(Riga)— RUSSIA (U.S.S.R.) Daily unless otherwise stated
(See Tables 43, 46 and 112)

(See local Tables for names of Airports, etc.)

Miles	Airports of	K	D	T	Airports of	T	D	K
0	LONDON ... ...dep	8 30	10‡ 0	...	MOSCOW ... ...dep	9 0	...	...
260	AMSTERDAM ... ... arr	11 5	12‡15	...	WELIKIJE LUKI ... arr	11 30	...	...
	Hull (Table 47)... ...dep		...	...	... ...dep	12 0	...	...
260	AMSTERDAM ... ...dep		12 30	...	KAUNAS ... ,, ... arr	12 35	...	...
622	BERLIN ... ... arr		16 20	...	,, ...dep	12 55	...	...
	,, ...dep		...	7 0	KÖNIGSBERG ... arr	14 15	...	...
876	DANZIG ... ... arr		...	9 15	Leningrad (Tab.162)dep		...	...
	,, ...dep		...	9 30	Tallinn (Table 162) dep		...	...
963	KÖNIGSBERG ... arr		...	10 20	Riga (Table 162) ...dep		...	...
1192	Riga (Table 162) ... arr		...	...	KÖNIGSBERG ... dep	14 45	...	...
1391	Tallinn (Table 162)... arr		...	...	DANZIG ... ... arr	15 40	...	...
	Leningrad (Table 162) arr		...	...	,, ...dep	16 0	...	...
963	KÖNIGSBERG ... dep		...	10 45	BERLIN ... ... arr	18 15	...	...
1101	KAUNAS ... ... arr		...	12 5	,, ...dep	...	8 30	...
	,, ...dep		...	12 25	AMSTERDAM ... arr	...	11 0	
1608	WELIKIJE LUKI ... arr		...	17 0	Hull (Table 47) ... arr	...	...	
	,, ...dep		...	17 20	AMSTERDAM ... ...dep	...	11‡15	12 10
1887	MOSCOW ,, ... arr		...	19 50	LONDON ... ... arr	...	12‡50	14 15

‡—On Weekdays only D—Operated by D.L.H. K—Operated by K.L.M. T—Operated by DERULUFT

¶ FARES

¶ These fares are subject to modification according to the fluctuation in Exchange Rates

FROM LONDON TO	Single	Return 60 Days
	£ s. d.	£ s. d.
AMSTERDAM	5 10 0	9 7 0
BERLIN	10 10 0	17 17 0
DANZIG	14 14 9	25 1 1
KÖNIGSBERG	15 11 9	26 9 10
RIGA	...	...
TALLINN	. ...	...
LENINGRAD...		
KAUNAS	17 2 3	28 18 5
WELIKIJE LUKI	21 10 4	36 11 7
MOSCOW	25 15 1	43 15 10

57

LONDON—AMSTERDAM—(Copenhagen)—GERMANY—POLAND
(See Tables 43, 46 and 100). Daily unless otherwise stated
(See local Tables for names of Airports, etc.)

Miles	Airports of	K	D	L	Airports of	L	D	K
0	**LONDON** ... ...dep	8 30	10 ‡ 0	...	**WARSAW** ... ...dep	8 10	...	...
260	**AMSTERDAM** ... ...arr	11 5	12‡15	...	**POSEN** ... ...arr	9 45	...	...
502	Hamburg (Table 91). arr	14 5	...	...	,, ...dep	10 0	...	...
682	Copenhagen				**BERLIN** .... arr	11 15	...	...
	(Table 86)... ... arr	15 35	...	...	Breslau (Table 101) dep	...	..	...
260	**AMSTERDAM** ... ...dep	...	12 30	...	**BERLIN** ... ...dep	...	8 30	...
622	**BERLIN** ... ...arr	...	16 20	...	**AMSTERDAM** ... arr	...	11 0	...
804	Breslau (Table 101)... arr	...	...	...	Copenhagen			
622	**BERLIN** ... ...dep	...	...	12 15	(Table 86) ... ...dep	...	...	9 0
743	**POSEN** ... ...arr	...	...	13 30	Hamburg (Table 91)dep	...	...	10 10
	,, ...dep	...	...	13 50	**AMSTERDAM** ...dep	...	11‡15	12 10
939	**WARSAW** ... ...arr	...	...	15 20	**LONDON** ... ... arr	...	12‡50	14 15

L—Operated by ' LOT '   K—Operated by K.L.M. and A.B.A.   D—Operated by D.L.H.
‡—On Weekdays only

¶ FARES

¶ These fares are subject to modification according to the fluctuation in Exchange Rates

FROM LONDON TO	Single	Return 60 Days
	£ s. d.	£ s. d.
AMSTERDAM	5 10 0	9 7 0
HAMBURG	8 15 0	14 17 6
COPENHAGEN	12 10 0	21 5 0
BERLIN	10 10 0	17 17 0
BRESLAU	......	......
POSEN	12 17 6	21 17 8
WARSAW	14 14 9	25 1 1

58

(Belfast)—LIVERPOOL—HULL—AMSTERDAM—(Paris, Berlin)—
COPENHAGEN
(Service suspended during Winter)
(See local Tables for names of Airports, etc.)

Miles	Airports of			Airports of		
	Belfast (Table 25) ...dep			**Malmö** (Table 86)... dep		
	Isle of Man (Table 25) dep			**COPENHAGEN** ...dep		
	LIVERPOOL ... ...dep			**AMSTERDAM** ... arr		
	HULL ... ... arr			**Chemnitz** (Tab. 110) dep		
	,, ... dep			**Dresden** (Table 110)dep		
	AMSTERDAM ... ... arr			**Berlin** (Table 83) ...dep		
	Rotterdam (Table 66).arr			**Hanover** (Table 83). dep		
	Brussels (Table 70)... arr			**Paris** (Table 66) ...dep		
	Paris (Table 66) ... arr			**Brussels** (Table 70).. dep		
	Hanover (Table 83)... arr			**Rotterdam** (Tab. 66)dep		
	Berlin (Table 83) ... arr			**AMSTERDAM** ...dep		
	Dresden (Table 110).. arr			**HULL**... ... ... arr		
	Chemnitz (Table 110) arr			,, ...dep		
	AMSTERDAM ... ...dep			**LIVERPOOL** ... ... arr		
	COPENHAGEN ... arr			**Isle of Man** (Table 25)arr		
	Malmö (Table 86) ... arr			**Belfast** (Table 25)... arr		

All times given in the Tables are local times, see page 22
Conveyance between an Airport and the Town Terminus is free unless otherwise indicated in the Table
The full names and addresses, etc., of the Companies will be found on pages 30 and 31

60   PARIS—VIENNA—CENTRAL EUROPE—ISTANBUL
(Weekdays only unless otherwise stated)
'Fleche d'Orient'—AIR FRANCE

Route 471

Miles	Airports of		M	T
0	PARIS ... ... dep		...	7 15
250	STRASBOURG ... ... arr	On Mon., Wed., & Fri.	...	9 30
	" ... dep		...	9 40
412	NÜRNBERG ... ... arr		...	12 10
	" ... dep		...	12 20
581	PRAGUE ... ... arr		...	13 55
581	Prague ... ... dep	10 15	...	
910	Warsaw ... ... arr	13 45		
581	PRAGUE ... ... dep	...	14 5	
754	VIENNA ... ... arr	...	15 45	
	" ... dep	8 0	...	
895	BUDAPEST ... ... arr	9 25	...	
	" ... dep	9 35	...	
1099	BELGRADE... ... ... arr	11 40	...	
1099	Belgrade ... ... dep	...	...	
1305	Sofia ... ... arr	...	...	
1099	BELGRADE... ... dep	11 50	...	
1393	BUCHAREST ... ... arr	15 50	...	
...	" ... dep	...	...	
...	ISTANBUL... ... ... arr	...	...	

(M column: On Tues. & Sat. — T column: On Tues., Thurs., & Sat.)

Airports of		M	T
ISTANBUL ... ... dep		...	...
BUCHAREST ... ... arr		...	...
" ... dep		...	9 45
BELGRADE ... ... arr		...	11 45
Sofia ... ... dep		...	...
Belgrade ... ... arr		...	...
BELGRADE ... ... dep	On Mon., Wed. & Fri.	...	11 55
BUDAPEST ... ... arr		...	14 0
" ... dep		...	14 10
VIENNA ... ... arr		...	15 35
" ... dep		8 15	...
PRAGUE ... ... arr		9 55	...
Warsaw ... ... dep		6 20	...
Prague ... ... arr		9 50	...
PRAGUE ... ... dep		10 10	...
NÜRNBERG ... ... arr		11 45	...
" ... dep		11 55	...
STRASBOURG ... arr		12 25	...
" ... dep		12 35	...
PARIS " ... ... arr		14 55	...

(T column: On Tues., Thurs. and Sat.)

Distance and Time allowance for conveyance between Airport and Town Terminus

TOWN	AIRPORT	TOWN TERMINUS	Miles	Minutes
PARIS	Le Bourget	Air France, Place Lafayette	6¾	35
STRASBOURG	Polygone	Grand Hotel Maison Rouge, Place Kléber	5¼	25
NÜRNBERG	Nürnberg	Grand Hotel and Württemburger Hof	2⅔	40
PRAGUE	Kbely	6 Narodni Trida	10½	45
WARSAW	Okecie	Al. Jerozolimska 35	5	50
VIENNA	Aspern	Kärntnerring 7	9¼	45
BUDAPEST	Matyasfold	Vorosmarty Ter 2	6¼	50
BELGRADE	Beograd (Zemun)..	36 Rue Kralja Petra§	9¼	45§
SOFIA	Bojourichte	5 Bd Dondoukoff	—	35
BUCHAREST	Banéasa	2 Rue Clémenceau	2½	50
ISTANBUL	Yechil Keuvy	Hotel Pera Palace	11¼	70

§—Motorboat from Belgrade to Zemun, thence Car to Airport

FARES

FROM PARIS	Single Francs	Return 15 Days Francs	Return 60 Days Francs	Excess Baggage per Kg (2·2 lbs) Francs
To STRASBOURG	320	...	544	3·20*
NÜRNBERG	620	...	1,054	6·20*
PRAGUE	935	...	1,590	9·35*
WARSAW	1,155	...	1,963·50	11·55*
VIENNA	1,050	...	1,785	10·50*
BUDAPEST	1,190	...	2,023	11·90*
BELGRADE	1,770	...	3,009	17·70*
SOFIA	2,100	...	3,570	21 *
BUCHAREST	2,240	...	3,808	22·40*
ISTANBUL	2,750	...	4,675	27·50*
FROM ISTANBUL	Turk. £	Turk. £	Turk. £	Turk. £
To BUCHAREST	42·95	...	73·00	0·45*
PARIS	229·35	...	391	2·30*

* After first 15 Kgs., half above rate is charged

61 (London)—PARIS—LYONS—(Marseilles—Cannes)—GENEVA
(Weekdays only)
AIR FRANCE

Routes 477, 477b

Miles	Airports of				Airports of			
	London (Table 30) ...dep	9	0		GENEVA ... ...dep	10	50	
0	PARIS ... ...dep	11	0		LYONS ... ...arr	10	40	
276½	LYONS ... ...arr	13	10		Cannes (Table 72)... dep	8	15	
454	Marseilles (Table 72) arr	14	45		Marseilles (Table 72)dep	9	15	
494	Cannes (Table 72) ... arr	15	45		LYONS ... ...dep	11	0	
276½	LYONS ... ...dep	13	30		PARIS ... ...arr	13	10	
347	GENEVA ... ...arr	15	10		London (Table 30)... arr	15	0	

Distance and Time allowance for conveyance between Airport and Town Terminus

TOWN	AIRPORT	TOWN TERMINUS	Miles	Minutes
PARIS	Le Bourget	Air France, Place Lafayette	6¾	35
LYONS	Bron	16 Rue de la Bourse	5¼	40
GENEVA	Cointrin	3 Place des Bergues	2½	30

FARES

FROM LONDON	Single	Week-end	Return 15 Days	Return 60 Days	Excess Baggage per Kg (2·2 lbs.)
	£ s. d.	£ s. d.	£ s. d.	£ s. d.	s. d.
To LYONS	8 13 0	...	...	14 14 0	1 4*
MARSEILLES	12 10 0	19 3 0	20 0 0	21 5 0	2 0*
CANNES	15 0 0	23 3 0	24 0 0	25 10 0	2 6*
GENEVA	9 17 0	14 18 0	15 15 0	16 15 0	1 6*
FROM GENEVA	S. Frs.	S. Frs.	S. Frs.	S. Frs.	S. Frs.
To LYONS	20	...	...	34	0·20*
PARIS	80	...	...	136	0·80*
LONDON	161·50	...	...	274·60	1·30*

* After first 15 Kgs, half above rate is charged.

62 PARIS—GENEVA—(Lausanne)
(Service suspended during Winter)
AIR FRANCE; SWISSAIR; ALPAR—BERN

Routes, 478 478a

Miles	Airports of				Airports of			
0	PARIS ... ...dep				GENEVA ... ...dep			
253½	GENEVA ... ...arr				PARIS ... ... arr			
291	Lausanne (Table 166) arr							

Distance and Time allowance for conveyance between Airport and Town Terminus.

TOWN	AIRPORT	TOWN TERMINUS	Miles	Minutes
PARIS	Le Bourget	Air France, Place Lafayette	6¾	35
GENEVA	Cointrin	3 Place des Bergues	2½	30

FARES

FROM PARIS TO	Single	Return 15 Days	Return 60 Days	Excess Baggage per Kg. (2·2 lbs.)
	Frs.	Frs.	Frs.	Frs.
GENEVA				
LAUSANNE				

MARSEILLES HOTEL DE NOAILLES
LA CANEBIERE.

63

PARIS—COLOGNE—BERLIN
(Weekdays only)
AIR FRANCE; D.L.H.

Route 6

Miles	Airports of					Airports of			
0	**PARIS** ... ...dep	9 40			**BERLIN** ... ...dep	11 35
252	**COLOGNE** ... ... arr	12 45			**COLOGNE** ... ... arr	14 5
	... ... dep	13 5			... ... dep	14 25
552	**BERLIN** ... ... arr	15 35			**PARIS** ... ... arr	15 30

Distance and Time allowance for conveyance between Airport and Town Terminus

TOWN	AIRPORT	TOWN TERMINUS	Miles	Minutes
PARIS	Le Bourget	Place Lafayette (116 rue Lafayette)	6¼	35
COLOGNE	Butzweiler Hof ...	Domhotel, Domhof	4¼	35
BERLIN.................	Tempelhof	Linden/Friedrichstrasse—No Special Conveyance	3	—

FARES

FROM PARIS	Single	Return 15 Days	Return 60 Days	Excess Baggage per Kg (2·2 lbs.)
	Frs.	Frs.	Frs.	Frs.
To COLOGNE	335	...	569·50	3·35*
BERLIN	695	...	1181·50	6·95*
FROM BERLIN	RM.	RM.	RM.	RM.
To COLOGNE	60	...	102	0·60*
PARIS	115	...	195·50	1·15*

* After first 15 Kgs., half above rate is charged

64

PARIS—BORDEAUX—BIARRITZ
(Service suspended during Winter)
AIR SERVICE

Miles	Airports of				Airports of	
0	**PARIS** ... ...dep				**BIARRITZ**... ... ...dep	
311	**BORDEAUX** ... ... arr				**BORDEAUX** ... ... arr	
	... ... dep				... ... dep	
419	**BIARRITZ** ... ... arr				**PARIS** ... ... arr	

Distance and Time allowance for conveyance between Airport and Town Terminus

TOWN	AIRPORT	TOWN TERMINUS	Miles	Minutes
PARIS	Le Bourget	Air France Office, Place Lafayette	4¼	30
BORDEAUX	Teynac...............	Air France Office, Place de La Comedie	8	—
BIARRITZ	Parme	Cassino de Biarritz	1¾	15

FARES

FROM PARIS TO	Single	Return 15 Days	Return 60 Days	Excess Baggage per Kg
	Frs.	Frs.	Frs.	Frs.
BORDEAUX...				
BIARRITZ				

All times given in the Tables are local times, see page 22
Conveyance between an Airport and the Town Terminus is free unless otherwise indicated in the Table
The full names and addresses, etc., of the Companies will be found on pages 30 and 31

65

PARIS—BASLE—ZÜRICH
(Service suspended during Winter)
AIR FRANCE; SWISSAIR

Miles	Airports of						Airports of				
0	**PARIS** ... ...dep						**ZÜRICH** ... ...dep				
256	**BASLE** ... ... arr						**BASLE** ... ... arr				
	,, ...dep						,, ...dep				
278	**ZÜRICH** ... ... arr						**PARIS** ... ... arr				

Distance and Time allowance for conveyance between Airport and Town Terminus

TOWN	AIRPORT	TOWN TERMINUS	Miles	Minutes
PARIS	Le Bourget	Air France, Place Lafayette	6¾	35
BASLE	Birsfelden	Luftreisebüro Swissair, Centralbahnplatz	2½	30
		(Central Station Square)		
ZÜRICH	Dübendorf	Hotel Schweizerhof Bahnhofplatz (Station		
		Square)	7½	40

FARES

FROM PARIS TO	Single	Return 15 Days	Return 60 Days	Excess Baggage per Kg (2·2 lbs.)
	Frs.	Frs.	Frs.	Frs.
BASLE				
ZÜRICH				

66

PARIS—ROTTERDAM—AMSTERDAM
(Daily)
K.L.M.

Miles	Miles	Airports of					Airports of				
0	0	**PARIS** ... ...dep	8 30				**AMSTERDAM** ...dep	12 10			
	238	**ROTTERDAM** arr	§				**ROTTERDAM** ... arr	§			
		,, dep					,, ...dep				
258½	273½	**AMSTERDAM** arr	11 5				**PARIS** ... ... arr	14 5			

§ Lands at Rotterdam if required

Distance and Time allowance for conveyance between Airport and Town Terminus

TOWN	AIRPORT	TOWN TERMINUS	Miles	Minutes
PARIS	Le Bourget	Air France, Place Lafayette	6¾	30
ROTTERDAM	Waalhaven	K.L.M. Office, Coolsingel 115.......................	4¼	40
AMSTERDAM	Schiphol	K.L.M. Office, Leidscheplein	8	40

FARES

FROM PARIS	Single	Return 15 Days	Return 60 Days	Excess Baggage per Kg (2·2 lbs.)
	Frs.	Frs.	Frs.	Frs.
To ROTTERDAM	300	...	510	3
AMSTERDAM...	330	...	561	3·30
FROM AMSTERDAM	Fl.	Fl.	Fl.	Fl.
To PARIS	30	...	51	0 30

All times given in the Tables are local times, see page 22
Conveyance between an Airport and the Town Terminus is ree unless otherwise indicated
in the Table
The full names and addresses, etc., of the Companies will be found on pages 30 and 31.

67 **SAARBRÜCKEN—FRANKFORT/O.M.—ERFURT—HALLE/LEIPZIG—BERLIN**

(Weekdays only)

D.L.H.

Route 11

Miles	Airports of						Airports of				
0	SAARBRÜCKEN	... dep	13	20		BERLIN	... ...	...dep	9	0
97½	FRANKFORT/M	... arr	14	10		HALLE/LEIPZIG	... arr	9	45
	...	... dep	14	25			...dep	10	0
221¼	ERFURT	... arr	15	25		ERFURT	... arr	10	35
	... ...	... dep	15	35			...dep	10	45
280½	HALLE/LEIPZIG	... arr	16	10		FRANKFORT/M	... arr	11	45
		... dep	16	25			...dep	12	0
371½	BERLIN	... arr	17	10		SAARBRÜCKEN	... arr	12	50

Distance and Time allowance for conveyance between Airport and Town Terminus or centre of Town.

TOWN	AIRPORT	TOWN TERMINUS	Miles	Minutes
SAARBRÜCKEN......	St. Arnual	No Special Conveyance—* By Tram...............	2¾	20*
FRANKFORT/M ...	Rebstock	Hauptbahnhof (Central Station)—No Special Conveyance	3	30
ERFURT	Erfurt	Hauptbahnhof (Central Station)...............	3⅝	25
		Halle— Postamt (Post Office), Thielenstrasse	—	40§ 35‡
HALLE/LEIPZIG	Schkeuditz	Hotel Hohenzollernhof, Hindenburgstr 65...	15	45§ 40‡
		Leipzig— Hotel Astoria, Blücherplatz 2	10	35§ 30‡
BERLIN..................	Tempelhof	Linden/Friedrichstrasse—No Special Conveyance	—	3

§—Towards Berlin   ‡—Towards Erfurt

FARES

FROM SAARBRÜCKEN	Single Frs.	Return 15 Days Frs.	Return 60 Days Frs.	Excess Baggage per Kg (2·2 lbs.) Frs.
To FRANKFORT/M	122	...	207·40	1·22
ERFURT	256	...	435·20	2·56
HALLE/LEIPZIG	305	...	518·50	3·05
BERLIN	425	...	722·50	4·25
FROM BERLIN	RM.	RM.	RM.	RM.
To HALLE/LEIPZIG	20	...	34	0·20
ERFURT	28	...	47·60	0·28
FRANKFORT/M	55	...	93·50	0·55
SAARBRÜCKEN	70	...	119	0·70

70

PARIS—BRUSSELS—ANTWERP—ROTTERDAM—AMSTERDAM
(Weekdays only)
AIR FRANCE ; SABENA

Miles	Airports of							Airports of						
0	**PARIS** ... ... dep	10 30	...				**AMSTERDAM**	... dep	8 0	...		
171	**BRUSSELS** ... ... arr	12 0	...				**ROTTERDAM**	... arr	8 25	...		
	,, ... dep	12 15	...				,,	... dep	8 35	...		
199	**ANTWERP** ... ... arr	...	...				**ANTWERP**	... arr	...	...		
	,, ... dep	...	...				,,	... dep	...	8 45		
248½	**ROTTERDAM** ... ... arr	13 20	...				**BRUSSELS**	... arr	9 0	9 5		
	,, ... dep	13 30	...				,,	... dep	9 15	9 15		
286	**AMSTERDAM** ... ... arr	13 55	...				**PARIS**	... arr	10 50	10 50		

Distance and Time allowance for conveyance between Airport and Town Terminus

TOWN	AIRPORT	TOWN TERMINUS	Miles	Minutes
PARIS	Le Bourget	Air France, Place Lafayette	6⅞	35
BRUSSELS	Haren	Sabena, Boulevard Adolphe Max 32/34............	3⅞	45
ANTWERP	Deurne	Sabena Offices, Zentralbahnhof (Central Station)	2½	45
ROTTERDAM	Waalhaven	K.L.M. Office, Coolsingel 115.......................	4¼	40
AMSTERDAM	Schiphol	K.L.M. Office, Leidscheplein	8	40

FARES

FROM PARIS	Single	Week-end	Return 60 Days	Excess Baggage per Kg (2·2 lbs.)
	Frs.	Frs.	Frs.	Frs.
To BRUSSELS	175	225	297·50	1·75*
ANTWERP	...	...	...	...
ROTTERDAM	300	...	510	3·00*
AMSTERDAM...	330	...	561	3·30*
FROM AMSTERDAM	Fl.	Fl.	Fl.	Fl.
To ANTWERP	...	...	...	...
BRUSSELS	15	...	25·50	0·15*
PARIS	30	...	51	0·30*

* After first 15 Kgs., half above rate is charged

72

(London)—LYONS—MARSEILLES—CANNES
(Weekdays only)
AIR FRANCE

Miles	Airports of				Airports of			
	London (Table 61) ...dep	9 0			**CANNES** ... ... dep	8 15	
0	**LYONS**... ... ... dep	13 25			**MARSEILLES** ... ... arr	9 5	
177	**MARSEILLES** ... ... arr	14 45			,, ... dep	9 15	
	,, ... dep	14 55			**LYONS** ... ... arr	10 45	
272	**CANNES** ... ... arr	15 45			London (Table 61) ... arr	15 0	

Distance and Time allowance for conveyance between Airport and Town Terminus

TOWN	AIRPORT	TOWN TERMINUS	Miles	Minutes
LYONS	Bron	16 Rue de la Bourse	5¼	4
MARSEILLES	Marignane	Air France, 1 Rue Papère	17½	0
CANNES	Mandelieu............	Air France, 4 Rue Bivouac Napoléon	3¼	15

FARES

FROM LYONS§	Single	Return 15 Days	Return 60 Days	Excess Baggage per Kg (2·2 lbs.)
	Frs.	Frs.	Frs.	Frs.
To MARSEILLES	350	...	595	3·50*
CANNES	575	...	977·50	5·75*
FROM MARSEILLES				
To CANNES	225	...	382·50	2·25*

* After first 15 Kgs., half above rate is charged § For Fares from London, see Table 61

TOULOUSE—(Marseilles)—BARCELONA—ALICANTE—TANGIER—RABAT—CASABLANCA
(Daily unless otherwise stated)
AIR FRANCE

Miles	Airports of				
0	**TOULOUSE** ...	...dep	6 0
186	**BARCELONA** ...	... arr	8 0
	Marseilles... ...	...dep	5 0
	Barcelona ...	... arr	8 0
186	**BARCELONA** ...	...dep	8 10
484	**ALICANTE** ...	... arr	10 30
	,, ...	...dep	10 50
901	**TANGIER**	... arr	13‡50
	,, ...	...dep	14‡ 5
1041	**RABAT**	... arr	15§15
	,, ...	...dep	15§20
1098	**CASABLANCA** ...	... arr	15 50

Airports of			
CASABLANCA ...	...dep	5 0
RABAT	... arr	5*30
,, ...	... dep	5*35
TANGIER ...	... arr	6 45
,, ...	... dep	7 0
ALICANTE ...	... arr	10 0
,, ...	... dep	10 20
BARCELONA ...	... arr	12 40
Barcelona ...	... dep	12 50
Marseilles ...	... arr	15 35
BARCELONA ...	... dep	12 50
TOULOUSE ...	... arr	14 50

*—Does not land on Mon† and Fri† ‡—Does not land on Sun §—Does not land on Sun, Wed† and Sat†
†—Company provides ground transport between Rabat and Casablanca on these days. Tickets issued at Rabat rates.

Distance and Time allowance for conveyance between Airport and Town Terminus or centre of Town

TOWN	AIRPORT	TOWN TERMINUS	Miles	Minutes
TOULOUSE	Montaudran	No Special Conveyance	1¾	8
BARCELONA	Pratt de Llobregat	Air France, 19 Paseo de Gracia	13¾	40
MARSEILLES	Marignane	Air France 1, Rue Papère	17½	60
ALICANTE	Campo de Aviacion	Paseo de los Martires 26	7¼	25
TANGIER	Tangier	No Special Conveyance	9⅓	25
RABAT	Rabat.................	No Special Conveyance	1⅜	10
CASABLANCA	Casablanca	Air France, 13 Rue Nolly	4¼	30

FARES

FROM TOULOUSE OR MARSEILLES TO	Single	Return 15 Days	Return 60 Days	Excess Baggage per Kg (2·2 lbs.)
	Frs.	Frs.	Frs.	Frs.
BARCELONA	330	...	561	3·30*
ALICANTE	675	...	1,147·50	6·75*
TANGIER	1,200	...	2,040	12·00*
RABAT	1,300	...	2,210	13·00*
CASABLANCA	1,350	...	2,295	13·50*

* After first 15 Kgs., half above rate is charged

All times given in the Tables are local times, see page 22
Conveyance between an Airport and the Town Terminus is free unless otherwise indicated in the Table
The full names and addresses, etc., of the Companies will be found on pages 30 and 31

74

MARSEILLES—ALCUDIA—ALGIERS
(Daily)
AIR FRANCE

Route 493

Miles	Airports of		§			Airports of		‡	
0	MARSEILLES	...	...dep	8 0		ALGIERS ...	... ...dep	7 30	
280	ALCUDIA ...	...	... arr	11 15		ALCUDIA...	... ... arr	10 0	
	"	...	...dep	11 45		"	... ...dep	10 30	
499	ALGIERS	... ...	... arr	14 15		MARSEILLES ...	... arr	13 45	

‡ Bookings only by special arrangement on Mons., Thurs. and Fri.
§ Bookings only by special arrangement on Mon., Wed. and Sat.

Distance and Time allowance for conveyance between Airport and Town Terminus

TOWN	AIRPORT	TOWN TERMINUS	Miles	Minutes
MARSEILLES	Marignane	Air France, 1 Rue Papère	17½	60
ALCUDIA	Alcudia Seaplane Station	No Special Conveyance	1¼	—
ALGIERS	Agha	Air France, 4 Boulevard Carnot....................	1¼	30

FARES

FROM MARSEILLES TO	Single	Return 15 Days	Return 60 Days	Excess Baggage per Kg (2·2 lbs.)
	Frs.	Frs.	Frs.	Frs.
ALCUDIA	500	...	850	5*
ALGIERS	850	...	1,445	8*

After first 15 Kgs., half above rate is charged

75

MARSEILLES—AJACCIO—TUNIS
(Weekdays only)
AIR FRANCE

Route 481

Miles	Airports of					Airports of			
0	MARSEILLES	...	...dep	7 45		TUNIS	... ...dep	8 0	
230	AJACCIO ...	...	... arr	10 15		AJACCIO ...	... ... arr	11 30	
	"	...	...dep	10 45		"	... ...dep	12 0	
621½	TUNIS ...	... ...	... arr	16 15		MARSEILLES ...	... arr	15 0	

Distance and Time allowance for conveyance between Airport and Town Terminus

TOWN	AIRPORT	TOWN TERMINUS	Miles	Minutes
MARSEILLES	Marignane	Air France, 1 Rue Papère	17½	60
AJACCIO	Seaplane Station ...	No Special Conveyance	1	5
TUNIS	Seaplane Station ...	Air France, Avenue Jules Ferry 46	7½	45

FARES

FROM MARSEILLES	Single	Return 15 Days	Return 60 Days	Excess Baggage per Kg (2·2 lbs.)
	Frs.	Frs.	Frs.	Frs.
To AJACCIO	400	...	680	4*
TUNIS	1,000	...	1,700	10*
FROM AJACCIO				
To TUNIS	600	...	1,020	6*

After first 15 Kgs., half above rate is charged

SAARBRÜCKEN—MANNHEIM/L/H—STUTTGART—
MUNICH—(Vienna—Budapest)
(Weekdays only)
D.L.H.

Miles	Airports of					Airports of	
0	SAARBRÜCKEN	...dep	10 0			Budapest (Table 194)dep	
69½	MANNHEIM/L/H	... arr	10 50			Vienna (Table 167) dep	
		...dep	11 0			MUNICH ... ...dep	12 55
128	STUTTGART ...	...arr	11 45			STUTTGART ... ... arr	14 10
	,,	...dep	12 0			... ...dep	14 25
247½	MUNICH	... arr	13 15			MANNHEIM/L/H... arr	15 10
413	Vienna (Table 167) ... arr		...			,, ...dep	15 20
553	Budapest (Table 194) arr		...			SAARBRÜCKEN ... arr	16 10

Distance and Time allowance for conveyance between Airport and Town Terminus or centre of Town

TOWN	AIRPORT	TOWN TERMINUS	Miles	Minutes
SAARBRÜCKEN......	St. Arnual	No Special Conveyance.................§ By Tram	2¾	20§
		Mannheim—		
		Verkehrsverein Mannheim e. V.N. 2, 4—On application	3	20
MANNHEIM/L H ...	Neuostheim ...	Palast Hotel, Augusta Anlage 4-8—On application......................................	—	15
		Ludwigshafen—		
		Verkehrsverein, Kaiser Wilhelm Strasses 31	5	30
		Heidelberg—		
		Städt. Verkehrsamt, Anlage I—On applica- tion	12½	40
STUTTGART	Böblingen	Luftverkehr Würtemberg A.G., Fürstenstrasse I	13¾	55
MUNICH	Oberwiesenfeld ...	Luftreisebüro, Ritter von Epp-Platz 6 (Hotel Bayerischerhof)	3½	40

FARES

FROM SAARBRÜCKEN	Single	Return 15 Days	Return 60 Days	Excess Baggage per Kg (2·2 lbs.)
	Frs.	Frs.	Frs.	Frs.
To MANNHEIM/L/H	80	...	136	0·80
STUTTGART	150	...	255	1·50
MUNICH...	290	...	493	2·90
FROM MUNICH	RM.	RM.	RM.	RM.
To STUTTGART	23	...	39·10	0·23
MANNHEIM/L/H	35	...	59·50	0·35
SAARBRÜCKEN	48	...	81·60	0·48

77 BRUSSELS—ANTWERP
(Weekdays only)
SABENA
Route 501a

Miles	Airports of								
0	**BRUSSELS** ... ...dep	10 55	15 15					
25	**ANTWERP** ... ...arr	11 15	15 35					

	Airports of								
	ANTWERP ... ...dep	8 45	14 45					
	BRUSSELS ... ...arr	9 5	15 5					

Distance and Time allowance for conveyance between Airport and Town Terminus

TOWN	AIRPORT	TOWN TERMINUS	Miles	Minutes
BRUSSELS	Haren	Sabena Office, Boulevard Adolphe Max 32/34...	3¾	45
ANTWERP	Deurne	Sabena Office, Zentralbahnhof (Central Station)	2½	30

FARES

FROM BRUSSELS TO	Single	Return 15 Days	Return 60 Days	Excess Baggage per Kg (2·2 lbs.)
	B. Frs.	B. Frs.	B. Frs.	B. Frs.
ANTWERP	60	96	...	1

80 OSTEND—KNOCKE-LE ZOUTE—ROTTERDAM—AMSTERDAM
(Weekdays only)
K.L.M.
Route 525

Miles	Airports of					Airports of				
0	**OSTEND** ... ...dep	...	...		**AMSTERDAM** ...dep	8 30		14 0
22	**KNOCKE—** { arr	...	...		**ROTTERDAM** ... arr	8 55		14 25
	LE ZOUTE { dep	...	...		...dep	9 5		14 35
35½	**FLUSHING** ... arr	...	...		**HAAMSTEDE** ... arr	9 35		15 5
	...dep	9 10	14 25		...dep	9 40		15 10
53½	**HAAMSTEDE** ... arr	9 25	14 40		**FLUSHING** ... ... arr	9 55		15 25
	...dep	9 30	14 45		...dep	...		...
87	**ROTTERDAM** ... arr	10 0	15 15		**KNOCKE—** { arr	...		...
	...dep	10 10	15 25		**LE ZOUTE** { dep	...		...
123	**AMSTERDAM** ... arr	10 35	15 50		**OSTEND** ... ... arr	...		...

Distance and Time allowance for conveyance between Airport and Town Terminus

TOWN	AIRPORT	TOWN TERMINUS	Miles	Minutes
OSTEND	Steene	Place Marie José...	3	30
KNOCKE	Zoute	Place Albert	2½	30
FLUSHING	Flushing	No Special Conveyance	—	—
HAAMSTEDE	West-Schouwen ...	Zierikzee, Kraanplein D 441	12½	40
ROTTERDAM	Waalhaven	K.L.M. Office, Coolsingel 115......................	4¼	40
AMSTERDAM	Schiphol	K.L.M. Office, Leidscheplein	8	40

FARES

FROM FLUSHING	Single	Return 15 Days	Return 60 Days	Excess Baggage per Kg (2·2 lbs.)
	Fl.	Fl.	Fl.	Fl.
To HAAMSTEDE	4	...	6·80	0·05
ROTTERDAM	8	...	13·60	0·10
AMSTERDAM...	11	...	18·70	0·10

OSTEND—KNOCKE-LE ZOUTE—ANTWERP—BRUSSELS
(Service suspended during Winter)

SABENA Route 507

Miles	Airports of				Airports of		
0	**OSTEND** ... ...de|				**BRUSSELS** ... ...de|	
25	**KNOCKE—** { ar|				**ANTWERP** ... ... ar|	
	LE ZOUTE... { dep				,, ...dep		
74½	**ANTWERP** ... ... arr				**KNOCKE—** { arr		
	,, ...dep				**LE ZOUTE** { dep		
96	**BRUSSELS** ... ...arr				**OSTEND** ... ... arr		

Distance and Time allowance for conveyance between Airport and Town Terminus

TOWN	AIRPORT	TOWN TERMINUS	Miles	Minutes
OSTEND	Steene	Place Marie José..	3	30
KNOCKE	Zoute	Place Albert	2½	30
ANTWERP	Deurne	Sabena Office, Zentralbahnhof (Central Station)	2½	30
BRUSSELS	Haren	Sabena, Boulevard Adolphe Max 32/34............	3¾	45

FARES

FROM OSTEND TO	Single	Return 15 Days	Return 60 Days	Excess Baggage per Kg (2·2 lbs.)
	B. Frs.	B. Frs.	B. Frs.	B. Frs.
KNOCKE-LE ZOUTE ...				
ANTWERP				
BRUSSELS				

BRADSHAW'S CONTINENTAL HANDBOOK
FOR
Travellers Through Europe, etc.,
ALSO
Directory of Bathing Resorts.

COMPREHENSIVE DETAILS IN REGARD TO UPWARDS OF 40 COUNTRIES, INCLUDING THE WHOLE OF EUROPE, TOGETHER WITH ALGERIA, TUNISIA, EGYPT, SUDAN, PALESTINE, etc. :: :: :: :: ::

400 pages of descriptive details. 150 pages regarding Hotels.
A Pocket Encyclopædia of Travel.

Price 3s. 6d. Net.

LONDON :
HENRY BLACKLOCK & CO. LIMITED, Bradshaw House, Surrey Street, Strand, W.C. 2 ;
and Albert Square, Manchester.
MAY BE ORDERED THROUGH ANY BOOKSELLER OR RAILWAY BOOKSTALL.

All times given in the Tables are local times, see page 22
Conveyance between an Airport and the Town Terminus is free unless otherwise indicated in the Table
The full names and addresses, etc., of the Companies will be found on pages 30 and 31

ANTWERP—BRUSSELS—ESSEN/MÜLHEIM—BERLIN
(Weekdays only)
SABENA

Route 510

Miles	Airports of					Airports of				
0	**ANTWERP**	...	...dep	8	45	**BERLIN**	...dep	11	30	
22	**BRUSSELS**	... arr	9	5		**DORTMUND** ...	... arr	14	10	
	,, ...	...dep	9	15		,, ...	...dep	14	15	
128	**DÜSSELDORF** ...	... arr	11	15		**ESSEN/MÜLHEIM**	... arr	14	35	
	,, ...	...dep	11	30		,,	...dep	14	40	
147	**ESSEN/MÜLHEIM**	... arr	11	45		**DÜSSELDORF**	... arr	14	55	
	,,	...dep	11	50		,,	...dep	15	5	
167	**DORTMUND** ...	... arr	12	10		**BRUSSELS** ...	... arr	15	5	
	,, ...	...dep	12	15		,, ...	...dep	15	15	
428	**BERLIN**	... arr	14	45		**ANTWERP** ...	... arr	15	35	

Distance and Time allowance for conveyance between Airport and Town Terminus

TOWN	AIRPORT	TOWN TERMINUS	Miles	Minutes
ANTWERP	Deurne	Sabena Offices, Zentralbahnhof (Central Station)	2½	30
BRUSSELS	Haren	Sabena, Boulevard Adolphe Max 32/34............	3¾	45
DÜSSELDORF	Düsseldorf	Breidenbacher Hof and Parkhotel	—	25
		Hauptbahnhof (Central Station)	5½	30
ESSEN/MÜLHEIM ...	Essen/M.	Verkehrsverein Essen—opposite Hauptbahnhof (Central Station)	6¾	40
DORTMUND	Brackel	Hotel Fürstenhof—opposite Hauptbahnhof (Central Station). On application...............	—	30
		Verkehrsverein, Betenstrasse—opposite Stadthaus (Town Hall)	5	35
BERLIN..................	Tempelhof	Linden/Friedrichstrasse—No Special Conveyance	3	—

FARES

FROM ANTWERP	Single	Return 15 Days	Return 60 Days	Excess Baggage per Kg (2·2 lbs.)
	B. Frs.	B. Frs.	B. Frs.	B. Frs.
To BRUSSELS	60	96	...	1
DÜSSELDORF	215	344	366	2·15
ESSEN/MÜLHEIM	235	...	400	2·35
DORTMUND	250	...	425	2·50
BERLIN	730	...	1,241	7·30
FROM BERLIN	RM.	RM.	RM.	RM.
To DORTMUND	50	...	85	0·50
ESSEN/MÜLHEIM	55	...	93·50	0·55
DÜSSELDORF	60	...	102	0·60
BRUSSELS	85	...	144·50	0·85
ANTWERP	85	...	144·50	0·85

83

(London—Rotterdam)—AMSTERDAM—HANOVER—BERLIN
(Service suspended during Winter)
K.L.M.; D.L.H.

Route 2

Miles	Airports of				Airports of			
0	London (*Table 46*) ...dep				BERLIN ... ...dep			
216	Rotterdam (*Table 46*) dep				HANOVER ... ... arr			
252	AMSTERDAM ... ...dep				,, ...dep			
458	HANOVER... ... ... arr				AMSTERDAM ... arr			
	,, ...dep				Rotterdam(*Table 46*)arr			
617	BERLIN ... ... arr				London (*Table 46*)... arr			

Distance and Time allowance for conveyance between Airport and Town Terminus

TOWN	AIRPORT	TOWN TERMINUS	Miles	Minutes
AMSTERDAM	Schiphol	K.L.M. Office, Leidscheplein	8	40
HANOVER	Vahrenwalder	Hauptbahnhof (Central Station), Ernst-August		
	Heide	Platz. On application	4	25
BERLIN...................	Tempelhof	Linden/Friedrichstrasse—No Special Conveyance	3	—

FARES

FROM LONDON TO	Single	Return 15 Days	Return 60 Days	Excess Baggage per Kg (2·2 lbs.)
	£ s. d.	£ s. d.	£ s. d.	s. d.
ROTTERDAM				
AMSTERDAM				
HANOVER				
BERLIN				

84

AMSTERDAM—ROTTERDAM—EINDHOVEN
(Weekdays only)
K.L.M.

Route 528

Miles	Airports of				Airports of			
0	AMSTERDAM ... ...dep	...			EINDHOVEN... ...dep	8 10		
35½	ROTTERDAM ... ... arr				ROTTERDAM ... arr	8 50		
	,, ...dep	15 20			,, ...dep	...		
86	EINDHOVEN ... ... arr	16 0			AMSTERDAM ... arr			

Distance and Time allowance for conveyance between Airport and Town Terminus

TOWN	AIRPORT	TOWN TERMINUS	Miles	Minutes
AMSTERDAM	Schiphol	K.L.M. Office, Leidscheplein	8	40
ROTTERDAM	Waalhaven	K.L.M. Office, Coolsingel 115	4½	40
EINDHOVEN	Welschap	Stationsplein	3¾	25

FARES

FROM ROTTERDAM TO	Single	Return 15 Days	Return 60 Days	Excess Baggage per Kg (2·2 lbs.)
	Fl.	Fl.	Fl.	Fl.
EINDHOVEN	5·50	...	9·35	0·05

AMSTERDAM—ESSEN/MÜLHEIM—DÜSSELDORF—COLOGNE
(Service suspended during Winter)
D.L.H.

Route 29

Miles	Airports of				Airports of			
0	AMSTERDAM ... ...dep				COLOGNE ... ...dep			
112	ESSEN/MÜLHEIM ... arr				DÜSSELDORF ... arr			
	,, ... dep				,, ... dep			
130½	DÜSSELDORF ... ... arr				ESSEN/MÜLHEIM arr			
	,, ... dep				,, ... dep			
151½	COLOGNE ... ... arr				AMSTERDAM ... arr			

Distance and Time allowance for conveyance between Airport and Town Terminus				
TOWN	AIRPORT	TOWN TERMINUS	Miles	Minutes
AMSTERDAM	Schiphol	K.L.M. Office, Leidscheplein	8	40
ESSEN/MÜLHEIM ...	Essen/M.	Verkehrsverein Essen, opposite Hauptbahnhof (Central Station)	6¾	{ 35 § / 40 ‡
DÜSSELDORF	Düsseldorf ...... {	Breidenbacher Hof and Parkhotel	—	25
		Hauptbahnhof (Central Station)	5½	30
COLOGNE	Butzweiler Hof ...	Domhotel, Domhof	4¼	45

§—Towards Düsseldorf   ‡—Towards Amsterdam

FARES

FROM AMSTERDAM TO	Single	Return 15 Days	Return 60 Days	Excess Baggage per Kg (2·2 lbs.)
	Fl.	Fl.	Fl.	Fl.
ESSEN/MÜLHEIM				
DÜSSELDORF				
COLOGNE				

AMSTERDAM—COPENHAGEN—MALMÖ
(Daily)
K.L.M.; A.B.A.

Route 517

Miles	Airports of				Airports of			
0	AMSTERDAM ... ...dep	11 30			MALMÖ ... ...dep	...		
413	COPENHAGEN ... arr	15 35			COPENHAGEN ... arr	...		
	,, ... dep	...			,, ... dep	9 0		
432	MALMÖ ... ... arr	...			AMSTERDAM ... arr	11 45		

Distance and Time allowance for conveyance between Airport and Town Terminus				
TOWN	AIRPORT	TOWN TERMINUS	Miles	Minutes
AMSTERDAM	Schiphol	K.L.M. Office, Leidscheplein	8	40
COPENHAGEN	Kastrup..............	Passagebüro der D.D.L., Meldahlsgade 5	6½	45
MALMÖ	Bultofta..............	Zentralbahnhof (Central Station)	2	30

FARES

FROM AMSTERDAM	Single	Return 15 Days	Return 60 Days	Excess Baggage per Kg (2·2 lbs.)
	Fl.	Fl.	Fl.	Fl.
To COPENHAGEN ..	77	...	130·90	0·50
FROM COPENHAGEN	D. Kr.	D. Kr.	D. Kr.	D. Kr.
To AMSTERDAM...	155	...	294·50	0·75

90

AMSTERDAM—ROTTERDAM—ESSEN/MÜLHEIM—HALLE/LEIPZIG—PRAGUE
(Service suspended during Winter)
C.L.S.

Route 676

Miles	Airports of				Airports of			
0	AMSTERDAM ... ...dep				PRAGUE ... ...dep			
41	ROTTERDAM ... ... arr				HALLE/LEIPZIG ... arr			
	... ...dep				... dep			
164	ESSEN/MÜLHEIM ... arr				ESSEN/MÜLHEIM arr			
	... ...dep				dep			
418	HALLE/LEIPZIG ... arr				ROTTERDAM ... arr			
	... ...dep				... dep			
555	PRAGUE ... ... arr				AMSTERDAM ... arr			

Distance and Time allowance for conveyance between Airport and Town Terminus

TOWN	AIRPORT	TOWN TERMINUS	Miles	Minutes
AMSTERDAM	Schiphol	K.L.M. Office Leidscheplein..........................	8	40
ROTTERDAM	Waalhaven	K.L.M. Office Coolsingel 115	4	40
ESSEN/MÜLHEIM ...	Essen/M..............	Verkehrsverein Essen—opposite Hauptbahnhof (Central Station)	6¾	40§ / 30‡
HALLE/LEIPZIG	Schkeuditz	Halle— Postamt (Post Office). Thielenstrasse.........	—	40§ / 45‡
		Hotel Stadt Hamburg, Gr. Steinstrasse 73...	15	45§ / 50‡
		Leipzig— Hotel Astoria, Blücherplatz 2	10	35§ / 40‡
PRAGUE	Kbely	Luftreisebüro der Avioslava Vodičkova ul 38......	7½	50

§—Towards Prague   ‡—Towards Rotterdam

FARES

FROM AMSTERDAM TO	Single	Return 15 Days	Return 60 Days	Excess Baggage per Kg (2·2 lbs.)
	Fl.	Fl.	Fl.	Fl.
ROTTERDAM				
ESSEN/MÜLHEIM				
HALLE/LEIPZIG				
PRAGUE				

All times given in the Tables are local times, see page 22
Conveyance between an Airport and the Town Terminus is free unless otherwise indicated in the Table
The full names and addresses, etc., of the Companies will be found on pages 30 and 31
76

91

AMSTERDAM—HAMBURG—COPENHAGEN—MALMÖ
(Daily)
K.L.M.; A.B.A.
Route 511

Miles	Airports of			Airports of		
0	AMSTERDAM ...	...dep	11 25	MALMÖ	...dep	8 30
242	HAMBURG ...	...arr	14 5	COPENHAGEN	... arr	...
"		...dep	14 20		...dep	...
422½	COPENHAGEN	... arr	...	HAMBURG ...	... arr	9 55
		...dep	...		...dep	10 10
441	MALMÖ	...arr	15 50	AMSTERDAM	...arr	11 50

Distance and Time allowance for conveyance between Airport and Town Terminus

TOWN	AIRPORT	TOWN TERMINUS	Miles	Minutes
AMSTERDAM	Schiphol	K.L.M. Office, Leidscheplein, ...	8	40
HAMBURG	Fuhlsbüttel	Hauptbahnhof (Central Station), Hapag Reisebüro	7½	40
COPENHAGEN	Kastrup...............	Passagebüro der D.D.L., Meldahlsgade 5........	6¼	45
MALMÖ	Bultofta...............	Zentralbahnhof (Central Station)	2	30

FARES

FROM AMSTERDAM	Single	Return 15 Days	Return 60 Days	Excess Baggage per Kg (2·2 lbs.)
	Fl.	Fl.	Fl.	Fl.
To HAMBURG	32	...	54·40	0·30
COPENHAGEN	77	...	130·90	0·50
MALMÖ	81	...	137·70	0·50
FROM MALMÖ	S. Kr.	S. Kr.	S. Kr.	S. Kr.
To COPENHAGEN	10	...	17	0·10
HAMBURG	75	...	127·50	0·75
AMSTERDAM...	165	...	280·50	0·80

92

ROTTERDAM—AMSTERDAM
(Daily unless otherwise stated)
K.L.M.
Routes 516, 525

Miles	Airports of		W	W			
0	ROTTERDAM	...dep	10 10	10 40	15 25		
35½	AMSTERDAM	... arr	10 35	11 5	15 50		

	Airports of		W	W			
	AMSTERDAM	...dep	8 30	12 10	14 0		
	ROTTERDAM	... arr	8 55	12 35	14 25		

W—Not on Sunday

Distance and Time allowance for conveyance between Airport and Town Terminus

TOWN	AIRPORT	TOWN TERMINUS	Miles	Minutes
ROTTERDAM	Waalhaven	K.L.M., Office, Coolsingel 115	4¼	40
AMSTERDAM	Schiphol	K.L.M., Office, Leidscheplein......................	8	40

FARES

FROM ROTTERDAM TO	Single	Return 15 Days	Return 60 Days	Excess Baggage per Kg (2·2 lbs.)
	Fl.	Fl.	Fl.	Fl.
AMSTERDAM	6	...	10	0·05

93

ROTTERDAM—AMSTERDAM—GRONINGEN
(Service suspended during Winter)
K.L.M.

Route 526

Miles	Airports of					Airports of			
0	**ROTTERDAM** ...	...dep				**GRONINGEN**	...dep		
35½	**AMSTERDAM** ...	... arr				**AMSTERDAM**	... arr		
	,, ...	... dep				,,	... dep		
136	**GRONINGEN** ...	... arr				**ROTTERDAM**	... arr		

Distance and Time allowance for conveyance between Airport and Town Terminus

TOWN	AIRPORT	TOWN TERMINUS	Miles	Minutes
ROTTERDAM	Waalhaven	K.L.M. Office, Coolsingel 115	4¼	40
AMSTERDAM	Schiphol	K.L.M. Office, Leidscheplein	8	40
GRONINGEN	Eelde	Groote Markt	8	35

FARES

FROM ROTTERDAM TO	Single	Return 15 Days	Return 60 Days	Excess Baggage per Kg (2·2 lbs.)
	Fl.	Fl.	Fl.	Fl.
GRONINGEN				

94

ROTTERDAM—AMSTERDAM—TWENTE
(Service suspended during Winter)
K.L.M.

Route 527

Miles	Airports of					Airports of			
0	**ROTTERDAM** ...	...dep				**TWENTE**	...dep		
35½	**AMSTERDAM** ...	... arr				**AMSTERDAM**	... arr		
	,, ...	... dep				,,	... dep		
125	**TWENTE**	... arr				**ROTTERDAM**	... arr		

Distance and Time allowance for conveyance between Airport and Town Terminus

TOWN	AIRPORT	TOWN TERMINUS	Miles	Minutes
ROTTERDAM	Waalhaven	K.L.M. Office, Coolsingel 115	4¼	40
AMSTERDAM	Schiphol	K.L.M. Office, Leidscheplein	8	40
TWENTE	Twente	Loenshof, Enschede	3½	25
		Groote Straat, Oldenzaal	3	30

FARES

FROM ROTTERDAM TO	Single	Return 15 Days	Return 60 Days	Excess Baggage per Kg (2·2 lbs.)
	Fl.	Fl.	Fl.	Fl.
TWENTE				

95 EINDHOVEN—TWENTE—GRONINGEN
(Service suspended during Winter)
K.L.M.
Route 529

Miles	Airports of				Airports of		
0	EINDHOVEN ... ...dep				GRONINGEN ...dep		
86	TWENTE ... ... arr				TWENTE ... ... arr		
	... ...dep				... ...dep		
147	GRÖNINGEN ... ... arr				EINDHOVEN... ... arr		

Distance and Time allowance for conveyance between Airport and Town Terminus

TOWN	AIRPORT	TOWN TERMINUS	Miles	Minutes
EINDHOVEN	Welschap	Stationsplein	3¾	25
		Loenshof, Enschede	3¼	25
TWENTE	Twente			
		Groote Straat, Oldenzaal	3	30
GRONINGEN	Eelde	Groote Markt	8	35

FARES

FROM EINDHOVEN TO	Single	Return 15 Days	Return 60 Days	Excess Baggage per Kg (2·2 lbs.)
	Fl.	Fl.	Fl.	Fl.
TWENTE				
GRONINGEN				

96 BERLIN—STETTIN—STOLP—DANZIG—MARIENBURG
(Service suspended during Winter)
D.L.H.
Route 137

Miles	Airports of				Airports of		
0	BERLIN ... ...dep				MARIENBURG ...dep		
79½	STETTIN ... ... arr				DANZIG ... ... arr		
	... ...dep				... ...dep		
204	STÖLP ... ... arr				STÖLP ... ... arr		
	... ...dep				... ...dep		
271	DANZIG ... ... arr				STETTIN ... ... arr		
	... ...dep				... ...dep		
298	MARIENBURG ... arr				BERLIN ... ... arr		

Distance and Time allowance for conveyance between Airport and Town Terminus

TOWN	AIRPORT	TOWN TERMINUS	Miles	Minutes
BERLIN..................	Tempelhof	Linden,Friedrichstrasse—No Special Conveyance	3	—
STETTIN	Dammschen See ...	Brietestrasse 68—On application	5	30
STOLP	Stolp	No Special Conveyance	I	—
DANZIG	Langfuhr	No Special Conveyance	3½	—
MARIENBURG	Königshof	Hauptbahnhof (Central Station)	3¾	20

FARES

FROM BERLIN TO	Single	Return 15 Days	Return 60 Days	Excess Baggage per Kg (2·2 lbs.)
	RM.	RM.	RM.	RM.
STETTIN				
STOLP				
DANZIG				
MARIENBURG				

All times given in the Tables are local times, see page 22
Conveyance between an Airport and the Town Terminus is free unless otherwise indicated in the Table
The full names and addresses, etc., of the Companies will be found on pages 30 and 31

97

BERLIN—STETTIN—SWINEMÜNDE—SELLIN—STRALSUND—HIDDENSEE
(Service suspended during Winter)
D.L.H.

Routes 138, 139

Miles	Airports of						Airports of				
0	BERLIN	...	...	...dep			HIDDENSEE ...	...dep			
79½	STETTIN	...	...	...arr			STRALSUND ...	...arr			
	...	...	...	...dep			...	...dep			
115¼	SWINEMÜNDE		...	...arr			SELLIN	... ...arr			
			...	...dep			...	...dep			
155	SELLIN...	...	...	...arr			SWINEMÜNDE	...arr			
	...	...	...	...dep			...	...dep			
180	STRALSUND	...		...arr			STETTIN ...	... ...arr			
			...	...dep			... ...	...dep			
202	HIDDENSEE	...		...arr			BERLIN	... ...arr			

Distance and Time allowance for conveyance between Airport and Town Terminus

TOWN	AIRPORT	TOWN TERMINUS	Miles	Minutes
BERLIN..............	Tempelhof	Linden/Friedrichstrasse—No Special Conveyance	3	—
STETTIN	Dammschen See ...	Reisebüro, Breitestrasse 68—On application......	5	30
SWINEMÜNDE	Seeflughafen	Bollwerk (Motorboat)	⅝	30
SELLIN	Sellin	No Special Conveyance	¼	—
STRALSUND	Stralsund	No Special Conveyance	1	—
HIDDENSEE	Hiddensee	No Special Conveyance	½	—

FARES

FROM BERLIN TO	Single	Return 15 Days	Return 60 Days	Excess Baggage per Kg (2·2 lbs.)
	RM.	RM.	RM.	RM.
STETTIN				
SWINEMÜNDE				
SELLIN				
STRALSUND				
HIDDENSEE				

100

BERLIN—POSEN—WARSAW
(Daily)
'LOT'

Route 13

Miles	Airports of						Airports of				
0	BERLIN	...	...	...dep	12 15		WARSAW	...	...dep	8 10	
121	POSEN	...	...	...arr	13 30		POSEN	...	... ...arr	9 45	
			...	...dep	13 50			...	... ...dep	10 0	
317	WARSAW	...	...	...arr	15 20		BERLIN	...	... ...arr	11 15	

Distance and Time allowance for conveyance between Airport and Town Terminus

TOWN	AIRPORT	TOWN TERMINUS	Miles	Minutes
BERLIN..............	Tempelhof	Linden,Freidrichstrasse—No Special Conveyance	3	—
POSEN	Lawica	Hotel Bazar, Al. Marcinkowskiego 10	4½	40
WARSAW	Okecie	Stadtbüro Al. Jerozolimskie 35	5	40

FARES

FROM BERLIN	Single	Return 15 Days	Return 60 Days	Excess Baggage per Kg (2·2 lbs.)
	RM.	RM.	RM.	RM.
To POSEN	28	...	47·60	0·28
WARSAW	50	...	85	0·50
FROM WARSAW	Zl.	Zl.	Zl.	Zl.
To POSEN	46	...	78·20	0·45
BERLIN	105	...	178·50	1·05

101

BERLIN—BRESLAU—GLEIWITZ
(Weekdays only)
D.L.H.

Route 15

Miles	Airports of					Airports of				
0	BERLIN	...	...	...dep	12 30	GLEIWITZ	...	...dep	8 20	
182	BRESLAU	...	...	...arr	14 25	BRESLAU	...	...arr	9 20	
	,,	...	...	...dep	14 40	,,	...	...dep	9 30	
273	GLEIWITZ	...	...	...arr	15 40	BERLIN	...	...arr	11 25	

Distance and Time allowance for conveyance between Airport and Town Terminus

TOWN	AIRPORT	TOWN TERMINUS	Miles	Minutes
BERLIN..................	Tempelhof	Linden/Friedrichstrasse—No Special Conveyance	3	—
BRESLAU	Gandau	Central Stn.—No Special Conveyance * By Tram	5	30*
GLEIWITZ	Gleiwitz	Hotel Haus Oberschlesien, Helmuth-Brückner Strasse 5—On application	2¾	30

FARES

FROM BERLIN	Single	Return 15 Days	Return 60 Days	Excess Baggage per Kg (2·2 lbs.)
	RM.	RM.	RM.	RM.
To BRESLAU	30	...	51	0·30
GLEIWITZ	39	...	66·30	0·39
FROM BRESLAU				
To GLEIWITZ	13	...	22·10	0·13

102

BERLIN—STETTIN—DANZIG—KÖNIGSBERG
(Weekdays only)
D.L.H.

Route 4

Miles	Airports of					Airports of				
0	BERLIN	...	...	...dep	13 10	KÖNIGSBERG	...dep	8 0		
80	STETTIN	...	...	...arr	13 55	DANZIG	...	...arr	8 50	
	,,	...	...	...dep	14 10	,,	...	...dep	9 10	
258	DANZIG	...	...	...arr	15 45	STETTIN	...	...arr	10 45	
	,,	...	...	...dep	16 0	,,	...	...dep	11 0	
345	KÖNIGSBERG	...	...arr	16 50	BERLIN	...	...arr	11 45		

Distance and Time allowance for conveyance between Airport and Town Terminus or centre of Town

TOWN	AIRPORT	TOWN TERMINUS	Miles	Minutes
BERLIN..................	Tempelhof	Linden/Friedrichstrasse—No Special Conveyance	3	—
STETTIN	Dammschen See ...	Reisebüro, Bréitestr. 68—on request	5	30
DANZIG	Langfuhr	No Special Conveyance ...... * By Tram.........	3¾	40*
KÖNIGSBERG/Pr ...	Devau	No Special Conveyance ...... * By Tram.........	2½	30*

FARES

	STETTIN			DANZIG			KÖNIGSBERG		
	RM.			RM.			RM.		
	Single	Ret.	Ex. Bag.	Single	Ret.	Ex. Bag.	Single	Ret.	Ex. Bag
BERLIN	15	25·50	0·15	50	85	0·50	60	102	0·60
STETTIN	...	...	...	35	59·50	0·35	45	76·50	0·45
DANZIG	...	...	...	...	...	...	20	34	0·20

Ret.—Return 60 days.   Ex. Bag.—Excess Baggage per Kg (2·2 lbs.).

103

BERLIN—MUNICH—VENICE—ROME
(Weekdays only)
D.L.H.; A.L.S.A.

Route 9

Miles	Airports of						Airports of				
0	**BERLIN**	...	...	...dep	8 0		**ROME**	...	...	...dep	8 0
313	**MUNICH**	...	...	...arr	10 50		**VENICE**	...	...	...arr	10 15
		...	...	...dep	11 20			...	...	...dep	10 45
588	**VENICE**	...	...	...arr	13 20		**MUNICH**	...	...	...arr	12 45
		...	...	...dep	13 50			...	...	...dep	13 15
844	**ROME** ...	...	...	...arr	16 5		**BERLIN**	...	...	...arr	16 5

Distance and Time allowance for conveyance between Airport and Town Terminus

TOWN	AIRPORT	TOWN TERMINUS	Miles	Minutes
BERLIN.................	Tempelhof	Linden/Friedrichstrasse—No Special Conveyance	3	—
MUNICH	Oberwelsenfeld ...	Ritter von Epp-Platz 6 (Hotel Bayerischerhof)...	3½	40
VENICE	San Nicolo di Lido {	Riva degli Schiavoni—opposite Hotel Danieli...	—	45 ‡
		Station. * 60 mins towards Rome.	—	70*
		‡ 30 mins towards Rome.		
ROME	Littorio..............	C.I.T. Piazza Esedra 64	—	30

FARES

FROM BERLIN	Single	Return 15 Days	Return 60 Days	Excess Baggage per Kg (2·2 lbs.)
	RM.	RM.	RM.	RM.
To MUNICH...	70	...	119	0·70
VENICE	100	...	170	1
ROME	130	...	221	1·30
FROM ROME	Lire	Lire	Lire	Lire
To VENICE	250	...	425	2·50
MUNICH...	420	...	714	4·20
BERLIN	610	...	1,037	6·10

104

BERLIN—COPENHAGEN—MALMÖ
(Daily)
D.L.H.

Route 7

Miles	Airports of						Airports of				
0	**BERLIN**	...	...	...dep	13 0		**MALMÖ**	...	...	...dep	8 30
293	**COPENHAGEN**		...	...arr	15 0		**COPENHAGEN**		...	...arr	8 45
			...	...dep	15 15				...	...dep	9 0
310	**MALMÖ**	...	...	...arr	15 30		**BERLIN**	...	...	...arr	11 0

Distance and Time allowance for conveyance between Airport and Town Terminus

TOWN	AIRPORT	TOWN TERMINUS	Miles	Minutes
BERLIN.................	Tempelhof	Linden/Friedrichstrasse—No Special Conveyance	3	—
COPENHAGEN	Kastrup..............	Passagebüro der D.D.L., Meldahlsgade 5.........	6½	45
MALMÖ	Bultofta..............	Zentralbahnhof (Central Station)	2½	30

FARES

FROM BERLIN TO	Single	Return 15 Days	Return 60 Days	Excess Baggage per Kg (2·2 lbs.)
	RM.	RM.	RM.	RM.
To COPENHAGEN	55	...	93·50	0·55
MALMÖ	62	...	104·40	0·62
FROM MALMÖ	S. Kr.	S. Kr.	S. Kr.	S. Kr.
To COPENHAGEN	10	...	17	0·10
BERLIN	85	...	144·50	0·85

105

BERLIN—DRESDEN—PRAGUE—VIENNA
(Weekdays only)
D.L.H.; C.L.S.; AUSTROFLUG

Route 32

Miles	Airports of					Airports of				
0	**BERLIN**	...	...	...dep	12 0	**VIENNA**	...	...	...dep	9 0
100	**DRESDEN**	...	...	...arr	13 0	**PRAGUE**	...	...	...arr	10 30
	,,	...	...	...dep	13 15	,,	...	...	...dep	10 50
174½	**PRAGUE**	...	...	...arr	14 5	**DRESDEN**	...	...	...arr	11 40
	,,	...	...	...dep	14 20	,,	...	...	...dep	11 55
332½	**VIENNA**	...	...	...arr	15 50	**BERLIN**	...	...	...arr	12 55

Distance and Time allowance for conveyance between Airport and Town Terminus

TOWN	AIRPORT	TOWN TERMINUS	Miles	Minutes
BERLIN..................	Tempelhof	Linden/Friedrichstrasse—No Special Conveyance	3	—
DRESDEN	Heller	Reisebüro, Hauptbahnhof (Central Station)......	5	30
PRAGUE	Kbely	Luftreisebüro der Avioslava Vodičkova ul 38 ...	7½	50
VIENNA	Aspern	Austroflug, Kärntnerring 5 (Hotel Bristol), Vienna I...	9¼	35

FARES

FROM BERLIN	Single RM.	Return 60 Days RM.	Excess Baggage per Kg (2·2 lbs.) RM.
To DRESDEN	22	37·40	0·20
PRAGUE	42	35·70 + Kc 285·60	0·40
VIENNA	82	69·70 + Sch 140·25	0·80
FROM VIENNA	Sch.	Sch.	Sch.
To PRAGUE	80	68 + Kc 272	0·80
DRESDEN	120	102 + RM. 51	1·20
BERLIN	165	140·25 + RM. 69·70	1·65

106

BERLIN—COPENHAGEN—GOTHENBURG—OSLO
(Service suspended during Winter)
D.L.H.; D.D.L.

Miles	Airports of				Airports of			
0	**BERLIN**	...	...	...dep	**OSLO**	...	...	...dep
293	**COPENHAGEM**		...	arr	**GOTHENBURG**		...	arr
			...	dep			...	dep
434	**GOTHENBURG**		...	arr	**COPENHAGEN**		...	arr
	,,		...	dep	,,		...	dep
593	**OSLO**	...	...	arr	**BERLIN**	...	...	arr

Distance and Time allowance for conveyance between Airport and Town Terminus

TOWN	AIRPORT	TOWN TERMINUS	Miles	Minutes
BERLIN..................	Tempelhof	Linden/Friedrichstrasse—No Special Conveyance	3	—
COPENHAGEN	Kastrup............	Passagebüro der D.D.L., Meldahlsgade 5.........	6½	45
GOTHENBURG	Torslanda............	Aerotransportkontor Hotellplatsen	10½	60
OSLO	Graesholmen	Brücke Ostbahnhof by Motorboat.................	—	45

FARES

FROM BERLIN TO	Single RM.	Return 15 Days RM.	Return 60 Days RM.	Excess Baggage per Kg (2·2 lbs.) RM.
COPENHAGEN				
GOTHENBURG				
OSLO				

107

BERLIN—VIENNA—BUDAPEST—BELGRADE—SOFIA—SALONICA
(Service suspended during Winter)
D.L.H.; AUSTROFLUG; 'MALERT'

Route 17

Miles	Airports of				Airports of	
0	**BERLIN** ... ...dep				**SALONICA** ... ...dep	
323	**VIENNA** ... ... arr				**SOFIA** ... ... arr	
	,, ...dep				,, ...dep	
522	**BUDAPEST** ... ... arr				**BELGRADE** ... ... arr	
	,, ...dep				,, ...dep	
721	**BELGRADE** ... ... arr				**BUDAPEST** ... ... arr	
	,, ...dep				,, ...dep	
926½	**SOFIA** ... ... arr				**VIENNA** ... ... arr	
	,, ...dep				,, ...dep	
1129½	**SALONICA** ... ... arr				**BERLIN** ... ... arr	

Distance and Time allowance for conveyance between Airport and Town Terminus

TOWN	AIRPORT	TOWN TERMINUS	Miles	Minutes
BERLIN..................	Tempelhof	Linden/Friedrichstrasse—No Special Conveyance	3	—
VIENNA	Aspern	Austroflug, Kärntnerring 5 (Hotel Bristol), Vienna I..	9½	35
BUDAPEST	Matyasföld	Luftreisebüro der Malert Váci ucca I................	7¾	40
BELGRADE	Beograd (Zemun)..	Special Conveyance on application to Airport Office	2½	—
		Or by Steamer from Save Hafen to Zemun§...	7	{25§
		Thence taxi to Airport‡	2½	{15‡
SOFIA	Bojourichte	Grand Hotel Bulgarie	8¾	50
SALONICA	Sedes	Angle Comninon-Mitropoleós	9¼	60

FARES

FROM BERLIN	Single RM.	Return 15 Days RM.	Return 60 Days RM.	Excess Baggage per Kg (2·2 lbs.) RM.
To VIENNA				
BUDAPEST				
BELGRADE				
SOFIA				
SALONICA				
FROM SALONICA	Drach.	Drach.	Drach.	Drach.
To SOFIA				
BELGRADE				
BUDAPEST				
VIENNA				
BERLIN				

All times given in the Tables are local times, see page 22
Conveyance between an Airport and the Town Terminus is free unless otherwise indicated in the Table
The full names and addresses, etc., of the Companies will be found on pages 30 and 31
84

110 BERLIN—DRESDEN—CHEMNITZ—ZWICKAU—PLAUEN
(Service suspended during Winter)
D.L.H.

Route 147

Miles	Airports of			Airports of	
0	**BERLIN** ... ...dep			**PLAUEN** ... ...dep	
100	**DRESDEN** ... ... arr			**ZWICKAU** ... ... arr	
	„ ... ...dep			... ...dep	
138½	**CHEMNITZ** ... ... arr			**CHEMNITZ** ... ... arr	
	... ... dep			... ... dep	
160	**ZWICKAU** ... ... arr			**DRESDEN**... ... ... arr	
	„ ... ... dep			„ ... ... dep	
182	**PLAUEN** ... ... arr			**BERLIN** ... ... arr	

Distance and Time allowance for conveyance between Airport and Town Terminus

TOWN	AIRPORT	TOWN TERMINUS	Miles	Minutes
BERLIN..................	Tempelhof	Linden/Friedrichstrasse—No Special Conveyance	3	—
DRESDEN	Heller	Reisebüro, Hauptbahnhof (Central Station)......	5	30
CHEMNITZ	Chemnitz	Bahnhofshotel (Continental)	3	30
		Verkehrsverein, Markt (corner of Ratskeller)...	—	25
ZWICKAU	Zwickau ....{	Reisebüro Meitzner	2¼	20
		Hauptbahnhof (Central Station)—On application	—	15
PLAUEN	Plauen ....{	Reisebüro Koch, Bahnhofstrasse 22—On application	3¾	30
		Hotel Kronprinz, opposite Postamt, 4 Pauserstrasse—On application	—	25

FARES

FROM BERLIN TO	Single	Return 15 Days	Return 60 Days	Excess Baggage per Kg (2·2 lbs.)
	RM.	RM.	RM.	RM.
DRESDEN				
CHEMNITZ				
ZWICKAU				
PLAUEN				

111 AIX LA CHAPELLE—COLOGNE
(Service suspended during Winter)
D.L.H.

Route 82

Miles	Airports of			Airports of	
0	**AIX LA CHAPELLE** dep			**COLOGNE** ... ...dep	
33	**COLOGNE** ... ... arr			**AIX LA CHAPELLE** arr	

Distance and Time allowance for conveyance between Airport and Town Terminus

TOWN	AIRPORT	TOWN TERMINUS	Miles	Minutes
AIX LA CHAPELLE	Aix la Chapelle {	Hauptbahnhof (Central Station), Vorplatz	6¼	30
		Theaterplatz 10-12	—	25
COLOGNE	Butzweiler Hof ...	Domhotel, Domhof	4¼	35

FARES

FROM AIX LA CHAPELLE TO	Single	Return 15 Days	Return 60 Days	Excess Baggage per Kg (2·2 lbs.)
	RM.	RM.	RM.	RM.
COLOGNE				

112 BERLIN—DANZIG—KÖNIGSBERG—KAUNAS—MOSCOW
(Daily)
DERULUFT

Routes 3, 3a

Miles	Airports of					Airports of				
0	BERLIN	...	...	...dep	7 0	MOSCOW	...	... dep	9 0	
253½	DANZIG	...	...	... arr	9 15	WELIKIJE LUKI	... arr	11 30		
		...	...	...dep	9 30		...dep	12 0		
340½	KÖNIGSBERG	...		... arr	10 20	KAUNAS ..."	...	... arr	12 35	
		...		... dep	10 45		... ... dep	12 55		
478½	KAUNAS	...	...	... arr	12 5	KÖNIGSBERG	... arr	14 15		
		...		... dep	12 25		...dep	14 45		
766	WELIKIJE LUKI		... arr	17 0	DANZIG ...	...	... arr	15 40		
	,,		... dep	17 20		,,	...dep	16 0		
1045	MOSCOW ..."	...	... arr	19 50	BERLIN	...	... arr	18 15		

Distance between Airport and Town

TOWN	AIRPORT	TOWN TERMINUS	Miles
BERLIN..................	Tempelhof	Linden/Freidrichstrasse—No Special Conveyance	3
DANZIG	Langfuhr	No Special Conveyance	3½
KÖNIGSBERG/Pr ...	Devau	No Special Conveyance	2½
KAUNAS	Linksmadvaris Aerostotis ...	No Special Conveyance	3
WELIKIJE LUKI	Welikije Luki	No Special Conveyance	4¼
MOSCOW	Chodynka	Hotel Boischaja Moskowskaja—On request......	1¾

FARES

FROM BERLIN	Single	Return 15 Days	Return 60 Days	Excess Baggage per Kg (2·2 lbs.)
	RM.	RM.	RM.	RM.
To DANZIG	50	...	85	0·50•
KÖNIGSBERG	60	...	102	0·60•
KAUNAS	78	...	132·60	0·78•
WELIKIJE LUKI	130	...	221	0·65§
MOSCOW	180	...	306	0·90§
FROM MOSCOW	Rbl.	Rbl.	Rbl.	Rbl.
To WELIKIJE LUKI	24	...	40·80	0·24•
KAUNAS	48	...	81·60	0·48•
KÖNIGSBERG	56	...	95·20	0·28§
DANZIG	60	...	102	0·30§
BERLIN	84	...	142·80	0·42§

•—After first 15 Kgs., half above rate is charged
§—30 Kgs. allowed free

113

BERLIN—HALLE/LEIPZIG—NÜRNBERG—MUNICH
(Weekdays only)
D.L.H.

Route 10

Miles	Airports of					Airports of				
0	**BERLIN**	...dep	12	45		**MUNICH** ...	...dep	8	40	
90	**HALLE/LEIPZIG**	... arr	13	35		**NÜRNBERG** ...	... arr	9	30	
	,,	... dep	13	45		,,	... dep	9	40	
234	**NÜRNBERG** ...	... arr	15	5		**HALLE/LEIPZIG**	... arr	11	0	
	,,	... dep	15	20		,,	... dep	11	15	
327½	**MUNICH**	... arr	16	10		**BERLIN**	... arr	12	5	

Distance and Time allowance for conveyance between Airport and Town Terminus

TOWN	AIRPORT	TOWN TERMINUS	Miles	Minutes
BERLIN..................	Tempelhof	Linden/Freidrichstrasse—No Special Conveyance	3	—
HALLE/LEIPZIG......	Schkeuditz	Halle— Postamt (Post Office), Thielenstrasse	—	{ 40§ { 35‡
		Hotel Hohenzollernhof, Hindenburg Str 65	15	{ 45§ { 40‡
		Leipzig— Hotel Astoria, Blücherplatz 2	10	{ 35§ { 30‡
NÜRNBERG	Nürnberg	Grand Hotel	2¾	25
MUNICH	Oberwiesenfeld ...	Ritter von Epp-Platz 6 (Hotel Bayerischer Hof)	3¼	40

§—Towards Nürnberg   ‡—Towards Berlin

FARES

	HALLE/LEIPZIG RM.			NÜRNBERG RM.			MUNICH RM.		
	Single	Ret.	Ex. Bag.	Single	Ret.	Ex. Bag.	Single	Ret.	Ex. Bag.
BERLIN	20	34	0·20	49	83·30	0·49	70	119	0·70
HALLE/LEIPZIG ..	...	...	...	29	49·30	0·29	50	85	0·50
NÜRNBERG ...				...	...	...	21	35·70	0·21

Ret.—Return 60 days   Ex. Bag.—Excess Baggage per Kg (2·2 lbs.)

114

CREFELD—COLOGNE
(Service suspended during Winter)
D.L.H.

Route 81

Miles	Airports of				Airports of	
0	**CREFELD**	...dep			**COLOGNE** ...	...dep
32	**COLOGNE** ...	... arr			**CREFELD**	... arr

Distance and Time allowance for conveyance between Airport and Town Terminus

TOWN	AIRPORT	TOWN TERMINUS	Miles	Minutes
CREFELD	Borkum	Reisebüro Esser, Ostwall 60	4½	25
COLOGNE	Butzweller Hof ...	Dom Hotel, Domhof..................................	4½	40

FARES

FROM CREFELD TO	Single	Return 15 Days	Return 60 Days	Excess Baggage per Kg (2·2 lbs.)
	RM.	RM.	RM.	RM.
COLOGNE				

115

CREFELD—DÜSSELDORF
(Service suspended during Winter)
D.L.H.

Route 80

Miles	Airports of				Airports of		
0	CREFELD ... ...dep				DÜSSELDORF ...dep		
12½	DÜSSELDORF ... ... arr				CREFELD ... ... arr		

Distance and Time allowance for conveyance between Airport and Town Terminus

TOWN	AIRPORT	TOWN TERMINUS	Miles	Minutes
CREFELD	Borkum	Reisebüro Esser, Ostwall 60	4½	25
DÜSSELDORF	Düsseldorf	Breidenbacher Hof and Parkhotel	—	55
		Hauptbahnhof (Central Station)	5½	60

FARES

FROM CREFELD TO	Single	Return 15 Days	Return 60 Days	Excess Baggage per Kg (2·2. lbs)
	RM.	RM.	RM.	RM.
DÜSSELDORF				

116

DÜSSELDORF—ESSEN/MÜLHEIM—MÜNSTER—BERLIN
(Service suspended during Winter)
D.L.H.

Route 18

Miles	Airports of				Airports of		
0	DÜSSELDORF ... ... dep				BERLIN ... ... dep		
19	ESSEN/MÜLHEIM ... arr				MÜNSTER ... ... arr		
	,, ... dep				,, ... dep		
—	MÜNSTER ... ... arr				ESSEN/MÜLHEIM... arr		
	... ... dep				,, ... dep		
301	BERLIN ... ... arr				DÜSSELDORF ... arr		

Distance and Time allowance for conveyance between Airport and Town Terminus

TOWN	AIRPORT	TOWN TERMINUS	Miles	Minutes
DÜSSELDORF	Lohausen	Hauptbahnhof (Central Station)	5½	30
ESSEN/MÜLHEIM ...	Mülheim/Rachr ...	Verkehrsverein Essen, opposite Hauptbahnhof		
		(Central Station)—On application	6¾	30
MÜNSTER	Polizle—Flugwache	Verkehrsverein Prinzipalmarkt	2¾	30
		Hauptbahnhof (Central Station)	—	20
BERLIN.................	Tempelhof	Linden/Freidrichstrasse—No Special Conveyance	3	—

FARES

	ESSEN/M.			MÜNSTER			BERLIN		
	RM.			RM.			RM.		
	Single	Ret.	Ex. Bag.	Single	Ret.	Ex. Bag	Singl:	Ret.	Ex. Bag.
DÜSSELDORF ...									
ESSEN/M.									
MÜNSTER									

Ret.—Return 60 days.   Ex. Bag.—Excess Baggage per Kg (2·2 lbs.).

All times given in the Tables are local times, see page 22
Conveyance between an Airport and the Town Terminus is free unless otherwise indicated in the Table
The full names and addresses, etc., of the Companies will be found on pages 30 and 31

117

DÜSSELDORF—COLOGNE—SAARBRÜCKEN
(Service suspended during Winter)
D.L.H.

Route 88

Miles	Airports of				Airports of		
0	DÜSSELDORF ... ...dep				SAARBRÜCKEN ...dep		
21	COLOGNE ... ... arr				COLOGNE ... ... arr		
	,, ...dep				,, ... dep		
139	SAARBRÜCKEN ... arr				DÜSSELDORF ... arr		

Distance and Time allowance for conveyance between Airport and Town Terminus

TOWN	AIRPORT	TOWN TERMINUS	Miles	Minutes
DÜSSELDORF	Düsseldorf ...... {	Breidenbacher Hof and Parkhotel	—	25
		Hauptbahnhof (Central Station)	5½	30
COLOGNE	Butzweiler Hof ...	Domhotel, Domhof	4¼	{ 25§ 15‡
SAARBRÜCKEN......	St. Arnual	No Special Conveyance. Trams.....................	2¾	20

§—Towards Saarbrücken ‡—Towards Düsseldorf

FARES

FROM DÜSSELDORF TO	Single	Return 15 Days	Return 60 Days	Excess Baggage per Kg (2·2 lbs.)
	RM.	RM.	RM.	RM.
COLOGNE				
SAARBRÜCKEN				

120

DÜSSELDORF—ERFURT—(Halle/Leipzig—Berlin)
(Service suspended during Winter)
D.L.H.

Route 142

Miles	Airports of				Airports of		
0	DÜSSELDORF ... ...dep				Berlin (Table 134)... dep		
186½	ERFURT ... ... arr				Halle/Leipzig		
245½	Halle/Leipzig				(Table 134) ... ... dep		
	(Table 134) ... ... arr				ERFURT ... ...dep		
335½	Berlin (Table 134) ... arr				DÜSSELDORF ... arr		

Distance and Time allowance for conveyance between Airport and Town Terminus

TOWN	AIRPORT	TOWN TERMINUS	Miles	Minutes
DÜSSELDORF	Düsseldorf ...... {	Hauptbahnhof (Central Station)	5½	30
		Breidenbacher Hof and Parkhotel	—	25
ERFURT	Erfurt	Hauptbahnhof (Central Station), Hauptausgang	3¾	25

FARES

FROM DÜSSELDORF TO	Single	Return 15 Days	Return 60 Days	Excess Baggage per Kg (2·2 lbs.)
	RM.	RM.	RM.	RM.
ERFURT				

121

DÜSSELDORF—COLOGNE—DORTMUND—HALLE/LEIPZIG—DRESDEN (Weekdays only)
D.L.H.

Miles	Airports of			Airports of		
0	DÜSSELDORF ...	...dep	12 45	DRESDEN... ...	...dep	...
21	COLOGNE ...	...arr	13 0	HALLE/LEIPZIG ...	arr	...
	,, ...	...dep	13 10	,,	...dep	11 20
68	DORTMUND ...	...arr	13 40	DORTMUND ...	...arr	13 35
	,, ...	...dep	13 50	,,	...dep	13 45
274	HALLE/LEIPZIG ...	...arr	16 5	COLOGNE ...	...arr	14 15
	,,	...dep	...	,,	...dep	14 25
344	DRESDEN	...arr	...	DÜSSELDORF	...arr	14 40

Distance and Time allowance for conveyance between Airport and Town Terminus

TOWN	AIRPORT	TOWN TERMINUS	Miles	Minutes
DÜSSELDORF	Lohausen...	Hauptbahnhof (Central Station)	5½	30
COLOGNE	Butzweiler Hof ...	Domhotel, Domhof	4¼	40§ / 35‡
DORTMUND	Brackel	Verkehrsverein, Betenstrasse—opposite Town Hall	5	35
		Hotel Fürstenhof—opposite Hauptbahnhof (Central Station)	—	30
HALLE/LEIPZIG	Schkeuditz	Halle—Postamt (Post Office), Thielenstrasse	—	40
		Hotel Hohenzozzernhof, Hindenburgstr. 65	15	45
		Leipzig—Hotel Astoria, Blücherplatz 2	10	35
DRESDEN	Heller	Reisebüro, Hauptbahnhof (Central Station)......	5	30

§—Towards Dortmund ‡—Towards Düsseldorf

FARES

	COLOGNE RM.			DORTMUND RM.			HALLE/LEIPZIG RM.			DRESDEN RM.		
	Single	Ret.	Ex. Bg.	Single	Ret.	Ex. Bg.	Single	Ret.	Ex. Bg.	Single	Ret.	Ex. Bg.
DÜSSELDORF ...	10	17	0·15	12	20·40	0·15	44	74·80	0·44	58	98·60	0·58
COLOGNE ...	...	...	...	12	20·40	0·15	43	73·10	0·43	57	96·90	0·15
DORTMUND ...	...	...	...	...	...	...	38	64·60	0·15	52	88·04	0·52
HALLE/L ...	...	...	...	...	...	...	...	...	...	14	23·80	0·15

Ret.—Return 60 days.   Ex. Bg.—Excess Baggage per Kg (2·2 lbs.).

122

COLOGNE—ESSEN/MÜLHEIM.
(Service suspended during Winter)
D.L.H.

Route 83

Miles	Airports of			Airports of		
0	COLOGNE... ...	...dep		ESSEN/MÜLHEIM.. dep		
36	ESSEN/MÜLHEIM ... arr			COLOGNE ... ... arr		

Distance and Time allowance for conveyance between Airport and Town Terminus

TOWN	AIRPORT	TOWN TERMINUS	Miles	Minutes
COLOGNE	Butzweiler Hof ...	Domhotel, Domhof	4¼	30
ESSEN/M.	Essen/M.	Verkehrsverein Essen, opposite Hauptbahnhof (Central Station)	6¾	35

FARES

FROM COLOGNE TO	Single	Return 15 Days	Return 60 Days	Excess Baggage per Kg (2·2 lbs.)
	RM.	RM.	RM.	RM.
ESSEN/MÜLHEIM				

123

COLOGNE—FRANKFORT.O.M.—BERLIN
(Service suspended during Winter)
D.L.H.

Route 19 (Ultra Rapid)

Miles	Airports of				Airports of				
0	**COLOGNE** ...	...dep			**BERLIN**	...dep			
92½	**FRANKFORT/M**	... arr			**FRANKFORT/M**	... arr			
		... ...dep			...	...dep			
355	**BERLIN**	... arr			**COLOGNE** ...	... arr			

Distance and Time allowance for conveyance between Airport and Town Terminus

TOWN	AIRPORT	TOWN TERMINUS	Miles	Minutes
COLOGNE	Butzweiler Hof ...	Domhotel, Domhof	4¼	35
FRANKFORT/M. ...	Rebstock	Hauptbahnhof (Central Station)—No Special	3	30
		Conveyance		
BERLIN..................	Tempelhof	Linden/Freidrichstrasse—No Special Conveyance	3	—

FARES

FROM COLOGNE TO	Single	Return 15 Days	Return 60 Days	Excess Baggage per Kg (2·2 lbs.)
	RM.	RM.	RM.	RM.
FRANKFORT/M				
BERLIN				

124

COLOGNE—HAMBURG—BERLIN
(Service suspended during Winter)
D.L.H.

Route 16 (Ultra Rapid)

Miles	Airports of				Airports of				
0	**COLOGNE** ...	...dep			**BERLIN**	...dep			
222	**HAMBURG** ...	... arr			**HAMBURG** ...	... arr			
		... ...dep			...	...dep			
380	**BERLIN**	... arr			**COLOGNE** ...	... arr			

Distance and Time allowance for conveyance between Airport and Town Terminus

TOWN	AIRPORT	TOWN TERMINUS	Miles	Minutes
COLOGNE	Butzweiler Hof ...	Domhotel, Domhof	4¼	30
HAMBURG	Fuhlsbüttel	Hauptbahnhof (Central Station), Hapag Reise-	7½	30
		büro		
BERLIN..................	Tempelhof	Linden/Freidrichstrasse—No Special Conveyance	3	—

FARES

FROM COLOGNE TO	Single	Return 15 Days	Return 60 Days	Excess Baggage per Kg (2·2 lbs.)
	RM.	RM.	RM.	RM.
HAMBURG				
BERLIN				

125 COLOGNE—DORTMUND—HANOVER—HAMBURG
D.L.H. (Service suspended during Winter)
Route 103

Miles	Airports of			Airports of		
0	COLOGNE ... ...dep			HAMBURG ... ...dep		
46½	DORTMUND ... ...arr			HANOVER ... ...arr		
	... ...dep			... ...dep		
160	HANOVER... ... ...arr			DORTMUND ... ...arr		
	... ...dep			......dep		
243	HAMBURG ... ...arr			COLOGNE ... ...arr		

Distance and Time allowance for conveyance between Airport and Town Terminus

TOWN	AIRPORT	TOWN TERMINUS	Miles	Minutes
COLOGNE	Butzweiler Hof ...	Domhotel, Domhof	4¼	35
DORTMUND	Brackel	Hotel Fürstenhof, opposite Hauptbahnhof (Central Station)—On application	—	30
		Verkehrsverein, Betenstrasse, opposite Stadthaus (Town Hall)................................	5	35
HANOVER	Vahrenwalder Heide	Hauptbahnhof (Central Station), Ernst-August, Platz—On application	4	{ 30§ 20‡
HAMBURG	Fuhlsbüttel	Hauptbahnhof (Central Station) Hapag Reisebüro	7½	40

§—Towards Hamburg   ‡—Towards Dortmund

FARES

FROM COLOGNE TO	Single	Return 15 Days	Return 60 Days	Excess Baggage per Kg (2·2 lbs.)
	RM.	RM.	RM.	RM.
DORTMUND				
HANOVER				
HAMBURG				

126 DORTMUND—BORKUM
D.L.H. (Service suspended during Winter)
Route 85

Miles	Airports of			Airports of		
0	DORTMUND ... ...dep			BORKUM ... ...dep		
148	BORKUM ... ...arr			DORTMUND ... ...arr		

Distance and Time allowance for conveyance between Airport and Town Terminus

TOWN	AIRPORT	TOWN TERMINUS	Miles	Minutes
DORTMUND	Brackel	Hotel Fürstenhof, opposite Hauptbahnhof (Central Station)—On application	—	30
		Verkehrsverein, Betenstrasse, opposite Stadthaus (Town Hall)................................	5	35
BORKUM	Borkum	Corner of Prinz Heinrich Kaiserstrasse............	1½	40
		Bahnhof (Station)—Strandstrasse	—	35

FARES

FROM DORTMUND TO	Single	Return 15 Days	Return 60 Days	Excess Baggage per Kg (2.2 lbs.)
	RM.	RM.	RM.	RM.
BORKUM				

All times given in the Tables are local times, see page 22
Conveyance between an Airport and the Town Terminus is free unless otherwise indicated in the Table
The full names and addresses, etc., of the Companies will be found on pages 30 and 31

127 ESSEN/MÜLHEIM—OSNABRÜCK—NORDERNEY—BORKUM
(Service suspended during Winter)
D.L.H.

Route 84

Miles	Airports of				Airports of	
0	ESSEN/MÜLHEIM ... dep				BORKUM ... ...dep	
77	OSNABRÜCK ... ... arr				NORDERNEY ... arr	
	,, ...dep				...dep	
184	NORDERNEY ... ... arr				OSNABRÜCK ... arr	
	,, ...dep				...dep	
206	BORKUM ... ... arr				ESSEN/MÜLHEIM .. arr	

Distance and Time allowance for conveyance between Airport and Town Terminus

TOWN	AIRPORT	TOWN TERMINUS	Miles	Minutes
ESSEN/M...............	Essen/M.	Verkehrsverein Essen, opposite Hauptbahnhof (Central Station)	6¾	40
OSNABRÜCK	Osnabrück	Städt. Reisebüro, Möserstrasse 20	3	20
NORDERNEY	Norderney	No Special Conveyance	⅛	—
JUIST	Juist	No Special Conveyance	—	—
BORKUM	Borkum .... {	Corner of Prinz Heinrich Kaiserstrasse............	1¾	40
		Bahnhof (Station)—Strandstrasse	—	35

FARES

FROM ESSEN/MÜLHEIM TO	Single	Return 15 Days	Return 60 Days	Excess Baggage per Kg (2·2 lbs.)
	RM.	RM.	RM.	RM.
OSNABRÜCK				
NORDERNEY				
JUIST				
BORKUM				

130 ESSEN/MÜLHEIM—DORTMUND—FRANKFORT.O.M.— NÜRNBERG—MUNICH
D.L.H. (Weekdays only)

Route 99

Miles	Airports of			Airports of		
0	ESSEN/MÜLHEIM ...dep	...		MUNICH ... ...dep	10 15	
20½	DORTMUND ... ... arr	...		NÜRNBERG ... ... arr	11 20	
	,, ...dep	...		...dep	11 35	
130	FRANKFORT/M. ... arr	...		FRANKFORT/M. ... arr	13 0	
	,, ...dep	12 10		...dep	...	
258½	NÜRNBERG ... ... arr	13 35		DORTMUND ... ... arr	...	
	,, ...dep	13 50		...dep	...	
352	MUNICH ... ... arr	14 55		ESSEN/MÜLHEIM... arr	...	

Distance and Time allowance for conveyance between Airport and Town Terminus

TOWN	AIRPORT	TOWN TERMINUS	Miles	Minutes
ESSEN/M...............	Essen/M.	Verkehrsverein Essen, opposite Hauptbahnhof (Central Station)	6¾	30
DORTMUND	Brackel .... {	Hotel Fürstenhof, opposite Hauptbahnhof (Central Station)—On application	—	30
FRANKFORT/M. ...	Rebstock	Verkehrsverein, Betenstrasse, opposite Stadthaus (Town Hall).................................	5	35
		Hauptbahnhof (Central Station)—No Special Conveyance	3	30
NÜRNBERG	Nürnberg	Grand Hotel	2⅘	25
MUNICH	Oberwiesenfeld ...	Ritter von Epp-Platz 6 (Hotel Bayerischer Hof)	3½	40

FARES

FROM FRANKFORT	Single	Return 15 Days	Return 60 Days	Excess Baggage per Kg (2·2 lbs.)
	RM.	RM.	RM.	RM.
To NÜRNBERG	23	...	39·10	0·23
MUNICH...	44	...	74·80	0·44
FROM NÜRNBERG				
To MUNICH...	21	...	35·70	0·21

131 ESSEN/MÜLHEIM—DÜSSELDORF—COLOGNE—FRANKFORT.O.M. NÜRNBERG—MUNICH
D.L.H. (Weekdays only)
Route 53

Miles	Airports of					Airports of				
0	ESSEN/MÜLHEIM	... dep	13 45		MUNICH	...	...dep	...	
19	DÜSSELDORF ...	... arr	14 0		NÜRNBERG ...	...	arr	...	
		... dep	14 5			...	...dep	...	
40	COLOGNE	... arr	14 20		FRANKFORT ...	...	arr	...	
		... dep	14 25			...	...dep	9 0	
132	FRANKFORT ...	... arr	15 25		COLOGNE	...	arr	10 0	
		... dep	...			,,	...dep	13 5	
261	NÜRNBERG ...	... arr	...		DÜSSELDORF		... arr	13 20	
		... dep	...			,,	...dep	13 25	
355	MUNICH ...	...	... arr	...	ESSEN/MÜLHEIM		arr	13 40	

Distance and Time allowance for conveyance between Airport and Town Terminus

TOWN	AIRPORT	TOWN TERMINUS	Miles	Minutes
ESSEN/M.	Mülheim/Ruhr	Verkehrsverein Essen, opposite Hauptbahnhof (Central Station)	6¾	30
DÜSSELDORF	Lohausen	Hauptbahnhof (Central Station)	5½	30
COLOGNE	Butzweile Hof ...	Domhotel, Domhof	4¼	35
FRANKFORT/M. ...	Rebstock	Hauptbahnhof (Central Station)—No Special Conveyance	3	30
NÜRNBERG	Nürnberg	Grand Hotel	2⅜	25
MUNICH	Oberwiesenfeld ...	Ritter von Epp-Platz 6 (Hotel Bayerischer Hof)	3½	40

FARES

FROM ESSEN/M TO	Single	Return 15 Days	Return 60 Days	Excess Baggage per Kg (2·2 lbs.)
	RM.	RM.	RM.	RM.
DÜSSELDORF	10	...	17	0·15
COLOGNE	10	...	17	0·15
FRANKFORT	27	...	45·90	0·25
NÜRNBERG...	...	...	...	...
MUNICH	...	...	...	...

---

132 FRANKFORT.O.M.—STUTTGART
(Service suspended during Winter)
D.L.H.
Route 43

Miles	Airports of					Airports of		
0	FRANKFORT/M	...dep				STUTTGART ...	...dep	
101	STUTTGART ...	... arr				FRANKFORT/M	... arr	

Distance and Time allowance for conveyance between Airport and Town Terminus

TOWN	AIRPORT	TOWN TERMINUS	Miles	Minutes
FRANKFORT/M. ...	Rebstock	Hauptbahnhof (Central Station)—No Special Conveyance	3	30
STUTTGART	Böblingen	Luftverkehr Würtemberg A.G., Fürstenstrasse I	13¾	55

FARES

FROM FRANKFORT/M TO	Single	Return 15 Days	Return 60 Days	Excess Baggage per Kg (2·2 lbs.)
	RM.	RM.	RM.	RM.
STUTTGART				

FRANKFORT.O.M.—DARMSTADT—MANNHEIM/L/H—
KARLSRUHE—BADEN/BADEN
(Service suspended during Winter)
D.L.H.

133

Route 50

Miles	Airports of				Airports of		
0	FRANKFORT/M	...dep			BADEN-BADEN	..dep	
17½	DARMSTADT ...	... arr			KARLSRUHE ...	... arr	
	,, ...	...dep			,, ...	...dep	
45	MANNHEIM/L/H	... arr			MANNHEIM/L/H...	arr	
	,, ...	...dep			,, ...	...dep	
79	KARLSRUHE ...	... arr			DARMSTADT ...	... arr	
	,, ...	...dep			,, ...	...dep	
97½	BADEN-BADEN	... arr			FRANKFORT/M	... arr	

Distance and Time allowance for conveyance between Airport and Town Terminus

TOWN	AIRPORT	TOWN TERMINUS	Miles	Minutes
FRANKFORT/M ...	Rebstock	Hauptbahnhof (Central Station)—No Special Conveyance	3	30
DARMSTADT	Darmstadt	Verkehrsverein, Adolf Hitler Platz 4..............	3¾	25
		Mannheim—		
		Verkehrsverein Mannheim e. V.N. 2, 4—On application	3	20
		Palast Hotel, Augusta Anlage 4–8—On application	—	15
MANNHEIM/L/H ...	Neuostheim ...	Ludwigshafen—		
		Verkehrsverein, Kaiser Wilhelm Strasse 31	5	30
		Heidelberg—		
		Städt. Verkehrsamt, Anlage I—On application	12½	40
		Schlosshotel am Hauptbahnhof (Central Station)	3½	35
KARLSRUHE	Karlsruhe	Hotel Germania am Ettlinger Tor	2¾	30
BADEN-BADEN ...	Baden Oos	Reisebüro der Hapag, Sophienstrasse I—On application	4¼	30

FARES

FROM FRANKFORT/M TO	Single	Return 15 Days	Return 60 Days	Excess Baggage per Kg (2·2 lbs.)
	RM.	RM.	RM.	RM.
DARMSTADT				
MANNHEIM				
KARLSRUHE				
BADEN-BADEN				

134 FRANKFORT.O.M.—ERFURT—HALLE/LEIPZIG—(Berlin)
(Service suspended during Winter)
D.L.H.

Route 104

Miles	Airports of				Airports of			
0	**FRANKFORT/M** ... dep				**Berlin** (*Table 173*)... dep			
122½	**ERFURT** ... ... arr				**HALLE/LEIPZIG** ... dep			
	„ ... ... dep				**ERFURT** ... ... arr			
181½	**HALLE/LEIPZIG** ... arr				„ ... ... dep			
271½	**Berlin** (*Table 173*) ... arr				**FRANKFORT/M** ... arr			

Distance and Time allowance for conveyance between Airport and Town Terminus

TOWN	AIRPORT	TOWN TERMINUS	Miles	Minutes
FRANKFORT/M. ...	Rebstock	Hauptbahnhof (Central Station)—No Special Conveyance	3	30
ERFURT	Erfurt	Hauptbahnhof (Central Station), Haputausgang	3¾	25
HALLE/LEIPZIG	Schkeuditz	Halle— Postamt (Post Office), Thielenstrasse	—	35
		Hotel Stadt Hamburg, Gr. Steinstrasse 73...	15	40
		Leipzig— Hotel Astoria, Blücherplatz 2	10	30

FARES

FROM FRANKFORT/M TO	Single	Return 15 Days	Return 60 Days	Excess Baggage per Kg (2·2 lbs.)
	RM.	RM.	RM.	RM.
ERFURT				
HALLE/LEIPZIG				
BERLIN				

135 FRANKFORT.O.M.—STUTTGART—ZÜRICH
(Service suspended during Winter)
D.L.H.

Route 48

Miles	Airports of				Airports of			
0	**FRANKFORT/M** ... dep				**ZÜRICH** ... ... dep			
101	**STUTTGART** ... ... arr				**STUTTGART** ... ... arr			
	„ ... ... dep				„ ... ... dep			
202½	**ZÜRICH** ... ... arr				**FRANKFORT/M** ... arr			

Distance and Time allowance for conveyance between Airport and Town Terminus

TOWN	AIRPORT	TOWN TERMINUS	Miles	Minutes
FRANKFORT/M ...	Rebstock	Hauptbahnhof (Central Station)—No Special Conveyance	3	30
STUTTGART	Böblingen	Luftverkehr Würtemberg A.G., Fürstenstrasse I	13¾	50
ZÜRICH	Dübendorf	Hotel Schweizerhof, Bahnhofplatz	7⅛	40

FARES

FROM FRANKFORT/M TO	Single	Return 15 Days	Return 60 Days	Excess Baggage per Kg (2·2 lbs.)
	RM.	RM.	RM.	RM.
STUTTGART				
ZÜRICH				

136 BREMEN—WANGEROOGE—LANGEOOG—NORDERNEY
(Service suspended during Winter)
D.L.H.

Route 113

Miles	Airports of				Airports of			
0	**BREMEN** ... ...dep				**NORDERNEY** ...dep			
62	**WANGEROOGE** ... arr				**LANGEOOG** ... ... arr			
	„ ...dep				„ ... ...dep			
80	**LANGEOOG** ... ... arr				**WANGEROOGE** ... arr			
	„ ...dep				„ ...dep			
94½	**NORDERNEY** ... ... arr				**BREMEN** ... ...arr			

Distance and Time allowance for conveyance between Airport and Town Terminus

TOWN	AIRPORT	TOWN TERMINUS	Miles	Minutes
BREMEN	Neuenland	Hotel Columbus, Bahnhofstrasse 35	3¼	30
		(Temporarily Suspended)		
WANGEROOGE ...	Wangerooge	No Special Conveyance	1	—
SPIEKEROOG	Spiekeroog	No Special Conveyance	—	—
LANGEOOG	Langeoog	No Special Conveyance	½	—
NORDERNEY	Norderney	No Special Conveyance	1½	—

FARES

FROM BREMEN TO	Single	Return 15 Days	Return 60 Days	Excess Baggage per Kg (2·2 lbs.)
	RM.	RM.	RM.	RM.
WANGEROOGE				
SPIEKEROOG				
LANGEOOG				
NORDERNEY				

137 BREMEN—HAMBURG—BERLIN.
(Weekdays only)
D.L.H.

Route 14

Miles	Airports of				Airports of			
0	**BREMEN** ... ...dep	9 10			**BERLIN** ... ...dep	14 0		
58¼	**HAMBURG** ... ... arr	9 45			**HAMBURG** ... ... arr	15 25		
	„ ...dep	9 55			„ ...dep	15 35		
217	**BERLIN** ... ... arr	11 20			**BREMEN** ... ...arr	16 10		

Distance and Time allowance for conveyance between Airport and Town Terminus

TOWN	AIRPORT	TOWN TERMINUS	Miles	Minutes
BREMEN	Neuenland	No Special Conveyance.................................	3¼	—
HAMBURG	Fuhlsbüttel	Hauptbahnhof (Central Station), Hapag Reise-		
		büro	7½	40
BERLIN..................	Tempelhof	Linden/Freidrichstrasse—No Special Conveyance	3	—

FARES

FROM BREMEN	Single	Return 15 Days	Return 60 Days	Excess Baggage per Kg (2.2 lbs.)
	RM.	RM.	RM.	RM.
To HAMBURG	12	...	20·40	0·12
BERLIN	30	...	51	0·30
FROM HAMBURG				
To BERLIN	25	...	42·50	0·25

All times given in the Tables are local times, see page 22
Conveyance between an Airport and the Town Terminus is free unless otherwise indicated in the Table
The full names and addresses, etc., of the Companies will be found on pages 30 and 31

138 ESSEN/MÜLHEIM—DÜSSELDORF—COLOGNE—FRANKFORT.O.M.—MANNHEIM/L/H—KARLSRUHE
(Weekdays only)
D.L.H.

Miles	Airports of			Airports of		
0	ESSEN/MÜLHEIM	...dep	10 0	KARLSRUHE ...	...dep	11 50
19	DÜSSELDORF ...	...arr	10 15	MANNHEIM/L/H...	arr	12 15
	...	...dep	10 25	,,	...dep	12 25
40	COLOGNE ...	...arr	10 40	FRANKFORT/M	...arr	13 0
	...	...dep	10 55	,,	... ...dep	13 15
133	FRANKFORT/M	...arr	11 55	COLOGNE ...	...arr	14 15
	...	...dep	12 10	,,	...dep	14 30
177½	MANNHEIM/L/H	...arr	12 45	DÜSSELDORF	...arr	14 45
	,,	...dep	12 55	...	...dep	14 55
211¼	KARLSRUHE ...	...arr	13 20	ESSEN/MÜLHEIM	arr	15 10

Distance and Time allowance for conveyance between Airport and Town Terminus

TOWN	AIRPORT	TOWN TERMINUS	Miles	Minutes
ESSEN/MÜLHEIM ...	Mülheim/Ruhr	Essen:—Verkehrsverein, opposite the Station...	7	30
		Mülheim:—Hauptpost (General Post Office)—On application	3	20
DÜSSELDORF	Lohausen	Hauptbahnhof (Central Station)	5½	30
COLOGNE	Butzweiler Hof ...	Domhotel, Domhof	4⅛	40
FRANKFORT/M	Rebstock	Hauptbahnhof (Central Station)—No Special Conveyance	3	30
MANNHEIM/L/H ...	Neuostheim ...	Mannheim—		
		Verkehrsverein Mannheim e. V.N. 24—On application	3	20
		Palast Hotel, Augusta Anlage 4-8—On application	—	15
		Ludwigshafen—		
		Verkehrsverein, Kaiser Wilhelm Strasse 31...	5	30
		Heidelberg—		
		Städt Verkehrsamt, Anlage I—On application	12½	40
KARLSRUHE	Karlsruhe	Schlosshotel at the Central Station	3½	25
		Hotel Germania am Ettlinger Tor—On application	2½	20

FARES

FROM ESSEN/M. TO	Single	Return 15 Days	Return 60 Days	Excess Baggage per Kg (2·2 lbs.)
	RM.	RM.	RM.	RM.
DÜSSELDORF	10	...	17	0·10
COLOGNE	10	...	17	0·10
FRANKFORT	27	...	45·90	0·27
MANNHEIM/L/H	36	...	61·20	0·36
KARLSRUHE	43	...	73·10	0·43

140 BREMEN—HANOVER—HALLE/LEIPZIG—CHEMNITZ
(Weekdays only)
D.L.H.

Miles	Airports of					Airports of			
0	**BREMEN** ... ...dep	9 5				**CHEMNITZ** ... ...dep	...		
62	**HANOVER**... ... ... arr	9 50				HALLE/LEIPZIG ... arr	...		
	,, ... dep	...				,, ... dep	...		
188	**HALLE/LEIPZIG** ... arr	...				**HANOVER** ... ... arr	...		
	,, ... dep	...				,, ...dep	15 5		
237	**CHEMNITZ** ... ... arr	...				BREMEN ... ... arr	15 50		

Distance and Time allowance for conveyance between Airport and Town Terminus

TOWN	AIRPORT	TOWN TERMINUS	Miles	Minutes
BREMEN	Neuenland	No special Conveyance. * By tram from Station.	3¼	3¼*
HANOVER	Stader Chaussee	Hauptbahnhof (Central Station), Ernst-August Platz—On application	4	{ 20§ { 25‡
HALLE/LEIPZIG	Schkeuditz	Halle— Postamt (Post Office), Thielenstrasse ...... Hotel Hohenzollernhof, Hindenburgstr. 65...	— 15	35 40
CHEMNITZ	Chemnitz	Leipzig— Hotel Astoria, Blucherplatz 2 .... Bahnhofshotel (Continental) .... Verkehrsverein, Markt (corner of Ratskeller)...	10 3 —	30 30 25

§—Towards Halle/Leipzig   ‡—Towards Bremen

FARES

FROM BREMEN TO	Single	Return 15 Days	Return 60 Days	Excess Baggage per Kg (2·2 lbs.)
	RM.	RM.	RM.	RM.
HANOVER	15	...	25·50	0·15
HALLE/LEIPZIG	...	...	...	...
CHEMNITZ	...	...	...	...

141 BREMEN—HANOVER—ERFURT—BAYREUTH—NÜRNBERG
(Service suspended during Winter)
D.L.H.

Route 101

Miles	Airports of				Airports of	
0	**BREMEN** ... ...dep				**NÜRNBERG** ... ...dep	
62	**HANOVER**... ... ...arr				**BAYREUTH** ... ...arr	
	... ...dep				... ...dep	
174½	**ERFÜRT** ... ...arr				**ERFÜRT** ... ...arr	
	... ...dep				... ...dep	
279½	**BAŸREUTH** ... ...arr				**HANOVER** ... ...arr	
	... ...dep				... ...dep	
321	**NÜRNBERG** ... ... arr				**BREMEN** ... ...arr	

Distance and Time allowance for conveyance between Airport and Town Terminus

TOWN	AIRPORT	TOWN TERMINUS	Miles	Minutes
BREMEN	Neuenland	Hotel Columbus, Bahnhofstrasse 35 .... (Temporarily Suspended)	3½	30
HANOVER	Vahrenwalder	Hauptbahnhof (Central Station), Ernst-August Platz—On application	4	20
ERFURT	Erfurt	Hauptbahnhof (Central Station), Hauptausgang...	3¾	25
BAYREUTH	Bayreuth	No Special Conveyance	3	—
NÜRNBERG	Nürnberg	Grand Hotel	2¾	25

FARES

FROM BREMEN TO	Single	Return 15 Days	Return 60 Days	Excess Baggage per Kg (2.2 lbs.)
	RM.	RM.	RM.	RM.
HANOVER				
ERFURT				
BAYREUTH				
NÜRNBERG...				

MANNHEIM/L/H—KARLSRUHE—BADEN/BADEN—FREIBURG—
CONSTANCE—ZÜRICH
142
(Service suspended during Winter)
D.L.H.

Route 49

Miles	Airports of				Airports of	
0	**MANNHEIM/L/H**	...dep			**ZÜRICH**	...dep
33½	**KARLSRUHE** ...	... arr			**CONSTANCE**...	... arr
	,, ...	... dep			,, ...	... dep
52	**BADEN-BADEN**	... arr			**FREIBURG** ...	... arr
		... dep			,, ...	... dep
107	**FREIBURG**	... arr			**BADEN-BADEN**	... arr
	,, ...	... dep			,, ...	... dep
172	**CONSTANCE** ...	... arr			**KARLSRHUE** ...	... arr
	...	... dep			,, ...	... dep
207½	**ZÜRICH**	... arr			**MANNHEIM/L/H**...	arr

Distance and Time allowance for conveyance between Airport and Town Terminus

TOWN	AIRPORT	TOWN TERMINUS	Miles	Minutes
MANNHEIM/L/H ...	Neuostheim ...	Mannheim— Verkehrsverein Mannheim e. V.N. 2, 4—On application	3	20
		Palast Hotel, Augusta Anlage 4-8—On application	—	15
		Ludwigshafen— Verkehrsverein, Kaiser Wilhelm Strasse 31...	5	30
		Heidelberg— Städt. Verkehrsamt, Anlage I—On applica-tion	12½	40
KARLSRHUE	Karlsruhe	Schlosshotel am Hauptbahnhof (Central Station)	3½	35
BADEN-BADEN	Baden Oos	Hotel Germania am Ettlinger Tor	2¾	30
		Reisebüro der Hapag, Sophienstrasse I—On application	4¼	30
FREIBURG	Freiburg	Reisebüro des Nordd Lloyd, Rottecksplatz 11...	1¾	25
CONSTANCE	Constance	Verkehrsvrein, opposite Hauptpost (General Post Office)	1¾	30
ZÜRICH	Dübendorf	Hotel Schweizerhof Bahnhofplatz	7½	40

FARES

FROM MANNHEIM TO	Single	Return 15 Days	Return 60 Days	Excess Baggage per Kg (2·2 lbs.)
	RM.	RM.	RM.	RM.
KARLSRUHE				
BADEN-BADEN				
FREIBURG				
CONSTANCE				
ZÜRICH				

All times given in the Tables are local times, see page 22
Conveyance between an Airport and the Town Terminus is free unless otherwise indicated in the Table
The full names and addresses, etc., of the Companies will be found on pages 30 and 31
101

143 MANNHEIM/L/H—KARLSRUHE—STUTTGART—MUNICH
D.L.H. (Service suspended during Winter) Route 44

Miles	Airports of				Airports of	
0	MANNHEIM/L/H ...dep				MUNICH ... ...dep	
33½	KARLSRUHE ... ... arr				STUTTGART ... ... arr	
	„ ... ...dep				„ ... ...dep	
69½	STUTTGART ... ... arr				KARLSRUHE ... ... arr	
	„ ... ...dep				„ ... ...dep	
189	MUNICH ... ... arr				MANNHEIM/L/H... arr	

Distance and Time allowance for conveyance between Airport and Town Terminus

TOWN	AIRPORT	TOWN TERMINUS	Miles	Minutes
		Mannheim—		
		Verkehrsverein Mannheim e. V.N. 2, 4—On application	3	20
		Palast Hotel, Augusta Anlage 4-8—On application	—	15
MANNHEIM/L/H ...	Neuostheim ...	Ludwigshafen—		
		Verkehrsverein, Kaiser Wilhelm Strasse 31...	5	30
		Heidelberg—		
		Städt. Verkehrsamt, Anlage I—On application	12½	40
KARLSRUHE	Karlsruhe	Schlosshotel am Hauptbahnhof (Central Station)	3½	35
		Hotel Germania am Ettlinger Tor	2¾	30
STUTTGART	Böblingen	Luftverkehr Würtemberg A.G., Fürstenstrasse I	13¾	50
MUNICH	Oberwiesenfeld ...	Ritter von Epp-Platz 6 (Hotel Bayerischer Hof)...	3¼	40

FARES

FROM MANNHEIM TO	Single	Return 15 Days	Return 60 Days	Excess Baggage per Kg (2·2 lbs.)
	RM.	RM.	RM.	RM.
KARLSRUHE				
STUTTGART				
MUNICH				

144 HAMBURG—COPENHAGEN—MALMÖ
D.L.H. (Weekdays only) Routes 7, 8

Miles	Airports of			Airports of	
0	HAMBURG ... ...dep	13 15		MALMÖ ... ...dep	8 30
180	COPENHAGEN ... arr	14 55		COPENHAGEN ... arr	8 45
	„ ... dep	15 15		„ ... dep	9 5
197	MALMÖ ... ... arr	15 30		HAMBURG ... ... arr	10 45

Distance and Time allowance for conveyance between Airport and Town Terminus

TOWN	AIRPORT	TOWN TERMINUS	Miles	Minutes
HAMBURG	Fuhlsbüttel	Hauptbahnhof (Central Station), Hapag Reisebüro	7½	40
COPENHAGEN	Kastrup................	Passagebüro der D.D.L., Meldahlsgade 5	6¼	45
MALMÖ	Bultofta...............	Zentralbahnhof (Central Station)	2¼	30

FARES

FROM HAMBURG	Single	Return 15 Days	Return 60 Days	Excess Baggage per Kg (2·2 lbs.)
	RM.	RM.	RM.	RM.
To COPENHAGEN	50	...	85	0·50
MALMÖ	57	...	96·90	0·60
FROM MALMÖ	S. Kr.	S. Kr.	S. Kr.	S. Kr.
To COPENHAGEN	10	...	17	0·10
HAMBURG	75	...	127·50	0·75

145

(Berlin)—HAMBURG—BREMERHAVEN/WESERMUNDE— WANGEROOGE—LANGEOOG—NORDERNEY—BORKUM
(Service suspended during Winter)
D.L.H.

Route 125

Miles	Airports of Berlin (Table 137) ...dep			Airports of		
				BORKUM ... ...dep		
0	**HAMBURG** ... ...dep			**NORDERNEY** ... arr		
57	**BREMERHAVEN/** { arr			,, ...dep		
	WESERMUNDE { dep			**LANGEOOG** ... ... arr		
96	**WANGEROOGE** ... arr			... ...dep		
	,, ... dep			**WANGEROOGE** ... arr		
114	**LANGEOOG** ... ... arr			... dep		
	... ...dep			**BREMERHAVEN/** { arr		
128	**NORDERNEY** ... ... arr			**WESERMUNDE** { dep		
	... ...dep			**HAMBURG** ... ... arr		
147	**BORKUM** ... ... arr			Berlin (Table 137) arr		

Distance and Time allowance for conveyance between Airport and Town Terminus

TOWN	AIRPORT	TOWN TERMINUS	Miles	Minutes
HAMBURG	Fuhlsbüttel	Hauptbahnhof (Central Station), Hapag Reise-büro	$7\frac{1}{2}$	40
		Bahnhof (Station), Wesermunder/Bremerhaven	$4\frac{1}{2}$	40
BREMERHAVEN/W	Bremerhaven/W {	Hotel Excelsior, Bürgermeister Smidt-Strasse...	—	30
WANGEROOGE ...	Wangerooge	No Special Conveyance	1	—
SPIEKEROOG	Spiekeroog	No Special Conveyance	—	—
LANGEOOG	Langeoog	No Special Conveyance	$\frac{1}{2}$	—
NORDERNEY	Norderney	No Special Conveyance	$\frac{1}{2}$	—
JUIST	Juist	No Special Conveyance	—	—
		Corner of Prinz Heinrich Kaiserstrasse............	$1\frac{3}{4}$	40
BORKUM	Borkum ....{	Bahnhof (Station)—Strandstrasse	—	35

FARES

FROM HAMBURG TO	Single	Return 15 Days	Return 60 Days	Excess Baggage per Kg (2·2 lbs.)
	RM.	RM.	RM.	RM.
BREMERHAVEN/W				
WANGEROOGE				
SPIEKEROOG				
LANGEOOG				
NORDERNEY				
JUIST				
BORKUM				

146

HAMBURG—HANOVER—FRANKFORT.O.M.—STUTTGART
(Weekdays only)
D.L.H.

Route 121

Miles	Airports of						Airports of				
0	**HAMBURG**	...	... dep	9 10			**STUTTGART** ...	... dep	12 5		
83	**HANOVER**...	...	... arr	9 55			**FRANKFORT/M**	... arr	12 55		
	,,	...	... dep	10 15			,,	...	... dep	13 20	
247	**FRANKFORT/M**		... arr	11 40			**HANOVER**	...	... arr	14 45	
	,,	...	... dep	12 5			,,	...	... dep	15 0	
348	**STUTTGART**	...	... arr	12 55			**HAMBURG**	...	... arr	15 45	

Distance and Time allowance for conveyance between Airport and Town Terminus

TOWN	AIRPORT	TOWN TERMINUS	Miles	Minutes
HAMBURG	Fuhlsbüttel	Hauptbahnhof (Central Station), Hapag Relse-büro	7½	40
HANOVER	Stader Chaussee...	Hauptbahnhof (Central Station), Ernst-August Platz—On application	4	{25§ / 20‡
FRANKFURT/M. ...	Rebstock	Hauptbahnhof (Central Station)—No Special Conveyance	3	30
STUTTGART	Böblingen	Luftverkehr Würtemberg A.G., Fürstenstrasse I	13¾	55

§—Towards Frankfort   ‡—Towards Hamburg

FARES

	HANOVER			FRANKFORT/M.			STUTTGART		
	RM.			RM.			RM.		
	Single	Ret.	Ex. Bag.	Single	Ret.	Ex. Bag.	Single	Ret.	Ex. Bag.
HAMBURG ...	20	34	0·20	55	93·50	0·55	76	129·20	0·76
HANOVER ...	...	...	...	35	59·50	0·35	56	95·20	0·56
FRANKFORT/M	...	...	...	...	...	...	21	35·70	0·21

Ret.—Return 60 days.   Ex. Bag.—Excess Baggage per Kg (2·2 lbs.).

147

STUTTGART—FRIEDRICHSHAFEN
(Service suspended during Winter)
D.L.H.

Route 40

Miles	Airports of					Airports of		
						FRIEDRICHS-		
0	**STUTTGART**	...	... dep			**HAFEN** ...	... dep	
74½	**FRIEDRICHSHAFEN**	arr				**STUTTGART** ...	... arr	

Distance and Time allowance for conveyance between Airport and Town Terminus

TOWN	AIRPORT	TOWN TERMINUS	Miles	Minutes
STUTTGART	Böblingen	Luftverkehr Würtemberg A.G., Fürstenstrasse I	13¾	55
FRIEDRICHSHAFEN	Löwental	Kurgarten Hotel	1½	30

FARES

FROM STUTTGART TO	Single	Return 15 Days	Return 60 Days	Excess Baggage per Kg (2·2 lbs.)
	RM.	RM.	RM.	RM.
FRIEDRICHSHAFEN				

150 HAMBURG—KIEL—FLENSBURG—WYK—WESTERLAND
(Service suspended during Winter)
D.L.H.

Route 123

Miles	Airports of					Airports of			
0	HAMBURG ... ...dep					WESTERLAND ...dep			
56	KIEL ... ...arr					WYK ... ...arr			
	,, ...dep					,, ...dep			
99½	FLENSBURG ... ...arr					FLENSBURG ... ...arr			
	,, ...dep					,, ...dep			
136	WYK ... ...arr					KIEL ... ...arr			
	,, ...dep					,, ...dep			
153	WESTERLAND... ...arr					HAMBURG ... ...arr			

Distance and Time allowance for conveyance between Airport and Town Terminus				
TOWN	AIRPORT	TOWN TERMINUS	Miles	Minutes
HAMBURG	Fuhlsbüttel	Hauptbahnhof (Central Station), Hapag Reise-büro	7½	40
KIEL	Holtenau	Hauptbahnhof (Central Station), opposite Hansa Hotel	5¼	35
		Dreiecksplatz, opposite the Capitol-licht-spielen	—	30
		Opposite Holstenbrauerie	—	25
		Reisebüro im Zentraiomnibus Station	3	25
FLENSBURG	Schäferhaus	Reichsbahnhof or Bahnhof (Station) Harrislee—On application		
WYK....................	Wyk	Hapag Seebäderdienst, Sandwall.....................	1¾	30
WESTERLAND	Westerland	Postamt (Post Office)	2¼	30

FARES

FROM HAMBURG TO	Single	Return 15 Days	Return 60 Days	Excess Baggage per Kg (2·2 lbs.)
	RM.	RM.	RM.	RM.
KIEL				
FLENSBURG				
WYK				
WESTERLAND				

151 STUTTGART—FREIBURG
(Weekdays only)
D.L.H.

Route 46

Miles	Airports of			Airports of		
	STUTTGART ... .. dep	14 20		FREIBURG ... ...dep	10 30	
71½	FREIBURG ... ... arr	15 15		STUTTGART ... ...arr	11 25	

Distance and Time allowance for conveyance between Airport and Town Terminus				
TOWN	AIRPORT	TOWN TERMINUS	Miles	Minutes
STUTTGART	Böblingen	Luftverekhr Würtemberg A.G., Fürstenstrasse I	13¾	50
FREIBURG	Freiburg	Reisebüro des Nordd Lloyd, Rottecksplatz II	1¾	25

FARES

FROM STUTTGART TO	Single	Return 15 Days	Return 60 Days	Excess Baggage per Kg (2·2 lbs.)
	RM.	RM.	RM.	RM.
FREIBURG	18	...	30·60	0·20

All times given in the Tables are local times, see page 22
Conveyance between an Airport and the Town Terminus is free unless otherwise indicated in the Table
The full names and addresses, etc., of the Companies will be found on pages 30 and 31

152
STUTTGART—NÜRNBERG—BAYREUTH—PLAUEN— CHEMNITZ—DRESDEN
D.L.H.—(Service suspended during Winter)

Route 145

Miles	Airports of					Airports of			
0	STUTTGART	...	...dep			DRESDEN...	...	...dep	
106	NÜRNBERG	...	...arr			CHEMNITZ	...	...dep	
		...	...dep				...	...dep	
147	BAYREUTH	...	...arr			PLAUEN ...	...	...arr	
		...	...dep				...	...dep	
191	PLAUEN	...	...arr			BAYREUTH	...	...arr	
		...	...dep				...	...dep	
233	CHEMNITZ	...	...arr			NÜRNBERG	...	...arr	
		...	...dep				...	...dep	
271½	DRESDEN ...	...	...arr			STUTTGART	...	...arr	

Distance and Time allowance for conveyance between Airport and Town Terminus

TOWN	AIRPORT	TOWN TERMINUS	Miles	Minutes
STUTTGART	Böblingen	Luftverkehr Würtemberg A.G., Fürstenstrasse I	13¾	45
NÜRNBERG	Nürnberg	Grand Hotel	2¼	25
BAYERUTH	Bayreuth	No Special Conveyance	3	—
PLAUEN	Plauen .... {	Reisebüro Koch, Bahnhofstrasse 22—On application	3¾	30
		Hotel Kronprinz, opposite Postamt (Post Office), 4, Pauserstrasse—On application	—	25
CHEMNITZ	Chemnitz .... {	Bahnhofshotel (Continental)	3	30
		Verkehrsverein, Markt (corner of Ratskeller)...	—	25
DRESDEN	Heller	Reisebüro, Hauptbahnhof (Central Station)......	5	30

FARES

FROM STUTTGART TO	Single	Return 15 Days	Return 60 Days	Excess Baggage per Kg (2·2 lbs.)
	RM.	RM.	RM.	RM.
NÜRNBERG...				
BAYREUTH				
PLAUEN				
CHEMNITZ				
DRESDEN				

153
STUTTGART—GENEVA—MARSEILLES—BARCELONA
(Weekdays only)
D.L.H.

Route 22

Miles	Airports of					Airports of			
0	STUTTGART	...	...dep	9 30		BARCELONA		...dep 8 45	
219	GENEVA	...	...arr	11 20		MARSEILLES ...		...arr 10 45	
		...	...dep	11 40			...	...dep 11 5	
455	MARSEILLES	...	...arr	12 30		GENEVA ...	...	...arr 13 45	
		...	...dep	12 50			...	...dep 14 5	
733	BARCELONA	...	...arr	15 0		STUTTGART ...	...	...arr 15 45	

Distance and Time allowance for conveyance between Airport and Town Terminus

TOWN	AIRPORT	TOWN TERMINUS	Miles	Minutes
STUTTGART	Böblingen	Luftverkehr Würtemberg A.G., Fürstenstrasse I	13¾	50
GENEVA	Cointrin	Place des Bergues, 3	2½	30
MARSEILLES	Marignane	Air France, I Rue Papère	17½	70
BARCELONA	Barcelona	Diputación, 260	15½	45

FARES

FROM STUTTGART TO	Single	Return 15 Days	Return 60 Days	Excess Baggage per Kg (2·2 lbs.)
	RM.	RM.	RM.	RM.
GENEVA	45	...	76·50	0·45
MARSEILLES...	90	...	153·0	0·90
BARCELONA	135	...	229·50	1·35

154

KIEL—BERLIN
D.L.H.—(Service suspended during Winter)

Miles	Airports of				Airports of			
0	KIEL ... ...dep				BERLIN ... ...dep			
180	BERLIN ... ... arr				KIEL ... ... arr			

Distance and Time allowance for conveyance between Airport and Town Terminus

TOWN	AIRPORT	TOWN TERMINUS	Miles	Minutes
KIEL	Holtenau	Hauptbahnhof (Central Station), opposite Hansa Hotel	5¼	35
		Dreiecksplatz, opposite the Capitol-licht-spielen	—	30
		Opposite Holstenbruerle	—	25
BERLIN..................	Tempelhof	Linden/Freidrichstrasse—No Special Conveyance	3	—

FARES

FROM KIEL TO	Single	Return 15 Days	Return 60 Days	Excess Baggage per Kg (2·2 lbs.)
	RM.	RM.	RM.	RM.
BERLIN				

155

(Berlin)—KIEL—FLENSBURG—WESTERLAND—WYK
D.L.H.—(Service suspended during Winter)

Miles	Airports of				Airports of			
	Berlin (Table 154) ...dep				WYK ... ...dep			
					WESTERLAND ... arr			
0	KIEL ... ...dep				" ... ...dep			
43½	FLENSBURG ... ... arr				FLENSBURG ... ... arr			
	" ... ...dep				" ... ...dep			
89½	WESTERLAND... ... arr				KIEL ... ... arr			
	" ... ...dep				Berlin (Table 154) ... arr			
107½	WYK ... ... arr							

Distance and Time allowance for conveyance between Airport and Town Terminus

TOWN	AIRPORT	TOWN TERMINUS	Miles	Minutes
KIEL	Holtenau	Hauptbahnhof (Central Station), opposite Hansa Hotel	5¼	35
		Dreiecksplatz, opposite the Capitol-lichtspielen	—	30
		Opposite Holstenbruerie	—	25
		Reisebüro im Zentralomnibus Station.............	3	25
FLENSBURG	Schäferhaus	Reichsbahnhof or Bahnhof (Station) Harrislee—On application	—	—
WESTERLAND	Westerland	Postamt (Post Office)	2¾	30
WYK....................	Wyk	Hapag-Seebäderdienst, Sandwall	1½	30

FARES

FROM BERLIN TO	Single	Return 15 Days	Return 60 Days	Excess Baggage per Kg (2·2 lbs.)
	RM.	RM.	RM.	RM.
KIEL				
FLENSBURG				
WESTERLAND				
WYK				

156 HALLE/LEIPZIG—CHEMNITZ—KARLSBAD—MARIENBAD
(Service suspended during Winter)
D.L.H.; C.L.S.

Route 149

Miles	Airports of				Airports of		
0	HALLE/LEIPZIG ... ...dep				MARIENBAD ... ...dep		
49	CHEMNITZ ... ... arr				KARLSBAD ... ... arr		
	,, ... dep				... ... dep		
91	KARLSBAD... ... ... arr				CHEMNITZ ... ... arr		
	... ... dep				,, ... dep		
110	MARIENBAD ... ... arr				HALLE/LEIPZIG ... arr		

Distance and Time allowance for conveyance between Airport and Town Terminus

TOWN	AIRPORT	TOWN TERMINUS	Miles	Minutes
HALLE/LEIPZIG	Schkeuditz	Halle—		
		Postamt (Post Office), Thielenstrasse	—	35
		Hotel Stadt Hamburg, Gr. Steinstrasse 73...	15	40
		Leipzig—		
		Hotel Astoria, Blücherplatz 2	10	30
CHEMNITZ	Chemnitz	Bahnhofshotel (Continental)	3	30
		Verkehrsverein, Markt (corner of Ratskeller)...	—	25
KARLSBAD	Karlsbad	Städtisches Flugverkehrsbüro, Theaterplatz......	5½	30
MARIENBAD	Sklare	Haus Sanssouci	4¼	30

FARES

FROM HALLE/LEIPZIG TO	Single	Return 15 Days	Return 60 Days	Excess Baggage per Kg (2·2 lbs.)
	RM.	RM.	RM.	RM.
CHEMNITZ				
KARLSBAD				
MARIENBAD				

157 MUNICH—MILAN
(Service suspended during Winter)
D.L.H.; A.L.I.

Route 42

Miles	Airports of				Airports of		
0	MUNICH ... ...dep				MILAN ... ...dep		
283	MILAN ... ... arr				MUNICH ... ... arr		

Distance and Time allowance for conveyance between Airport and Town Terminus

TOWN	AIRPORT	TOWN TERMINUS	Miles	Minutes
MUNICH	Oberwiesenfeld ...	Ritter von Epp-Platz 6 (Hotel Bayerischer Hof)...	3½	40
MILAN	Milan	A.L.I. Via Sta. Margherita 16 (Hotel Regina)...	3¾	30

FARES

FROM MUNICH TO	Single	Return 15 Days	Return 60 Days	Excess Baggage per Kg (2·2 lbs.)
	RM.	RM.	RM.	RM.
MILAN				

All times given in the Tables are local times, see page 22
Conveyance between an Airport and the Town Terminus is free unless otherwise indicated in the Table
The full names and addresses, etc., of the Companies will be found on pages 30 and 31

160

HALLE/LEIPZIG—GERA—ZWICKAU—PLAUEN
(Service suspended during Winter)
D.L.H.

Miles	Airports of					Airports of			
0	**HALLE/LEIPZIG**	...dep				**PLAUEN**	...dep		
36	**GERA**	...arr				**ZWICKAU** ...	...arr		
	... ...	...dep				,, ...	...dep		
59	**ZWICKAU** ...	...arr				**GERA**	...arr		
	,, ...	...dep				,, ...	...dep		
81	**PLAUEN**	...arr				**HALLE/LEIPZIG**	...arr		

Distance and Time allowance for conveyance between Airport and Town Terminus

TOWN	AIRPORT	TOWN TERMINUS	Miles	Minutes
		Halle—		
HALLE/LEIPZIG ...	Schkeuditz	Postamt (Post Office), Thielenstrasse	—	35
		Hotel Stadt Hamburg, Gr. Steinstrasse 73...	15	40
		Leipzig—		
		Hotel Astoria, Blücherplatz 2	10	30
GERA	Gera	Rathaus Reklamelaterne—On application.........	2½	20
		Reisebüro Meitzner	2½	20
ZWICKAU	Zwickau			
		Hauptbahnhof (Central Station)—On application	—	15
		Reisebüro Koch, Bahnhofstrasse 22—On appli-		
PLAUEN	Plauen	cation	3¾	30
		Hotel Kronprinz, opposite Postamt (Post Office),		
		4, Pauserstrasse—On application	—	25

FARES

FROM HALLE/LEIPZIG TO	Single	Return 15 Days	Return 60 Days	Excess Baggage per Kg (2·2 lbs.)
	RM.	RM.	RM.	RM.
GERA ... ...:				
ZWICKAU ... ...:				
PLAUEN ... ...:				

161 (Berlin)—DRESDEN—GÖRLITZ—RIESENGEBIRGE/HIRSCHBERG—BRESLAU
(Service suspended during Winter)
D.L.H.

Route 160

Miles	Airports of										
	Berlin (Table 110) ... dep										
0	DRESDEN ... ... dep										
55	GÖRLITZ ... ... arr										
	,, ... dep										
91	RIESENGEBIRGE/H ... arr										
	... dep										
150	BRESLAU ... ... arr										

Miles	Airports of										
0	BRESLAU ... ... dep										
59	RIESENGEBIRGE/H ... arr										
	,, dep										
95	GÖRLITZ ... ... arr										
	,, ... dep										
150	DRESDEN ... ... arr										
	Berlin (Table 110) ... arr										

Distance and Time allowance for conveyance between Airport and Town Terminus

TOWN	AIRPORT	TOWN TERMINUS	Miles	Minutes
DRESDEN	Heller	Reisebüro, Hauptbahnhof (Central Station)......	5	30
GÖRLITZ	Görlitz	Verkehrsverein, Adolf-Hitler-Strasse 29	2½	30
		Reisebüro O. Ringert, Adolf-Hitler-Strasse 2 ...	—	25
RIESENGEBIRGE/H.	Hartau	Hirschberger Reisebüro, Adolf-Hitler-Platz ...	2½	25
BRESLAU	Gandau	Nordhotel—No Special Conveyance	5	—

FARES

FROM BERLIN TO	Single	Return 15 Days	Return 60 Days	Excess Baggage per Kg (2·2 lbs.)
	RM.	RM.	RM.	RM.
GÖRLITZ				
RIESENBGEIRGE/H				
BRESLAU				

162

(Berlin—Danzig)—KÖNIGSBERG—TILSIT—RIGA—
TALLINN—LENINGRAD
(Service suspended during Winter)
DERULUFT

Miles	Airports of				Airports of			
0	**Berlin** (*Table 112*) ... dep				**LENINGRAD** ... ...dep			
253½	**Danzig** (*Table 112*) ... dep				**TALLINN** ... ... dep			
340¼	**KÖNIGSBERG** ... ...dep				,, ...dep			
401	**TILSIT** ... ... arr				**RIGA** ... ... arr			
	,, ... dep				,, ...dep			
569	**RIGA** ... ... arr				**TILSIT** ... ... arr			
	,, ... dep				,, ...dep			
768½	**TALLINN** ... ... arr				**KÖNIGSBERG** ... arr			
	,, ... dep				**Danzig** (*Table 112*) , arr			
985	**LENINGRAD** ... ... arr				**Berlin** (*Table 112*)... arr			

Distance and Time allowance for conveyance between Airport and Town Terminus or Centre of Town

TOWN	AIRPORT	TOWN TERMINUS	Miles	Minutes
KÖNIGSBERG/Pr ...	Devau	No Special Conveyance—*By Tram	2	30*
TILSIT	Splitter	Post Office	5	30
		Bahnhof (Station)	—	25
RIGA	Spilve	No Special Conveyance	4¼	—
TALLINN	Tallinna lennujaam	No Special Conveyance	3	—
LENINGRAD	Korpusny	Hotel Europejskaja Gostiniza—On application...	3¾	—

FARES

FROM BERLIN TO	Single	Return 15 Days	Return 60 Days	Excess Baggage per Kg (2·2 lbs.)
	RM.	RM.	RM.	RM.
DANZIG				
KÖNIGSBERG				
TILSIT				
RIGA				
TALLINN				
LENINGRAD				

163 BASLE—BERNE—LAUSANNE—GENEVA
(Service suspended during Winter)
ALPAR—BERN
Routes 537, 536, 535

Miles	Airports of					Airports of			
0	BASLE ... ...dep					GENEVA ... ...dep			
50	BERNE... ... ... arr					LAUSANNE ... ... arr			
	,, ...dep					,, ...dep			
101	LAUSANNE ... ... arr					BERNE ... ... arr			
	,, ...dep					,, ...dep			
138	GENEVA ... ... arr					BASLE ... ... arr			

Distance and Time allowance for conveyance between Airport and Town Terminus				
TOWN	AIRPORT	TOWN TERMINUS	Miles	Minutes
BASLE	Birsfelden	Luftreisebüro Swissair, Centralbahnplatz (Central Station Square)	2½	30
BERNE	Belpmoos	Bahnhofplatz (Station Square)	6¼	30
LAUSANNE............	La Blecherette...{	Place St. Francois 12....................................	1¾	25
GENEVA	Cointrin	Bahnhof, C.F.F. (Station)	2	30
		Place des Bergues	2⅛	30

FARES

FROM BASLE TO	Single	Return 15 Days	Return 60 Days	Excess Baggage per Kg (2·2 lbs.)
	S. Frs.	S. Frs.	S. Frs.	S. Frs.
BERNE				
LAUSANNE				
GENEVA				

164 BERNE—ZÜRICH—ST. GALLEN
(Service suspended during Winter)
ALPAR—BERN ; AERO ST. GALLEN
Routes 533, 534

Miles	Airports of					Airports of			
0	BERNE... ... ...dep					ST. GALLEN ... ...dep			
59	ZÜRICH ... ... arr					ZÜRICH ... ... arr			
	,, ...dep					,, ...dep			
109	ST. GALLEN ... ... arr					BERNE ... ... arr			

Distance and Time allowance for conveyance between Airport and Town Terminus				
TOWN	AIRPORT	TOWN TERMINUS	Miles	Minutes
BERNE	Belpmoos	Bahnhofplatz (Station Square)	6¼	30
ZÜRICH	Dübendorf	Hotel Schweizerhof, Bahnhofplatz (Station Square)	7½	40
ST. GALLEN	Altenrhein	Oeffentl. Verkehrsbüro	10	50

FARES

FROM BERNE TO	Single	Return 15 Days	Return 60 Days	Excess Baggage per Kg (2·2 lbs.)
	S. Frs.	S. Frs.	S. Frs.	S. Frs.
ZÜRICH				
ST. GALLEN				

All times given in the Tables are local times, see page 22
Conveyance between an Airport and the Town Terminus is free unless otherwise indicated in the Table
The full names and addresses, etc., of the Companies will be found on pages 30 and 31

165 BASLE—LA CHAUX DE FONDS—BERNE—LAUSANNE—GENEVA
(Service suspended during Winter)
ALPAR—BERN
Route 532

Miles	Airports of				Airports of	
0	BASLE ... ...dep				GENEVA ... ...dep	
50	LA CHAUX ... ... arr				LAUSANNE ... ... arr	
	DE FONDS ...dep				,, ...dep	
91	BERNE ... ... arr				BERNE ... ... arr	
	,, ...dep				... ...dep	
142	LAUSANNE ... ... arr				LA CHAUX ... ... arr	
	,, ...dep				DE FONDS ...dep	
179	GENEVA ... ... arr				BASLE ... ... arr	

Distance and Time allowance for conveyance between Airport and Town Terminus

TOWN	AIRPORT	TOWN TERMINUS	Miles	Minutes
BASLE	Birsfelden	Luftreisebüro Swissair, - Centralbahnplatz (Central Station Square)	2½	30
LA CHAUX DE FONDS	La Chaux de Fonds	J. Veron, Grauer & Cie, Place de la Gare (Station Square)	1½	30 .
BERNE	Belpmoos	Bahnhofplatz (Station Square)	6¼	30
		Place St. Francois 12....................................	1¾	25
LAUSANNE...........	La Blecherette...{			
		Bahnhof, C.F.F. (Station)	2	30
GENEVA	Cointrin	Place des Bergues	2½	30

FARES

FROM BASLE TO	Single	Return 15 Days	Return 60 Days	Excess Baggage per Kg (2·2 lbs.)
	S. Frs.	S. Frs.	S. Frs.	S. Frs.
LA CHAUX DE FONDS ...				
BERNE				
LAUSANNE				
GENEVA				

166 GENEVA—LAUSANNE
(Service suspended during Winter)
ALPAR—BERN
Route 478a

Miles	Airports of				Airports of	
0	GENEVA ... ...dep				LAUSANNE ... ...dep	
37	LAUSANNE ... ... arr				GENEVA ... ... arr	

Distance and Time allowance for conveyance between Airport and Town Terminus

TOWN	AIRPORT	TOWN TERMINUS	Miles	Minutes
GENEVA	Cointrin	Place des Bergues	2½	30
		Place St. Francois 12....................................	1¾	25
LAUSANNE...........	La Blècherette...{			
		Bahnhof (Station) C.F.F.	2	30

FARES

FROM GENEVA TO	Single	Return 15 Days	Return 60 Days	Excess Baggage per Kg (2.2 lbs.)
	S. Frs.	S. Frs.	S. Frs.	S. Frs.
LAUSANNE				

167

BASLE—(Geneva)—ZÜRICH—MUNICH—VIENNA
(Service suspended during Winter)
SWISSAIR

Routes 541b, 541

Miles	Airports of					Airports of		
0	**BASLE** ... ... **...dep**					**VIENNA** ... ... **...dep**		
50	**ZÜRICH** ... ... **arr**					**MUNICH** ... **... arr**		
	Geneva (Table 170)... dep					... **...dep**		
50	**ZÜRICH** ... ... **...dep**					**ZÜRICH** ... ... **... arr**		
200	**MUNICH** ... ... **... arr**					Geneva (Table 170) arr		
	„ ... ... **...dep**					**ZÜRICH** ... ... **...dep**		
429	**VIENNA** ... ... **... arr**					**BASLE** ... ... **... arr**		

Distance and Time allowance for conveyance between Airport and Town Terminus				
TOWN	AIRPORT	TOWN TERMINUS	Miles	Minutes
BASLE	Birsfelden	Luftreisebüro Swissair, Centralbahnplatz (Central Station Square)	2½	30
ZÜRICH	Dübendorf	Hotel Schweizerhof, Bahnhofplatz (Station Square)	7½	40
MUNICH	Oberwiesenfeld ...	Luftreisebüro, Ritter von Epp-Platz 6 (Hotel Bayerischerhof)	3½	40
VIENNA	Aspern	Austroflug, Kärntnerring 5 (Hotel Bristol), Vienna I.................................	9½	35

FARES

FROM BASLE TO	Single	Return 15 Days	Return 60 Days	Excess Baggage per Kg (2·2 lbs.)
	S. Frs.	S. Frs.	S. Frs.	S. Frs.
ZÜRICH				
MUNICH				
VIENNA				

170

GENEVA—BERNE—ZÜRICH
(Service suspended during Winter)
SWISSAIR

Route 541a

Miles	Airports of					Airports of		
0	**GENEVA** ... ... **...dep**					**ZÜRICH** ... ... **...dep**		
78	**BERNE** ... ... **arr**					**BERNE** ... ... **... arr**		
	„ ... ... **...dep**					„ ... ... **...dep**		
137	**ZÜRICH** ... ... **... arr**					**GENEVA** ... ... **... arr**		

Distance and Time allowance for conveyance between Airport and Town Terminus				
TOWN	AIRPORT	TOWN TERMINUS	Miles	Minutes
GENEVA	Cointrin	Place des Bergues	2½	30
BERNE	Belpmoos	Bahnhofplatz (Station Square)	6¼	30
ZÜRICH	Dübendorf	Hotel Schweizerhof, Bahnhofplatz (Station Square)	7½	40

FARES

FROM GENEVA TO	Single	Return 15 Days	Return 60 Days	Excess Baggage per Kg (2·2 lbs.)
	S. Frs.	S. Frs.	S. Frs.	S. Frs.
BERNE				
ZÜRICH				

171

ZÜRICH—MUNICH—VIENNA
(Service suspended during Winter)
D.L.H.

Route 41

Miles	Airports of					Airports of		
0	ZÜRICH ... ...dep					VIENNA ... ...dep		
150	MUNICH ... ... arr					MUNICH ... ... arr		
	,, ... dep					... ...dep		
375	VIENNA ... ... arr					ZÜRICH ... ... arr		

Distance and Time allowance for conveyance between Airport and Town Terminus

TOWN	AIRPORT	TOWN TERMINUS	Miles	Minutes
ZÜRICH	Dübendorf	Hotel Schweizerhof, Bahnhofplatz (Station Square)	7½	40
MUNICH	Oberwiesenfeld ...	Ritter von Epp-Platz 6 (Hotel Bayerischerhof)	3½	40
VIENNA	Aspern	Austroflug, Kärntnerring 5 (Hotel Bristol), Vienna I...	9½	35

FARES

FROM ZÜRICH TO	Single	Return 15 Days	Return 60 Days	Excess Baggage per Kg (2·2 lbs.)
	S. Frs.	S. Frs.	S. Frs.	S. Frs.
MUNICH				
VIENNA				

172

ZÜRICH—MILAN
(Service suspended during Winter)
A.L.I.

Route 347a

Miles	Airports of					Airports of		
0	ZÜRICH ... ...dep					MILAN ... ...dep		
152	MILAN ... ... arr					ZÜRICH ... ... arr		

Distance and Time allowance for conveyance between Airport and Town Terminus

TOWN	AIRPORT	TOWN TERMINUS	Miles	Minutes
ZÜRICH	Dübendorf...........	Hotel Schweizerhof, Bahnhofplatz (Station Square)	7½	40
MILAN	Milan	A.L.I. Via Sta. Margherita 16 (Hotel Regina)...	3¾	30

FARES

FROM ZÜRICH TO	Single	Return 15 Days	Return 60 Days	Excess Baggage per Kg (2·2 lbs.)
	S. Frs.	S. Frs.	S. Frs.	S. Frs.
MILAN				

173

ZÜRICH—STUTTGART—HALLE/LEIPZIG—BERLIN
(Weekdays only)
D.L.H.

Route 12

Miles	Airports of				Airports of			
0	**ZÜRICH**	... dep	10 50		**BERLIN**	... dep	11 15	
102	**STUTTGART** ...	... arr	11 40		**HALLE/LEIPZIG**	... arr	12 0	
	,,	... dep	12 0		,,	... dep	12 10	
345	**HALLE/LEIPZIG** ...	... arr	13 50		**STUTTGART** ...	... arr	14 0	
	,,	... dep	14 5		,,	... dep	14 20	
435	**BERLIN**	... arr	14 50		**ZÜRICH**	... arr	15 10	

Distance and Time allowance for conveyance between Airport and Town Terminus

TOWN	AIRPORT	TOWN TERMINUS	Miles	Minutes
ZÜRICH	Dübendorf	Hotel Schweizerhof, Bahnhofplatz (Station Square)...	7½	40
STUTTGART	Böblingen	Luftverkehr Würtemberg A.G., Fürstenstrasse 1	13¾	50
HALLE/LEIPZIG	Schkeuditz	Halle—		
		Postamt (Post Office), Thielenstrasse	—	40
		Hotel Hohenzollernhof, Hindenburgstr. 65...	15	45
		Leipzig—		
		Hotel Astoria, Blücherplatz 2	10	35
BERLIN	Tempelhof	Linden/Friedrichstrasse—No Special Conveyance	3	—

FARES

FROM ZÜRICH	Single	Return 15 Days	Return 60 Days	Excess Baggage per Kg (2·2 lbs.)
	S. Frs.	S. Frs.	S. Frs.	S. Frs.
To STUTTGART	31	...	52·70	0·31
HALLE/LEIPZIG	94	...	159·80	0·94
BERLIN	120	...	204	1·20
FROM BERLIN	RM.	RM.	RM.	RM.
To HALLE/LEIPZIG	20	...	34	0·20
STUTTGART	70	...	119	0·70
ZÜRICH	95	...	161·50	0·95

174

TURIN—MILAN
(Service suspended during Winter)
A.L.I.

Route 346

Miles	Airports of				Airports of			
0	**TURIN**	... dep			**MILAN**	... dep		
87	**MILAN**	... arr			**TURIN**	... arr		

Distance and Time allowance for conveyance between Airport and Town Terminus

TOWN	AIRPORT	TOWN TERMINUS	Miles	Minutes
TURIN	Turin	C.I.T. Via XX Settembre 3............................	3¾	—
MILAN	Milan	A.L.I. Via Sta. Margherita 16 (Hotel Regina) ...	3¾	30

FARES

FROM TURIN TO	Single	Return 15 Days	Return 60 Days	Excess Baggage per Kg (2·2 lbs.)
	Lire	Lire	Lire	Lire
MILAN				

All times given in the Tables are local times, see page 22
Conveyance between an Airport and the Town Terminus is free unless otherwise indicated in the Table
The full names and addresses, etc., of the Companies will be found on pages 30 and 31

175

ROME—NAPLES—SYRACUSE—MALTA—TRIPOLI

A.L.S.A.

Route 362

Miles	Airports of		T	M	Airports of		T	M
0	**ROME**	...dep	7 20	9 0	**TRIPOLI**	...dep	7 20	7 20
	NAPLES	... arr	8 40	...	**MALTA**	... arr	...	9 35
	,, ...	...dep	9 10	...	,, ...	...dep	...	10 5
	SYRACUSE... ...	... arr	12 0	12 15	**SYRACUSE** ...	... arr	10 5	11 5
	,, ...	...dep	12 40	13 15	,, ...	...dep	11 5	11 45
	MALTA	... arr	13 40	...	**NAPLES**	... arr	...	14 35
	,, ...	...dep	14 10	...	,, ...	...dep	...	15 5
	TRIPOLI	... arr	16 25	16 0	**ROME**	... arr	14 20	16 25

T On Tuesday, Thursday and Saturday.　**M** On Monday, Wednesday and Friday.

Distance and Time allowance for conveyance between Airport and Town Terminus

TOWN	AIRPORT	TOWN TERMINUS	Miles	Minutes
ROME	Lido Seaplane Stn.	C.I.T. Piazza Esedra	—	30
NAPLES	Molo Beverello ...	No Special Conveyance	—	—
SYRACUSE	Seaplane Station...	No Special Conveyance	—	—
MALTA	Marsasciroceo	14 Strada Mezzodi	—	60
TRIPOLI	Seaplane Station...	No Special Conveyance	—	—

FARES

	NAPLES			SYRACUSE			MALTA			TRIPOLI		
	Lire			Lire			Lire			Lire		
	Single	Ret.	Ex. Bg.	Single	Ret.	Ex.Bg.	Single	Ret.	Ex.Bg.	Single	Ret.	Ex. Bg.
ROME	120	§	1·20	400	§	4	540	§	5·40	780	§	7·80
NAPLES	...	...	...	280	§	2.80	420	§	4·20	660	§	6·60
SYRACUSE	...	...	...	...	...	...	140	§	1·40	380	§	3·80
MALTA*	...	...	...	...	...	...	...	...	...	...	...	...

* See Supplementary List of Fares.　§ Return (60 days), 30% reduction on homeward journey.
Ex. Bg.—Excess Baggage per Kg (2·2 lbs.)

176

MILAN—ROME
(Daily)
A.L.I.

Route 347

Miles	Airports of				Airports of			
0	**MILAN**	...dep	12 15		**ROME**	...dep	9 0	
323	**ROME**	... arr	15 15		**MILAN**	... arr	12 0	

Distance and Time allowance for conveyance between Airport and Town Terminus

TOWN	AIRPORT	TOWN TERMINUS	Miles	Minutes
MILAN	Milan	A.L.I. Via Sta. Margherita 16 (Hotel Regina) ...	3¾	30
ROME	Rome	C.I.T., Piazza Esedra	3¾	30

FARES

FROM MILAN TO	Single	Return 15 Days	Return 60 Days	Excess Baggage per Kg (2·2 lbs.)
	Lire	Lire	Lire	Lire
ROME	250	...	450	2·50

177 ROME—NAPLES—PALERMO—TUNIS
A.L.S.A.
Route 363

Miles	Airports of		M		Airports of		T
	ROME ... ...dep	9 30			TUNIS ... ...dep	8 30	
	NAPLES ... ... arr	10 50			PALERMO ... ... arr	10 40	
	,, ...dep	11 20			,, ...dep	11 10	
	PALERMO ... ... arr	13 20			NAPLES ... ... arr	13 10	
	,, ...dep	13 50			,, ...dep	13 40	
	TUNIS ... ... arr	16 0			ROME ... ... arr	15 0	

M On Monday, Wednesday, and Friday.   T On Tuesday, Thursday, and Saturday.

Distance and Time allowance for conveyance between Airport and Town Terminus

TOWN	AIRPORT	TOWN TERMINUS	Miles	Minutes
ROME	Lido Seaplane Stn.	C.I.T. Piazza Esedra	—	70
NAPLES	Molo Beverello	No Special Conveyance	—	—
PALERMO	Molo Santa Lucia	No Special Conveyance	—	—
TUNIS	Khereddine	C.I.T. Avenue Jules Ferry 19	7½	60

FARES

	NAPLES			PALERMO			TUNIS		
	Lire			Lire			Lire		
	Single	Ret.	Ex. Bag.	Single	Ret.	Ex. Bag.	Single	Ret.	Ex. Bag.
ROME	120	§	1·20	320	§	3·20	440	§	4·40
NAPLES	...	...	...	200	§	2	320	§	3·20
PALERMO	200	§	2	...	...	...	200	§	2

Ex. Bag.—Excess Baggage per Kg (2.2 lbs.)
§ Return (60 days), 30% reduction on homeward journey

180 ROME—CAGLIARI—TUNIS
A.L.S.A.
Route 334

Miles	Airports of		T	W	Airports of		M	W
0	ROME ... ...dep		8 45	8 45	TUNIS ... ...dep		8 30	...
292	CAGLIARI ... ... arr		11 15	11 15	CAGLIARI ... ... arr		10 15	...
	,, ...dep		11 45	...	,, ...dep		10 45	10 45
483	TUNIS ... ... arr		13 30	...	ROME ... ... arr		13 15	13 15

M On Monday, Wednesday and Friday.   T On Tuesday, Thursday and Saturday.   W Weekdays only.

Distance and Time allowance for conveyance between Airport and Town Terminus

TOWN	AIRPORT	TOWN TERMINUS	Miles	Minutes
ROME	Lido Seaplane Stn.	C.I.T. Piazza Esedra	—	70
CAGLIARI	Elmas	C.I.T. Via Roma 53	3¾	45
TUNIS	Khereddine	C.I.T. Avenue Jules Ferry 19	7½	60

FARES

FROM ROME	Single	Return 15 Days	Return 60 Days	Excess Baggage per Kg (2·2 lbs.)
	Lire	Lire	Lire	Lire
To CAGLIARI	240	...	§	2·40
TUNIS	440	...	§	4·40
FROM TUNIS	Frs.	Frs.	Frs.	Frs.
To CAGLIARI	260	...	§	2·60
ROME	575	...	§	5·75

§ 30% reduction allowed on homeward journey.

181 ROME—BARI—BRINDISI—TIRANA—SALONICA
A.L.S.A.
Route 387

Miles	Airports of		M		Airports of		T	
0	ROME ... ... dep		7 30		SALONICA ... ... dep		10 0	
252	BARI ... ... arr		9 40		TIRANA ... ... arr		11 0	
	,, ... dep		9 50		,, ... dep		11 45	
304½	BRINDISI ... ... arr		10 20		BRINDISI ... ... arr		13 0	
	,, ... dep		11 5		,, ... dep		13 45	
460	TIRANA ... ... arr		12 20		BARI ... ... arr		14 15	
	,, ... dep		13 5		,, ... dep		14 25	
674	SALONICA ... ... arr		16 5		ROME ... ... arr		16 35	

M On Monday, Wednesday and Friday.   **T** On Tuesday, Thursday and Saturday.

Distance and Time allowance for conveyance between Airport and Town Terminus.

TOWN	AIRPORT	TOWN TERMINUS	Miles	Minutes
ROME	Littorio	C.I.T., Piazza Esedra	—	30
BARI	Umberto di Savoia {	Hotel Oriente..	4½	50
		C.I.T. Via Piccini 94	—	45
		Hotel Internazionale	5	25
BRINDISI	Civil Airport ...{	C.I.T. Via Regina Margherita 16	—	20
TIRANA	Tirana	Ufficio C.I.T. Via Abdi Bey Toptani (Fare, 3 Gold Fr.)	2½	30
SALONICA	Sedes	Tour Blanche Misrahi Depots......................	9¼	60

FARES

	BARI			BRINDISI			TIRANA			SALONICA		
	Lire			Lire			Lire			Lire		
	Single	Ret.	Ex. Bg.	Single	Ret.	Ex. Bg.	Single	Ret.	Ex. Bg.	Single	Ret.	Ex. Bg.
ROME	250	§	2·50	300	§	3	500	§	5	750	§	7·50
BARI	...	...	...	100	§	1	300	§	3	550	§	5·50
BRINDISI	100	§	1	...	...	...	250	§	2·50	500	§	5
TIRANA	81	§	0·80	68	§	0·68	...	...	...	110	§	1·10

Ex. Bg.—Excess Baggage per Kg (2·2 lbs.)

§ Return (60 days). 30% reduction on homeward journey

182 VENICE⇌TRIESTE
(Weekdays only)
A.L.S.A.
Route 391

Miles	Airports of				Airports of			
0	VENICE ... ... dep		14 0		TRIESTE ... ... dep		8 55	
70	TRIESTE ... ... arr		15 0		VENICE ... ... arr		9 55	

Distance and Time allowance for conveyance between Airport and Town Terminus.

TOWN	AIRPORT	TOWN TERMINUS	Miles	Minutes
VENICE	San Andrea ......{	Riva degli Schiavoni, opposite Hotel Danieli ...	—	40
		Station	—	70
TRIESTE	Bacino S. Giorgio.	No Special Conveyance	½	—

FARES

FROM VENICE TO	Single	Return 15 Days	Return 60 Days	Excess Baggage per Kg (2·2 lbs.)
	Lire	Lire	Lire	Lire
TRIESTE	75	...	§	0.75

§ 30% reduction on homeward journey.

183

VENICE—POLA—ABBAZIA—FIUME
A.L.S.A.
Route 393

Miles	Airports of		W			Airports of		W
0	VENICE	... ...dep	14 20			FIUME	... ...dep	7 55
87	POLA	... ...arr	15 20			ABBAZIA	... ...arr	...
		... ...dep	15 45				... ...dep	...
134	ABBAZIA	... ...arr	...			POLA	... ...arr	8 30
		... ...dep	...				... ...dep	8 45
140	FIUME ...	... ...arr	16 20			VENICE	... ...arr	9 45

W Weekdays only.

Distance and Time allowance for conveyance between Airport and Town Terminus

TOWN	AIRPORT	TOWN TERMINUS	Miles	Minutes
VENICE	San Andrea	Riva degli Schiavoni, opposite Hotel Danieli	—	40
POLA	Seaplane Station	No Special Conveyance	—	—
ABBAZIA	Seaplane Station	No Special Conveyance	—	—
FIUME	Umberto M'dd'lena	No Special Conveyance	—	—

FARES

	POLA			ABBAZIA			FIUME		
	Lire			Lire			Lire		
	Single	Ret.	Ex. Bag.	Single	Ret.	Ex. Bag.	Single	Ret.	Ex. Bag.
VENICE	90	§	0.90	...	...	...	100	§	1
POLA	...	...	...	...	...	...	50	§	0.50
ABBAZIA	...	...	...	...	...	...	...	...	...

Ex. Bag.—Excess Baggage per Kg (2.2 lbs.)
§ Return (60 days), 30% reduction on homeward journey

184

VENICE—KLAGENFURT—BUDAPEST
(Service suspended during Winter)
'MALERT'
Route 423

Miles	Airports of				Airports of	
0	VENICE	... ...dep			BUDAPEST	... ...dep
155	KLAGENFURT	...arr			KLAGENFURT	...arr
		...dep				...dep
379	BUDAPEST	... ...arr			VENICE	... ...arr

Distance and Time allowance for conveyance between Airport and Town Terminus

TOWN	AIRPORT	TOWN TERMINUS	Miles	Minutes
VENICE	San Nicolo di Lido	Riva degli Schiavoni, opposite Hotel Danieli	—	45
KLAGENFURT	Annabichl	Hôtel Moser-Verdino	3¾	20
		Hauptbahnhof (Central Station)—On application to Airport Office	2½	—
BUDAPEST	Matyasföld	Luftreisebüro der Malert, Váci ucca I	7¾	40

FARES

FROM VENICE TO	Single	Return 15 Days	Return 60 Days	Excess Baggage per Kg (2.2 lbs.)
	Lire	Lire	Lire	Lire
KLAGENFURT				
BUDAPEST				

185 VENICE—KLAGENFURT—GRAZ—VIENNA
(Service suspended during Winter)
AUSTROFLUG
Route 401

Miles	Airports of				Airports of	
0	**VENICE** ... ...dep				**VIENNA** ... ...dep	
140	**KLAGENFURT** ... arr				**GRAZ** ... ... arr	
	,, ...dep				,, ...dep	
211	**GRAZ** ... ... arr				**KLAGENFURT** ... arr	
	,, ...dep				,, ...dep	
311	**VIENNA** ... ... arr				**VENICE** ... ... arr	

Distance and Time allowance for conveyance between Airport and Town Terminus

TOWN	AIRPORT	TOWN TERMINUS	Miles	Minutes
VENICE	San Nicolo di Lido	Riva degli Schiavoni, opposite Hotel Danieli ...	—	45
		Hotel Moser-Verdino	2¼	20
KLAGENFURT	Annabichl			
		Hauptbahnhof (Central Station)—On application to Airport Office	2½	—
GRAZ	Thalerhof	Reisebüro 'Opernring,' Opernring 22...........	11¼	35
VIENNA	Aspern	Austroflug, Kärntnerring 5 (Hotel Bristol), Vienna I.................................	9⅜	35

FARES

FROM VENICE TO	Single	Return 15 Days	Return 60 Days	Excess Baggage per Kg (2·2 lbs.)
	Lire	Lire	Lire	Lire
KLAGENFURT				
GRAZ				
VIENNA				

186 VENICE—VIENNA
A.L.S.A.
Route 332

Miles	Airports of		M		Airports of		T
0	**VENICE** ... ...dep		11 0		**VIENNA** ... ...dep		10 30
298	**VIENNA** ... ... arr		13 45		**VENICE** ... ... arr		13 15

M On Monday, Wednesday and Friday. **T** Tuesday, Thursday and Saturday.

Distance and Time allowance for conveyance between Airport and Town Terminus.

TOWN	AIRPORT	TOWN TERMINUS	Miles	Minutes
VENICE	San Nicolo di Lido	Riva degli Schiavoni, opposite Hotel Danieli ...	—	40
VIENNA	Aspern	Austroflug, Kärntnerring 5 (Hotel Bristol), Vienna I.................................	9¼	35

FARES

FROM VENICE	Single	Return 15 Days	Return 60 Days	Excess Baggage per Kg (2·2 lbs.)
	Lire	Lire	Lire	Lire
To VIENNA	325	...	§	3·25
FROM VIENNA	Sch.	Sch.	Sch.	Sch.
To VENICE	135	...	§	1·35

§ 30% reduction on homeward journey.

All times given in the Tables are local times, see page 22
Conveyance between an Airport and the Town Terminus is free unless otherwise indicated in the Table
The full names and addresses, etc., of the Companies will be found on pages 30 and 31

187

TRIESTE—ZARA—LAGOSTA—DURAZZO—BRINDISI
(A.L.S.A.)
Route 392

Miles	Airports of	M	W	Airports of	T	
0	**TRIESTE** ... ...dep	7 45	7 45	**BRINDISI** ... ...dep	8 15	...
62	**POLA** ... ...arr	8 20	8 20	**DURAZZO** ... ...arr	9 30	...
	,, ...dep	8 40	8 40	,, ...dep	9 55	...
107	**LUSSINO** ... ...arr	9 10	9 10	**LAGOSTA** ... ...arr	11 55	†
	,, ...dep	9 15	9 15	,, ...dep	12 20	†
156	**ZARA** ... ...arr	9 45	9 45	**ZARA** ... ...arr	14 5	W
	,, ...dep	10 15	†	,, ...dep	14 35	14 35
340	**LAGOSTA** ... ...arr	12 0	†	**LUSSINO** ... ...arr	15 5	15 5
	,, ...dep	12 25	...	,, ...dep	15 10	15 10
523	**DURAZZO** ... ...arr	14 25	...	**POLA** ... ...arr	15 40	15 40
	,, ...dep	14 50	...	,, ...dep	16 0	16 0
626	**BRINDISI** ... ...arr	16 5	...	**TRIESTE** ... ...arr	16 35	16 35

M—On Mon. and Fri. **T**—On Tues. and Sats. **W**—Weekdays only. **†**—To or from Ancona, see Table 190

Distance and Time allowance for conveyance between Airport and Town Terminus

TOWN	AIRPORT	TOWN TERMINUS	Miles	Minutes
TRIESTE	Bacino S. Giorgio...	No Special Conveyance	½	—
POLA	Pola Seaplane Sta...	No Special Conveyance	—	—
LUSSINO	Lussino Seaplane St	No Special Conveyance	—	—
ZARA	Zara Seaplane Sta.	No Special Conveyance	—	—
LAGOSTA	Lago Grande Seaplane Station	No Special Conveyance	—	—
DURAZZO	Durazzo Seaplane Station	No Special Conveyance	—	—
BRINDISI	Civil Airport	Motorboat from Quai, opposite Hotel Internazionale	—	25

FARES

FROM TRIESTE TO	Single	Return 15 Days	Return 60 Days	Excess Baggage per Kg (2·2 lbs.)
	Lire	Lire	Lire	Lire
POLA	50	...	§	0·50
LUSSINO	65	...	§	0·65
ZARA	100	...	§	1
LAGOSTA	185	...	§	1·85
DURAZZO	275	...	§	2·75
BRINDISI	375	...	§	3·75

§ 30% reduction on homeward journey

190

ANCONA—ZARA
A.L.S.A.
(Weekdays only)
Route 394

Miles	Airports of		Airports of	
0	**ANCONA** ... ...dep	9 40	**ZARA** ... ...dep	12 0
106	**ZARA** ... ...arr	10 55	**ANCONA** ... ...arr	13 15

Distance and Time allowance for conveyance between Airport and Town Terminus

TOWN	AIRPORT	TOWN TERMINUS	Miles	Minutes
ANCONA	Sanzio Andreoli	Piazza Roma 8	—	30
ZARA	Zara Seaplane Sta.	No Special Conveyance	—	—

FARES

FROM ANCONA TO	Single	Return 15 Days	Return 60 Days	Excess Baggage per Kg (2·2 lbs.)
	Lire	Lire	Lire	Lire
ZARA	75	...	§	0·75

§ 30 % reduction on homeward journey.

191 BRINDISI—ATHENS—RHODES
AERO ESPRESSO
Route 371

Miles	Airports of		W		Airports of		T
0	**BRINDISI** ... ...dep	7 0		**RHODES** ... ...dep	7 0
435	**ATHENS** ... ... arr	11 30		**ATHENS** ... ... arr	9 30
	,, ...dep	12 0		,, ...dep	10 30
736	**RHODES** ... ... arr	14 30		**BRINDISI** ... ... arr	13 0

T On Thursday only. **W** On Wednesday only.

Distance and Time allowance for conveyance between Airport and Town Terminus

TOWN	AIRPORT	TOWN TERMINUS	Miles	Minutes
BRINDISI	Seaplane Station...	Motorboat from Quai, opposite Hotel Internazionale	—	45
ATHENS	Falero	Hotel Grande Bretagne	—	60
RHODES	Seaplane Station...	No Special Conveyance	—	—

FARES

FROM BRINDISI	Single	Return 15 Days	Return 60 Days	Excess Baggage per Kg (2·2 lbs.)
	Lire	Lire	Lire	Lire
To ATHENS	500	...	§	5
RHODES	800	...	§	8
FROM ATHENS To RHODES	380	...	§	3.80

§ 30% reduction on homeward journey.

192 BRINDISI—ATHENS—ISTANBUL
AERO ESPRESSO
Route 372

Miles	Airports of		T		Airports of		W
0	**BRINDISI** ... ... dep	7 0		**ISTANBUL** ... ...dep	7 0
435	**ATHENS** ... ... arr	11 30		**ATHENS** ... ... arr	10 30
	,, ...dep	12 0		,, ...dep	11 0
906	**ISTANBUL** ... ... arr	16 0		**BRINDISI** ... ... arr	13 30

T On Monday and Friday. **W** On Tuesday and Saturday.

Distance and Time allowance for conveyance between Airport and Town Terminus

TOWN	AIRPORT	TOWN TERMINUS	Miles	Minutes
BRINDISI	Seaplane Station...	Motorboat from Quai, opposite Hotel Internazionale	—	45
ATHENS	Falero	Hotel Grande Bretagne	—	60
ISTANBUL	Buyukdere	Hotel Pera Palace and Tokatlian	—	60

FARES

FROM BRINDISI	Single	Return 15 Days	Return 60 Days	Excess Baggage per Kg (2·2 lbs.)
	Lire	Lire	Lire	Lire
To ATHENS	500	...	§	5
ISTANBUL	1,000	...	§	10
FROM ATHENS To ISTANBUL	500	...	§	5

§ 30% reduction on homeward journey.

194   **VIENNA—BUDAPEST**
(Service suspended during Winter)
' MALERT '   Route 421

Miles	Airports of					Airports of		
0	**VIENNA** ... ...dep					**BUDAPEST** ... ...dep		
143	**BUDAPEST** ... ... arr					**VIENNA** ... ... arr		

Distance and Time allowance for conveyance between Airport and Town Terminus

TOWN	AIRPORT	TOWN TERMINUS	Miles	Minutes
VIENNA	Aspern	Austroflug, Kärntnerring 5 (Hotel Bristol), Vienna I..	9½	35
BUDAPEST	Matyasföld	Luftreisebüro der Malert, Váci ucca I	7¾	40

FARES

FROM VIENNA TO	Single	Return 15 Days	Return 60 Days	Excess Baggage per Kg (2.2 lbs.)
	Sch.	Sch.	Sch.	Sch.
BUDAPEST				

BRADSHAW'S

FOREIGN PHRASE BOOKS

WILL FIT THE WAISTCOAT POCKET

		ENGLISH—FRENCH.		
		ENGLISH—GERMAN.		
		ENGLISH—SPANISH.		
		ENGLISH—ITALIAN.		

A Correspondent writes: "They are quite the best I have ever seen."

Bound in Red Cloth, 1/6 each.

Bradshaw's Guide Offices:—
LONDON : BRADSHAW HOUSE, SURREY STREET, STRAND, W.C.2.

MANCHESTER : Albert Square.   Henry Blacklock & Co. Ltd., Proprietors and Publishers.

195

VIENNA—GRAZ—ZAGREB—BELGRADE
(Service suspended during Winter)
AUSTROFLUG; 'AEROPOUT'

Route 405

Miles	Airports of					Airports of			
0	**VIENNA** ... ...dep					**BELGRADE** ... ...dep			
99½	**GRAZ** ... ... arr					**ZAGREB** ... ... arr			
	,, ...dep					,, ...dep			
193	**ZAGREB** ... ... arr					**GRAZ** ... ... arr			
	,, ...dep					,, ...dep			
422½	**BELGRADE** ... ... arr					**VIENNA** ... ... arr			

Distance and Time allowance for conveyance between Airport and Town Terminus

TOWN	AIRPORT	TOWN TERMINUS	Miles	Minutes
VIENNA	Aspern	Austroflug, Kärntnerring 5 (Hotel Bristol), Vienna I..	9½	35
GRAZ	Thalerhof	Reisebüro ' Opernring,' Opernring 22	11¼	35
ZAGREB	Borongaj	Jelacicew 6	4½	60
BELGRADE	Beograd (Zemun)..	Boat to Zemun, thence ' Aeropout ' conveyance to Airport*	2½*	45

FARES

FROM VIENNA TO	Single	Return 15 Days	Return 60 Days	Excess Baggage per Kg (2·2 lbs.)
	Sch.	Sch.	Sch.	Sch.
GRAZ				
ZAGREB				
BELGRADE				

196

INNSBRUCK—SALZBURG
(Service suspended during Winter)
AUSTROFLUG

Route 406

Miles	Airports of					Airports of			
0	**INNSBRUCK** ... ...dep					**SALZBURG** ... ...dep			
89½	**SALZBURG** ... ... arr					**INNSBRUCK** ... ... arr			

Distance and Time allowance for conveyance between Airport and Town Terminus

TOWN	AIRPORT	TOWN TERMINUS	Miles	Minutes
INNSBRUCK	Reichenau............	Tiroler Landesreisebüro, Bozener Platz	2	20
SALZBURG	Maxglan	Verkehrsbüro, Schwartzstrasse 1	3	25

FARES

FROM INNSBRUCK TO	Single	Return 15 Days	Return 60 Days	Excess Baggage per Kg (2·2 lbs.)
	Sch.	Sch.	Sch.	Sch.
SALZBURG				

197

VIENNA—BRNO—CRACOW—WARSAW
(Daily)
'LOT'

Route 632

Miles	Airports of						Airports of			
0	VIENNA ... ...dep	...				WARSAW ... ...dep	10 30			
86	BRNO ... ... arr	...				CRACOW... ... ... arr	12 15			
	... ...dep	...				... ...dep	...			
265	CRACOW ... ... arr	...				BRNO ... ... arr	...			
	... ...dep	8 15				... ...dep	...			
430½	WARSAW ... ... arr	10 0				VIENNA ... ... arr	...			

Distance and Time allowance for conveyance between Airport and Town Terminus

TOWN	AIRPORT	TOWN TERMINUS	Miles	Minutes
VIENNA	Aspern	Austroflug, Kärntnerring 5 (Hotel Bristol), Vienna I..	9¼	35
BRNO	Cernovice............	'Cedok,' Nam Svobody 4...........................	1½	40
CRACOW	Czyzyny	P.L.L. 'Lot' ul Szpitalna 32	4½	40
WARSAW	Okecie	Stadtbüro (Town Office), Al Jerozolimskie 35...	5	45

FARES

	BRNO			CRACOW			WARSAW		
	Zl.			Zl.			Zl.		
	Single	Ret.	Ex. Bag.	Single	Ret.	Ex. Bag.	Single	Ret.	Ex. Bag.
VIENNA	...	...	...	...	...	...	...	...	...
BRNO				...	...	...	...	...	...
CRACOW							35	59·50	0·35

Ret.—Return 60 days.   Ex. Bag.—Excess Baggage per Kg (2·2 lbs.).

200

KLAGENFURT—LJUBLJANA
(Service suspended during Winter)
'AEROPOUT'

Route 628

Miles	Airports of				Airports of			
0	KLAGENFURT ...dep				LJUBLJANA ... ...dep			
44½	LJUBLJANA ... ... arr				KLAGENFURT ... arr			

Distance and Time allowance for conveyance between Airport and Town Terminus

TOWN	AIRPORT	TOWN TERMINUS	Miles	Minutes
KLAGENFURT	Annabichl .... {	Hotel Moser-Verdino	3¾	20
		Hauptbahnhof (Central Station)—On application to Airport Office	2⅛	—
LJUBLJANA	Ljubljana (Lyoublyana)	No Special Conveyance	4	—

FARES

FROM KLAGENFURT TO	Single	Return 15 Days	Return 60 Days	Excess Baggage per Kg (2·2 lbs.)
	Sch.	Sch.	Sch.	Sch.
LJUBLJANA				

201 KLAGENFURT—GRAZ—VIENNA
(Service suspended during Winter)
AUSTROFLUG
Route 404

Miles	Airports of				Airports of	
0	**KLAGENFURT** ...dep				**VIENNA** ... ...dep	
71½	**GRAZ** ... ... arr				**GRAZ** ... ... arr	
	" ... ...dep				" ... ...dep	
171	**VIENNA** ... ... arr				**KLAGENFURT** ... arr	

Distance and Time allowance for conveyance between Airport and Town Terminus

TOWN	AIRPORT	TOWN TERMINUS	Miles	Minutes
KLAGENFURT	Annabichl	Hotel Moser-Verdino	2	20
		Hauptbahnhof (Central Station)—On application to Airport Office	2½	—
GRAZ	Thalerhof	Reisebüro "Opernring," Opernring 22...........	11¼	35
VIENNA	Aspern	Austroflug, Kärntnerring 5 (Hotel Bristol), Vienna I................................	9¼	35

FARES

FROM KLAGENFURT TO	Single	Return 15 Days	Return 60 Days	Excess Baggage per Kg (2·2 lbs.)
	Sch.	Sch.	Sch.	Sch.
GRAZ				
VIENNA				

202 PRAGUE—BRNO—BRATISLAVA—ZAGREB—SUŠAK
(Service suspended during Winter)
C.S.A
Route 654

Miles	Airports of				Airports of	
0	**PRAGUE** ... ...dep				**SUŠAK** ... ...dep	
122	**BRNO** ... ... arr				**ZAGREB** ... ... arr	
	" ... ...dep				" ... ...dep	
197½	**BRATISLAVA** ... ... arr				**BRATISLAVA** ... ... arr	
	" ... ...dep				" ... ...dep	
396	**ZAGREB** ... ... arr				**BRNO** ... ... arr	
	" ... ...dep				" ... ...dep	
474	**SUŠAK** ... ... arr				**PRAGUE** ... ... arr	

Distance and Time allowance for conveyance between Airport and Town Terminus

TOWN	AIRPORT	TOWN TERMINUS	Miles	Minutes
PRAGUE	Kbely	Luftreisebüro C.S.A., Jungmannova Str 18......	7½	45
BRNO	Czernowice	' Cedok ' Nam Svobody 4	—	40
BRATISLAVA	Vajnory	Hotel Carlton (Cedok)	5	40
ZAGREB	Borongaj	Jelačicév 6	4½	60
SUŠAK	Susak	Masarikovo Setaliste 9	7	60

FARES

FROM PRAGUE TO	Single	Return 15 Days	Return 60 Days	Excess Baggage per Kg (2·2 lbs.)
	Kc.	Kc.	Kc.	Kc.
BRNO				
BRATISLAVA				
ZAGREB				
SUSAK				

203

PRAGUE—BRNO—BRATISLAVA—KOŠICE—UŽHOROD—CLUJ—BUCHAREST
(Service suspended during Winter)
C.S.A.

Route 651

Miles	Airports of					Airports of		
0	PRAGUE ... ...dep					BUCHAREST ... ...dep		
122	BRNO ... ...arr					CLUJ ... ...arr		
	„ ... ...dep					„ ... ...dep		
197½	BRATISLAVA ... ...arr					UŽHOROD ... ...arr		
	... ...dep					... ...dep		
324	KOŠICE ... ...arr					KOŠICE ... ...arr		
	... ...dep					„ ... ...dep		
370½	UŽHOROD ... ...arr					BRATISLAVA ... ...arr		
	... ...dep					... ...dep		
519½	CLUJ„ ... ...arr					BRNO ... ...arr		
	... ...dep					„ ... ...dep		
749	BUCHAREST ... ...arr					PRAGUE ... ...arr		

Distance and Time allowance for conveyance between Airport and Town Terminus

TOWN	AIRPORT	TOWN TERMINUS	Miles	Minutes
PRAGUE	Kbely	Luftreisebüro C.S.A., Jungmannova Str. 18......	7½	45
BRNO	Czernowice	'Cedok,' Nam Svobody 4	—	40
BRATISLAVA	Vajnory	Hotel Carlton (Cedok)	5	40
KOSICE	Kosice	Hotel Salkhaz, Hlavna ul.	⅝	15
UZHOROD	Cernevice	Hotel Koruna, Nové nam	1¼	25
CLUJ	Cluj	I Piata Unirei	—	45
BUCHAREST	Baneasa	No Special Conveyance	—	—

FARES

FROM PRAGUE TO	Single	Return 15 Days	Return 60 Days	Excess Baggage per Kg (2·2 lbs.)
	Kc.	Kc.	Kc.	Kc.
BRNO				
BRATISLAVA				
KOSICE				
UZHOROD				
CLUJ				
BUCHAREST				

204

MARIENBAD—KARLSBAD—PRAGUE
(Service suspended during Winter)
C.S.A.

Route 652

Miles	Airports of					Airports of		
0	MARIENBAD ... ...dep					PRAGUE ... ...dep		
19	KARLSBAD... ... ...arr					KARLSBAD ... ...arr		
	„ ... ...dep					... ...dep		
99½	PRAGUE ... ...arr					MARIENBAD ... ...arr		

Distance and Time allowance for conveyance between Airport and Town Terminus

TOWN	AIRPORT	TOWN TERMINUS	Miles	Minutes
MARIENBAD	Sklare	Haus Sanssouci	4½	30
KARLSBAD	Karlsbad .... (Karlovy Vary)	Divadelni Namesti	5½	30
PRAGUE	Kbely	Luftreisebüro C.S.A., Jungmannova Str. 18......	7½	45

FARES

FROM MARIENBAD TO	Single	Return 15 Days	Return 60 Days	Excess Baggage per Kg (2·2 lbs.)
	Kc.	Kc.	Kc.	Kc.
KARLSBAD				
PRAGUE				

205

COPENHAGEN—MALMÖ
(Service suspended during Winter)
D.D.L.

Route 562

Miles	Airports of								
0	**COPENHAGEN** ... ...dep								
17	**MALMÖ** ... ...arr								

	Airports of								
	MALMÖ ... ... dep								
	COPENHAGEN ... ... arr								

Distance and Time allowance for conveyance between Airport and Town Terminus

TOWN	AIRPORT	TOWN TERMINUS	Miles	Minutes
COPENHAGEN	Kastrup...............	Passagebüro der D.D.L., Meldahlsgade 5	6½	45
MALMÖ	Bultofta...............	Zentralbahnhof (Central Station)	2	30

FARES

FROM COPENHAGEN TO	Single	Return 15 Days	Return 60 Days	Excess Baggage per Kg (2·2 lbs.)
	Kr.	Kr.	Kr.	Kr.
MALMÖ				

206

MALMÖ—COPENHAGEN—GOTHENBURG
(Service suspended during Winter)
A.B.A.

Route 575

Miles	Airports of			Airports of			
0	**MALMÖ** ... ... dep			**GOTHENBURG** ...dep			
17	**COPENHAGEN** ... arr			**COPENHAGEN** ... arr			
	... dep			... dep			
170	**GOTHENBURG** ... arr			**MALMÖ** ... ... arr			

Distance and Time allowance for conveyance between Airport and Town Terminus

TOWN	AIRPORT	TOWN TERMINUS	Miles	Minutes
MALMÖ	Bultofta...............	Zentralbahnhof (Central Station)	2	30
COPENHAGEN	Kastrup...............	Passagebüro der D.D.L., Meldahlsgade 5	6½	45
GOTHENBURG	Torslanda	Aerotransportkontor. Hotellplatsen	10½	60

FARES

FROM MALMÖ TO	Single	Return 15 Days	Return 60 Days	Excess Baggage per Kg (2·2 lbs.)
	S. Kr.	S. Kr.	S. Kr.	S. Kr.
COPENHAGEN				
GOTHENBURG				

All times given in the Tables are local times, see page 22
Conveyance between an Airport and the Town Terminus is free unless otherwise indicated in the Table
The full names and addresses, etc., of the Companies will be found on pages 30 and 31
Ft 1
129

STOCKHOLM—ÅBO—HELSINGFORS—TALLINN
(Daily)
A.B.A.; AERO O/Y.

Routes 571, 582

Miles	Airports of				A	B	Airports of			A	B
0	STOCKHOLM ...	...dep	..		9 30	9 30	TALLINN ...	...dep	11 30	..	..
165	ABO	...arr	..		12 0	..	HELSINGFORS	...arr	12 0	..	..
	"	...dep	..		12 15	..	"	...dep	..	13 45	13 20
269	HELSINGFORS	...arr	..		13 15	12 50	ABO "	...arr	..	14 45	..
	"	...dep	9 30	..	..	..	"	...dep	..	15 0	..
325	TALLINN	...arr	10 0	..	..	..	STOCKHOLM	...arr	..	15 30	14 40

A—Not after November 15th.   **B**—From November 16th.

Distance and Time allowance for conveyance between Airport and Town Terminus

TOWN	AIRPORT	TOWN TERMINUS	Miles	Minutes
STOCKHOLM	Lindarängen	A.B.A. Flugpavillon, Nybroplan	2	30
ABO	Abo (Turku)	Aero O/Y. Eriksgatan 12, Salutorget...............	4	45
HELSINGFORS	Helsingfors (Helsinki)	No Special Conveyance	1½	—
TALLINN	Tallinna lennujaam	No Special Conveyance	1¾	—

FARES

FROM STOCKHOLM	Single	Return 15 Days	Return 60 Days	Excess Baggage per Kg (2.2 lbs.)
	S. Kr.	S. Kr.	S. Kr.	S. Kr.
To ABO	59	...	100	0·50
HELSINGFORS	88	...	150	0·50
TALLINN	110	...	187	0·80
FROM TALLINN	E. Kr.	E. Kr.	E. Kr.	E. Kr.
To HELSINGFORS	22·50	...	38·25	0·45
ABO...	51	...	87	0·65
STOCKHOLM	110	...	187	0·80

STOCKHOLM—VISBY
(Service suspended during Winter)
A.B.A.

Route 572

Miles	Airports of				Airports of			
0	STOCKHOLM ...	...dep			VISBY	...dep		
119	VISBY	...arr			STOCKHOLM	...arr		

Distance and Time allowance for conveyance between Airport and Town Terminus

TOWN	AIRPORT	TOWN TERMINUS	Miles	Minutes
STOCKHOLM	Lindarängen	A.B.A. Flugpavillon, Nybroplan	2	·30
VISBY	Tingstäde	Anfartygs AB Gotlands Kontor	13¾	35

FARES

FROM STOCKHOLM TO	Single	Return 15 Days	Return 60 Days	Excess Baggage per Kg (2.2 lbs.)
	S. Kr.	S. Kr.	S. Kr.	S. Kr.
VISBY				

211

MARIEHAMN—STOCKHOLM
(Service suspended during Winter)
AERO O/Y,

Route 585

Miles	Airports of				Airports of		
0	**MARIEHAMN** ...	... dep			**STOCKHOLM**	... dep	
87	**STOCKHOLM** ...	... arr			**MARIEHAMN**	... arr	

Distance and Time allowance for conveyance between Airport and Town Terminus

TOWN	AIRPORT	TOWN TERMINUS	Miles	Minutes
MARIEHAMN	Mariehamn	No Special Conveyance	—	—
STOCKHOLM	Lindarängen	A.B.A. Flugpavillon, Nybroplan	2	30

FARES

FROM MARIEHAMN TO	Single	Return 15 Days	Return 60 Days	Excess Baggage per Kg (2·2 lbs.)
	F. Mk.	F. Mk.	F. Mk.	F. Mk.
STOCKHOLM				

212

MADRID—SEVILLE
(Weekdays only)
L.A.P.E.

Route 552

Miles	Airports of				Airports of		
0	**MADRID**	... dep	14 15		**SEVILLE**	... dep	7 0
261	**SEVILLE**	... arr	16 50		**MADRID**	... arr	9 40

Distance and Time allowance for conveyance between Airport and Town Terminus

TOWN	AIRPORT	TOWN TERMINUS	Miles	Minutes
MADRID	Barajas	Antonio Maura 2	9¼	45
SEVILLE ,..............	Tablada	Avenida de la Libertad 1.............................	3¾	30

FARES

FROM MADRID TO	Single	Return 15 Days	Return 60 Days	Excess Baggage Per Kg (2·2 lbs.)
	Ptas.	Ptas.	Ptas.	Ptas.
SEVILLE	125	...	212·50	1·25•

* After first 15 Kgs., half above rate is charged.

213

MADRID—VALENCIA
L.A.P.E.

Route 353

Miles	Airports of		M			Airports of		T	
0	MADRID	...dep	14 20			VALENCIA ... ...dep	7 40	
186	VALENCIA ...	... arr	16 10			MADRID ... ... arr	9 30	

M On Monday, Wednesday, Thursday and Saturday.   **T** On Monday, Tuesday, Thursday and Friday.

Distance and Time allowance for conveyance between Airport and Town Terminus

TOWN	AIRPORT	TOWN TERMINUS	Miles	Minutes
MADRID	Barajas	Antonio Maura 4	9½	40
VALENCIA	Manises	Paz 39	5	30

FARES

FROM MADRID TO	Single	Return 15 Days	Return 60 Days	Excess Baggage per Kg
		Ptas	Ptas	Ptas
VALENCIA	Ptas 110	...	187	1·10*

* After first 15 Kgs., half above rate is charged

214

BARCELONA—MADRID
(Weekdays only)
L.A.P.E.

Route 551

Miles	Airports of					Airports of			
0	BARCELONA ...	...dep	9 30			MADRID ... ...dep	10 0	
311	MADRID	... arr	12 45			BARCELONA ... arr	13 0	

Distance and Time allowance for conveyance between Airport and Town Terminus

TOWN	AIRPORT	TOWN TERMINUS	Miles	Minutes
BARCELONA	Prat de Lobregat...	Diputación 260	15½	45
MADRID	Barajas	Antonio Maura 2	9½	45

FARES

FROM BARCELONA TO	Single	Return 15 Days	Return 60 Days	Excess Baggage per Kg (2·2 lbs.)
	Ptas.	Ptas.	Ptas.	Ptas.
MADRID	150	...	255	1·50*

* After first 15 Kgs., half above rate is charged

215

BARCELONA—MARSEILLES—GENOA—ROME
A.L.S.A.
Route 361

Miles	Airports of		M		Airports of		T
0	**BARCELONA** ...	...dep	7 0		**ROME**	...dep	7 40
	MARSEILLES ...	... arr	8 50		**GENOA**	... arr	9 50
	,, ...	... dep	9 50		,, ...	... dep	10 35
	GENOA	... arr	12 50		**MARSEILLES** ...	... arr	11 35
	,, ...	... dep	13 35		,, ,,	... dep	12 35
	ROME	... arr	15 45		**BARCELONA**	... arr	14 25

M On Monday, Wednesday and Friday. **T** On Tuesday, Thursday and Saturday

Distance and Time allowance for conveyance between Airport and Town Terminus

TOWN	AIRPORT	TOWN TERMINUS	Miles	Minutes
BARCELONA	Rompeolas	No Special Conveyance	—	—
MARSEILLES	Marignane	Air France, I rue Papère	17½	60
GENOA	Bacino Mussolini...	C.I.T. Via XX Settembre 237r	—	30
ROME	Lido Seaplane Stn.	C.I.T. Piazza Esedra	—	70

FARES

FROM BARCELONA	Single	Return 15 Days	Return 60 Days	Excess Baggage Per Kg (2·2 lbs.)
	Ptas.	Ptas.	Ptas.	Ptas.
To MARSEILLES	125	...	§	1·25
GENOA	265	...	§	2·65
ROME	420	...	§	4·20
FROM ROME	Lire	Lire	Lire	Lire
To GENOA	240	...	§	2·40
MARSEILLES	460	...	§	4·60
BARCELONA...	660	...	§	6·60

§ 30% reduction allowed on homeward journey

216

SEVILLE—LAS PALMAS
L.A.P.E.
Route 554

Miles	Airports of		T		Airports of		H
0	**SEVILLE**	...dep	6 0		**LAS PALMAS**	...dep	7 0
870	**CABO JUBY** ...	... arr	...		**CABO JUBY** ...	... arr	...
	,, ...	... dep	...		,, ,,	...... dep	...
1025	**LAS PALMAS** ...	... arr	15 30		**SEVILLE**	... arr	17 0

T—On Tuesdays only **H**—On Thursdays only

Distance and Time allowance for conveyance between Airport and Town Terminus

TOWN	AIRPORT	TOWN TERMINUS	Miles	Minutes
SEVILLE	Tablada	Avenida de la Libertad I	3¾	30
CABO JUBY	Cabo Juby	No Special Conveyance	—	—
LAS PALMAS	Gando	Alameda de Colon.......................	23	45

FARES

FROM SEVILLE	Single	Return 15 Days	Return 60 Days	Excess Baggage per Kg (2·2 lbs.)
	Ptas.	Ptas.	Ptas.	Ptas.
To CABO JUBY	350	...	595	3·50•
LAS PALMAS	485	...	824·50	4·85•
FROM CABO JUBY				
To LAS PALMAS	135	...	229·50	1·35•

• After first 15 Kgs., half above rate is charged

217

WARSAW—LEMBERG—CERNAUTI—BUCHAREST
(Daily unless otherwise stated)
'LOT'

Route 634

Miles	Airports of		M		Airports of		T	
0	WARSAW ... ...dep	8 0	...		BUCHAREST ......dep	8 0	...	
230	LEMBERG ... ... arr	10 20	...		CERNAUTI ... ... arr	11 20	...	
	... ...dep	...	10 30		,, ...dep	11 45	...	
381½	CERNAUTI ... ... arr	...	13 5		LEMBERG ... ... arr	12 20	...	
	... ...dep	...	13 30		,, ...dep	...	12 45	
701½	BUCHAREST ... ... arr	...	16 50		WARSAW ... ... arr	...	15 5	

M—On Monday only.   T—On Thursday only.

Distance and Time allowance for conveyance between Airport and Town Terminus

TOWN	AIRPORT	TOWN TERMINUS	Miles	Minutes
WARSAW	Okecie	Stadtbüro (Town Office), Al Jerozolimskie 35...	5	45
LEMBERG	Sknilow,............	P.L.L. 'Lot' Plac Marjacki 5	7	30
CERNAUTI	Czachor	'Primaria,' Piata Uniril	1¾	50
BUCHAREST	Baneasa	A.R.P.A. P. Reg. Carol I..............................	2½	55

FARES

	LEMBERG			CERNAUTI			BUCHAREST		
	Zl.			Zl.			Zl.		
	Single	Ret	Ex Bag	Single	Ret	Ex Bag	Single	Ret	Ex Bag
WARSAW	45	76·50	0·45	80	136	0·80	130	221	1·30
LEMBERG	...	...	...	35	59·50	0·35	85	144·50	0·85
CERNAUTI ...	35	59·50	0·35	...	...	...	50	85	0·50

Ret—Return 60 days.   Ex Bag—Excess Baggage per Kg. (2·2 lbs.)

220

WARSAW—KATOWICE
(Daily)
'LOT'

Route 640

Miles	Airports of			Airports of		
0	WARSAW ... ...dep	12 50		KATOWICE ... ...dep	8 30	
174½	KATOWICE ... ... arr	14 40		WARSAW ... ... arr	10 20	

Distance and Time allowance for conveyance between Airport and Town Terminus

TOWN	AIRPORT	TOWN TERMINUS	Miles	Minutes
WARSAW	Okecie	Stadtbüro (Town Office), Al Jerozojimskie 35...	5	50
KATOWICE	Muchawiec	Square opposite the Central Station	1	30

FARES

FROM WARSAW TO	Single	Return 15 Days	Return 60 Days	Excess Baggage per Kg (2·2 lbs.)
	Zl.	Zl.	Zl.	Zl.
KATOWICE	30	...	51	0·30

All times given in the Tables are local times, see page 22
Conveyance between an Airport and the Town Terminus is free unless otherwise indicated
in the Table
The full names and addresses, etc., of the Companies will be found on pages 30 and 31

221 WARSAW—WILNO—RIGA—TALLINN
(Service suspended during Winter)
'LOT'

Route 641

Miles	Airports of				Airports of	
0	WARSAW ... ...dep				TALLINN ... ...dep	
270	WILNO ... ... arr				RIGA ... ... arr	
	... ...dep				... ...dep	
527	RIGA ... ... arr				WILNO ... ... arr	
	... ...dep				... ...dep	
718	TALLINN ... ... arr				WARSAW ... ... arr	

Distance and Time allowance for conveyance between Airport and Town Terminus

TOWN	AIRPORT	TOWN TERMINUS	Miles	Minutes
WARSAW	Okecie	Stadtbüro (Town Office), Al Jerozolimskie 35...	5	50
WILNO	Porubanek	Ul. Mickiewicza 20....................................	4	45
RIGA	Spilve	No Special Conveyance—Central Station	2½	15
TALLINN	Tallinna lennujaam	No Special Conveyance— ,, ,, ...	3¾	15

FARES

FROM WARSAW TO	Single	Return 15 Days	Return 60 Days	Excess Baggage per Kg (2·2 lbs.)
	Zl.	Zl.	Zl.	Zl.
WILNO				
RIGA				
TALLINN				

222 WARSAW—DANZIG/GDYNIA
(Service suspended during Winter)
'LOT'

Route 631

Miles	Airports of				Airports of	
0	WARSAW ... ...dep				DANZIG/GDYNIA dep	
200	DANZIG/GDYNIA ... arr				WARSAW .... arr	

Distance and Time allowance for conveyance between Airport and Town Terminus

TOWN	AIRPORT	TOWN TERMINUS	Miles	Minutes
WARSAW	Okecie	Stadtbüro (Town Office) Al Jerozolimskie 35...	5	45
DANZIG/GDYNIA...	Langfuhr	Danzig—No Special Conveyance, Central Stn....	3	—
		Gdynia—Pl. Kaszubski	10¾	55

FARES

FROM WARSAW TO	Single	Return 15 Days	Return 60 Days	Excess Baggage per Kg (2·2 lbs.)
	Zl.	Zl.	Zl.	Zl.
DANZIG/GDYNIA				

BELGRADE—SKOPLJÉ—SALONICA
(Service suspended during Winter)
' AEROPOUT '

Route 626

Miles	Airports of				Airports of		
0	**BELGRADE** ... ...dep				**SALONICA** ... ...dep		
225½	**SKOPLJÉ** ... ... arr				**SKOPLJÉ** ... ... arr		
	" ... ...dep				" ... ...dep		
362	**SALONICA** ... ... arr				**BELGRADE** ... ... arr		

Distance and Time allowance for conveyance between Airport and Town Terminus or centre of Town

TOWN	AIRPORT	TOWN TERMINUS	Miles	Minutes
BELGRADE	Beograd (Zemun)	Boat to Zemun; thence 'Aeropout' conveyance to Airport*	2¼*	45
SKOPLJÉ	Skopljé	No Special Conveyance	3	—
SALONICA	Sedes	Angle Comninon-Mitropo éos	9¼	60

FARES

FROM BELGRADE TO	Single	Return 15 Days	Return 60 Days	Excess Baggage per Kg (2·2 lbs.)
	Din.	Din.	Din.	Din.
SKOPLJE				
SALONICA				

LJUBLJANA—ZAGREB—SUSAK
(Service suspended during Winter)
' AEROPOUT '

Route 627

Miles	Airports of				Airports of		
0	**LJUBLJANA** ... ...dep				**SUSAK** ... ...dep		
73½	**ZAGREB** ... ... arr				**ZAGREB** ... ... arr		
	" ... ...dep				" ... ...dep		
158	**SUSAK** ... ... arr				**LJUBLJANA** ... ... arr		

Distance and Time allowance for conveyance between Airport and Town Terminus or centre of Town

TOWN	AIRPORT	TOWN TERMINUS	Miles	Minutes
LJUBLJANA	Ljubljana .... (Lyoubljana)	No Special Conveyance	4	—
ZAGREB	Borongaj	Jelacicew 6	4¼	60
SUSAK	Susak	Jelaclev	7	60

FARES

FROM LJUBLJANA TO	Single	Return 15 Days	Return 60 Days	Excess Baggage per Kg (2·2 lbs.)
	Din.	Din.	Din.	Din.
ZAGREB				
SUSAK				

225

BUDAPEST—PÉCS—KAPOSVÁR
(Service suspended during Winter)
'MALERT'

Route 422

Miles	Airports of					Airports of			
0	**BUDAPEST** ... ...dep					**KAPOSVÁR** ... ...dep			
115	**PÉCS** ... ...arr					**PÉCS** ... ...arr			
	,, ...dep					,, ...dep			
143	**KAPOSVÁR** ... ...arr					**BUDAPEST** ... ...arr			

Distance and Time allowance for conveyance between Airport and Town Terminus

TOWN	AIRPORT	TOWN TERMINUS	Miles	Minutes
BUDAPEST	Matyasfold	Luftreisebüro der Malert, Václ ucca 1...............	7¾	40
PÉCS	Pécs	No Special Conveyance	2¾	—
KAPOSVÁR	Kaposvár	No Special Conveyance	6¼	—

FARES

FROM BUDAPEST TO	Single	Return 15 Days	Return 60 Days	Excess Baggage per Kg (2·2 lbs.)
	Pen.	Pen.	Pen.	Pen.
PECS				
KAPOSVÁR				

226

TIRANA—PESKOPEJA—KUKUS
(Service suspended during Winter)
A.L.S.A.

Route 388a

Miles	Airports of					Airports of			
0	**TIRANA** ... ...dep					**KUKUS** ... ...dep			
·	**PESKOPEJA** ... ...arr					**PESKOPEJA** ... ...arr			
	... ...dep					,, ...dep			
	KUKUS ... ...arr					**TIRANA** ... ...arr			

Distance and Time allowance for conveyance between Airport and Town Terminus

TOWN	AIRPORT	TOWN TERMINUS	Miles	Minutes
TIRANA	Tirana	Ufficio C.I.T. Via Abdi Bey Toptani (Fare, 3 Gold Fr.)	2½	30
PESKOPEJA	Peskopeja	No Special Conveyance	—	—
KUKUS..................	Kukus	No Special Conveyance	—	—

FARES

FROM TIRANA TO	Single	Return 15 Days	Return 60 Days	Excess Baggage per Kg (2·2 lbs.)
	Alb. Gold Fr.	Alb. Gold Fr.	Alb. Gold Fr.	Alb. Gold Fr.
PESKOPEJA				
KUKUS				

227 TIRANA—SCUTARI
A.L.S.A.
Route 388

Miles	Airports of		T		Airports of			T	
0	**TIRANA**	... ...dep	9 55		**SCUTARI**	... ...dep	10 55	
59	**SCUTARI**	... ... arr	10 40		**TIRANA**	... ... arr	11 40	

T On Tuesday, Thursday and Friday

Distance and Time allowance for conveyance between Airport and Town Terminus.

TOWN	AIRPORT	TOWN TERMINUS	Miles	Minutes
TIRANA	Tirana	Ufficio C.I.T. Via Abdi Bey Toptani (Fare, 3 Gold Fr.).............................	2½	30
SCUTARI...............	Scutari	Agenzia 'Adria-Aerolloyd ' (Fare 3 Gold Fr.)...	—	60

FARES

FROM TIRANA TO	Single	Return 15 Days	Return 60 Days	Excess Baggage per Kg (2·2 lbs.)
	Alb. Gold Fr.	Alb. Gold Fr.	Alb. Gold Fr.	Alb. Gold Fr.
SCUTARI	22	...	§	0·22

§ 30% reduction on homeward journey

230 TIRANA—VALONA
A.L.S.A.
Route 390

Miles	Airports of		T		Airports of			T	
0	**TIRANA**	... ...dep	8 0		**VALONA**	... ...dep	9 0	
62	**VALONA**	... ... arr	8 50		**TIRANA**	... ... arr	9 50	

T On Tuesday, Thursday and Friday

Distance and Time allowance for conveyance between Airport and Town Terminus

TOWN	AIRPORT	TOWN TERMINUS	Miles	Minutes
TIRANA	Tirana	Ufficio C.I.T. Via Abdi Bey Toptani (Fare, 3 Gold Fr.), ...	2½	30
VALONA	Valona	Agenzia 'Adria Aerolloyd ' (Fare 3 Gold Fr.).....	—	30

FARES

FROM TIRANA TO	Single	Return 15 Days	Return 60 Days	Excess Baggage per Kg (2·2 lbs.)
	Alb. Gold Fr.	Alb. Gold Fr.	Alb. Gold Fr.	Alb. Gold Fr.
VALONA	32	...	§	0·32

§ 30% reduction on homeward journey

231 TIRANA—CORITZA
A.L.S.A.
Route 389

Miles	Airports of		M		Airports of			M	
0	**TIRANA**	... ...dep	8 0		**CORITZA**	... ...dep	9 10	
78	**CORITZA**	... ... arr	9 0		**TIRANA**	... ... arr	10 10	

M On Monday, Wednesday and Saturday

Distance and Time allowance for conveyance between Airport and Town Terminus.

TOWN	AIRPORT	TOWN TERMINUS	Miles	Minutes
TIRANA	Tirana	Ufficio C.I.T. Via Abdi Bey Toptani (Fare, 3 Gold Fr.), ...	2½	30
CORITZA	Coritza	Agenzia 'Adria Aerolloyd' (Fare, 3 Gold Fr.) ...	—	30

FARES

FROM TIRANA TO	Single	Return 15 Days	Return 60 Days	Excess Baggage per Kg (2·2 lbs.)
	Alb. Gold Fr.	Alb. Gold Fr.	Alb. Gold Fr.	Alb. Gold Fr.
CORITZA	35	...	§	0·35

§ 30% reduction on homeward journey

232 DRAMA—SALONICA—ATHENS
(Subject to confirmation)
S.H.C.A.
Route 443

Miles	Airports of		M	S		Airports of			M			M
0	**DRAMA**	...dep	13 30	...		**ATHENS**	...dep	6§30	8‡30	...		
	SALONICA ...	...arr	14 15	...		**SALONICA** ...	...arr	8 30	10 30	...		
	,, ...	...dep	15 30	15 30		,, ...	...dep	...	...	11 15		
230	**ATHENS**	...arr	17 30	17 30		**DRAMA**	...arr	...	...	12 0		

M—On Mondays, Wednesdays, and Fridays   **S**—On Weekdays only
‡—On Mondays, Thursdays, and Fridays   §—On Tuesdays, Wednesdays, and Saturdays

---

Distance and Time allowance for conveyance between Airport and Town Terminus

TOWN	AIRPORT	TOWN TERMINUS	Miles	Minute
DRAMA	Drama	Rue Alexandre le Grand	1¼	40
SALONICA	Sedes	Angle Comninon-Mitropóleos	9¼	60
ATHENS	Tatoi .... {	S.H.C.A. Place de la Constitution, 5 Rue Mitro-poléos	11½	—
		Hotel Grande Bretagne, Rue de Strade 64 ...	10½	60

FARES

FROM DRAMA	Single	Return 15 Days	Return 60 Days	Excess Baggage per Kg (2·2 lbs.)
	Drach.	Drach.	Drach.	Drach.
To SALONICA	500	...	850	7
ATHENS	1,500	...	2,550	23
FROM SALONICA				
To ATHENS	1,000	...	1,700	16

---

233 SALONICA—SOFIA—BUCHAREST
'LOT'
Route 635

Miles	Airports of		W		Airports of		T	
0	**SALONICA** ...	...dep	10 25		**BUCHAREST** ...	...dep	8 0	
178	**SOFIA**	...arr	12 15		**SOFIA**	...arr	10 15	
	,, ...	...dep	12 45		,, ...	...dep	10 45	
391½	**BUCHAREST** ...	...arr	15 0		**SALONICA** ...	...arr	12 35	

W—On Wednesday only   **T** On Tuesday only

Distance and Time allowance for conveyance between Airport and Town Terminus

TOWN	AIRPORT	TOWN TERMINUS	Miles	Minutes
SALONICA	Sedes................	Allalouf & Co., 10 Rue Metropole	11¼	60
SOFIA	Buzurisżcze	Hotel ' Bulgaria,' Lewski I............................	8¾	60
BUCHAREST	Baneasa	A.R.P.A. P. Reg. Carol I................................	2¼	55

FARES

FROM SALONICA	Single	Return 15 Days	Return 60 Days	Excess Baggage per Kg (2·2 lbs.)
	Zl.	Zl.	Zl.	Zl.
To SOFIA	80	...	136	0·80
BUCHAREST	150	...	255	1·50
FROM SOFIA				
To BUCHAREST	70	...	119	0·70

All times given in the Tables are local times, see page 22
Conveyance between an Airport and the Town Terminus is free unless otherwise indicated in the Table
The full names and addresses, etc., of the Companies will be found on pages 30 and 31

234   JANNINA—AGRINION—ATHENS
(Subject to confirmation)
S.H.C.A.
Route 442

Miles	Airports of			M	W	Airports of				T	F
0	JANNINA ... ...dep			12 0	12 0	ATHENS ... ...dep				8 0	8 0
84	AGRINION ... ...arr			...	12 45	AGRINION ... ...arr				...	9 30
	,, ...dep			...	13 15	,, ...dep				...	10 0
230	ATHENS ... ...arr			14 15	14 45	JANNINA ... ...arr				10 15	10 45

F—On Mon. & Fri.   M—On Mon., Thurs. & Fri.   T—On Wed., Thurs., & Sat.   W—On Wed. & Sat.

Distance and Time allowance for conveyance between Airport and Town Terminus

TOWN	AIRPORT	TOWN TERMINUS	Miles	Minutes
JANNINA	Jannina	S.H.C.A., 4 Rue Souliou	3	45
AGRINION	Agrinion	Place Centrale...	1½	30
ATHENS	Tatoi .... {	Acropole Palace, Place d'Amérique	11½	60
		Hotel Grande Bretagne, Rue de Strade 64	—	60

FARES

FROM JANNINA	Single	Return 15 Days	Return 60 Days	Excess Baggage per Kg (2·2 lbs.)
	Drach.	Drach.	Drach.	Drach.
To AGRINION	300	...	500	16
ATHENS	716	...	1.200	16
FROM AGRINION To ATHENS	600	...	1.000	16

235   TRIPOLI—SIRTE—BENGASI
NORD AFRICA AVIAZIONE S.A.
Route 366a

Miles	Airports of			T	Airports of				M
0	TRIPOLI ... ...dep			7 0	BENGASI ... ...dep				7 0
341	SIRTE ... ...arr			10 0	SIRTE ... ...arr				11 15
	,, ...dep			10 30	,, ...dep				11 45
579	BENGASI ... ...arr			14 45	TRIPOLI ... ...arr				14 45

T—On Tues., Thurs., and Sats.   M—On Mons., Weds., and Fris.

Distance and Time allowance for conveyance between Airport and Town Terminus

TOWN	AIRPORT	TOWN TERMINUS	Miles	Minutes
TRIPOLI	Mellaha	Grand Hotel. No Special Conveyance............	—	—
SIRTE	Sirte	No Special Conveyance	—	—
BENGASI	Campo Militare della Berka	Piazza del Re	—	30

FARES

FROM TRIPOLI	Single	Return 60 Days	Excess Baggage per Kg (2·2 lbs.)
	Lire	Lire	Lire
To SIRTE	250	...	2·35
BENGASI	466	...	4·0
FROM SIRTE To BENGASI	250	...	2·35

236

BENGASI—CIRENE—DERNA—TOBRUK
NORD—AFRICA AVIAZIONE S.A.

Route 366b

Miles	Airports of		W		Airports of		T	
0	BENGASI	... ...dep	6 0		TOBRUK	... ...dep	11 30	
134	CIRENE	... ... arr	7 45		DERNA	... ... arr	12 45	
	,,	... ...dep	8 0		,,	... ...dep	13 15	
176½	DERNA	... ... arr	8 45		CIRENE	... ... arr	14 0	
	,,	... ...dep	9 15		,,	... ...dep	14 15	
276	TOBRUK	... ... arr	10 30		BENGASI	... ... arr	16 0	

W—On Wednesday only   **T**—On Thursday only

Distance and Time allowance for conveyance between Airport and Town Terminus

TOWN	AIRPORT	TOWN TERMINUS	Miles	Minutes
BENGASI	Campo Militare della Berka	Plazza del Re	—	30
CIRENE	Apollonia	No Special Conveyance	—	—
DERNA	Feteiah	No Special Conveyance	—	—
TOBRUK	Campo Militare ...	No Special Conveyance	—	—

FARES

FROM BENGASI TO	Single	Return 60 Days	Excess Baggage per Kg (2·2 lbs.)
	Lire	Lire	Lire
CIRENE	130		0·95
DERNA	170		1·20
TOBRUK	266		1·90

MOUNT NELSON HOTEL, CAPETOWN.

● *The Premier Hotel of South Africa*

Accommodation for 175 Visitors.
Suites. Private Bathrooms. Extensive Grounds
Inclusive Terms:—
Oct. to April from 21/- per day.
May to Sept. ,, 17/6 ,, ,,
Telegrams—Hostel, Capetown.
Telephone—2-6771 Capetown.

London Office: 3, Fenchurch Street, London, E.C.3.
Telegrams: "Hostel, London"
Telephone: Royal **3000**.

WEST END
ORCHESTRA

●

SUPERB
DANCE
FLOOR

TORRS HOTEL

NAIROBI.

EXQUISITE
CUISINE

●

TELEGRAMS:
JET NAIROBI.
BOX 419 NAIROBI

GIBBS' AUTO TRANSPORT LTD.,

OFFICIAL TRANSPORT CONTRACTORS TO

Imperial Airways, Ltd. - - Wilson Airways, Ltd.
Thos. Cook & Son, Ltd.
Motor Tours arranged. - - - Complete Safari Outfitters.

STANLEY ARCADE, NAIROBI.

Telegrams: "Nafika" Nairobi. : : : : : : Box 1001, Nairobi.

RICHARDSON, TYSON, & MARTIN LTD.

Whiteaway's Building, Sixth Avenue,

Phone: 2441. **NAIROBI, KENYA COLONY.** Grams: "Managing"

STOCK AND SHARE BROKERS, LAND AND ESTATE AGENTS, SECRETARIES.

Representing leading Insurance Companies for

ALL TYPES OF INSURANCE BUSINESS.

Miles	Airports of					Airports of				
0	LONDON ... ...dep	Wed.	12 30			CAPETOWN ...dep	Tues.	7 30		
205	PARIS (Gare de					KIMBERLEY ...dep	,,	13 50	A	
	Lyon) § ... ...✈dep	,,	17 15			JOHANN-✈ { arr	,,	Even.	Sat.	
1352	BRINDISI § ... ...arr	Fri.	Morn.			ESBURG { dep	Wed.	6 0	9 0	
,,	... ...dep	,,	6 0			BULAWAYO ...dep	,,	11 15	14 30	
1721	ATHENS ... ...dep	,,	11 40			SALISBURY ... ...dep	,,	14 0	16 40	
2308	ALEXANDRIA ...dep	,,	19 0			BROKEN ✈ { arr	,,	Even.	———	
2426	CAIRO ... ...✈ arr	,,	Even.			HILL { dep	Thurs.	4 30		
,,	... ...dep	Sat.	5 0			DODOMA ... ...dep	,,	14 15		
3058	WADI HALFA ...dep	,,	13 0			NAIROBI ...✈ arr	,,	Even.		
3576	KHARTOUM...✈ arr	,,	Even.			,,	... ...dep	Fri.	9 0		
,,	... ...dep	Sun.	6 45			ENTEBBE ... ...dep	,,	13 40		
4335	JUBA ... ...✈ arr	,,	Even.			JUBA ... ...✈ arr	,,	Even.		
,,	... ...dep	Mon.	7 0			,,	... ...dep	Sat.	7 0		
4670	ENTEBBE ... ...dep	,,	13 0			KHARTOUM ✈ arr	,,	Even.		
5004	NAIROBI ...✈ arr	,,	Even.			,,	... ...dep	Sun.	5 45		
,,	... ...dep	Tues.	9 0			WADI HALFA ...dep	,,	13 0		
5376	DODOMA ... ...dep	,,	14 25			LUXOR ... ...✈ arr	,,	Even.		
5662	MBEYA ...✈ arr	,,	Even.			,,	... ...dep	Mon.	8 0		
,,	... ...dep	Wed.	9 0			CAIRO ... ...✈ arr	,,	Aftn.		
6175	BROKEN HILL ...dep	,,	14 0	A		,,	... ...dep	Tues.	4 0	A	
6475	SALISBURY ...✈ arr	,,	Even.	Tues		ALEXANDRIA ...dep	,,	6 0	Tues	
,,	... ...dep	Thurs.	7 30	8 0		ATHENS ... ...dep	,,	14 30	8 0	
6701	BULAWAYO ...dep	,,	9 55	10 35		BRINDISI ... ... arr	,,	Even.	16 25	
7153	JOHANNES-✈ { arr	,,	Aftn.	16 25		,,	§ ...✈ dep	,,	20 27		
	BURG { dep	Fri.	7 0	———		PARIS§(G.de Lyon) arr	Thurs.	6 40		
7425	KIMBERLEY ... ...dep	,,	10 15			,,	... ...dep	,,	9 30		
7963	CAPETOWN ...arr	,,	Aftn.			LONDON ... ... arr	,,	11 45		

Intermediate calls may be made at the following places:—**Assiut, Assuan, Luxor** (outward), **Kosti, Malakal, Kisumu, Moshi, Mpika, Mbeya** (return), **Pietersburg,** and **Victoria West.**
A—Local service; calls at Pietersburg. § By rail between Paris and Brindisi.
✈ A passenger spends the night at this port or in the train.

Distance and Time allowance for conveyance between Airport and Town Terminus.

TOWN	AIRPORT	TOWN TERMINUS	Miles	Minutes
LONDON	Croydon	Airway Terminus, Victoria Station, S.W. 1 ...	12	45
PARIS	Le Bourget	Airway Terminus, Rue des Italiens................	8	45
BRINDISI	Marine	Hotel Internationale	1	5
ATHENS	Phaleron Bay	Hotel Grande Bretagne	4	15
ALEXANDRIA	Ras-el-Tin (Marine)	Hotel Cecil	1¾	10
CAIRO	Heliopolis	Shepheards Hotel	6	20
LUXOR	Luxor	Luxor Hotel	9½	20
WADI HALFA	Wadi Halfa	Wadi Halfa Hotel	1½	5
KHARTOUM	Khartoum............	Grand Hotel	3	10
MALAKAL	Malakal	Imperial Airways Office	2	*
JUBA...................	Juba	Juba Hotel	¾	5
ENTEBBE	Entebbe	No Transport	—	—
KISUMU	Kisumu	Kisumu Hotel	4	15
NAIROBI	Nairobi	Avenue Hotel	5	15
MOSHI	Moshi	Mawenze Hotel	1¼	5
DODOMA	Dodoma	Railway Hotel	1½	7
MBEYA	Mbeya	No Transport	—	—
BROKEN HILL	Broken Hill	Boons Hotel	3	5
SALISBURY	Salisbury	Meikels Hotel	2½	10
BULAWAYO	Bulawayo	Grand Hotel	2½	12
JOHANNESBURG ...	Germiston	Carlton Hotel (Germiston)	10	20
KIMBERLEY	Kimberley	Queen's Hotel	5	15
CAPETOWN	Wingfield	Assembly Hotel	6	20

* 10 minutes by car in dry season, 45 minutes by launch.

Fares, etc., continued on next page

Quoted in English £ and inclusive of all accommodation, meals, surface transport and tips en route. As these fares include a proportion of expenditure in foreign currency they are liable to fluctuation without notice in accordance with the prevailing exchange rates.

CANCELLATIONS.—The fare less 10% will be refunded if not less than 14 days notice is given cancelling a reservation. Telegrams or other expenses incurred may be charged for.

RETURN TICKETS.—A reduction equivalent to 20% (twenty per cent) of the single fare for the homeward journey is allowed on return tickets taken in advance.

The fares given are based on the transport of a weight of 100 kgs. (221 lb.) a passenger (including baggage). The average passenger weighs 75 kgs. (166 lb.) and, therefore, normally 25 kgs. (55 lb.) of baggage may be carried free of additional charge. If the personal weight of a passenger be more than 85 kgs. (187 lb.) an allowance of 15 kgs. (33 lb.) of baggage free of charge is made irrespective of the weight of the passenger. Excess baggage at rate of ½% of single fare per kg. (2.2 lb.). Fractions of a kilogramme are charged to the nearest kilogramme, with a minimum of one kilogramme.

Passengers who wish to break their journey must pay the fares quoted for each section. Break of journey cannot be made on through tickets.

SINGLE FARES

	LONDON	PARIS	BRINDISI	ATHENS	ALEXANDRIA	CAIRO	ASSIUT	ASSUAN	WADI HALFA	KHARTOUM	KOSTI	MALAKAL	JUBA	ENTEBBE*	KISUMU	NAIROBI	MOSHI	DODOMA	MBEYA	MPIKA	BROKEN HILL	SALISBURY	BULAWAYO	PIETERSBURG	JOHANNESBURG	KIMBERLEY	VICTORIA WEST
ATHENS	32	30	12																								
ALEXANDRIA	40	38	23	14																							
CAIRO	42	40	25	16																							
ASSIUT	50	47	32	20																							
ASSUAN	64	68	47	33																							
WADI HALFA	70	70	55	43																							
KHARTOUM	70	70	55	43	33	30			10																		
KOSTI	70	70	55	43	33	30				10																	
MALAKAL	95	95	82	70	36	34																					
JUBA	105	105	92	80	61	59																					
ENTEBBE*	105	105	92	80	71	69							8														
KISUMU	105	105	92	80	71	69							11	7													
NAIROBI	109	109	96	84	71	69							14	10	4												
MOSHI	109	109	98	86	75	73							16	13	8	4											
DODOMA	109	109	98	86	77	75							22	19	14	10	6										
MBEYA	109	109	98	86	77	75							27	23	19	16	13	7									
MPIKA	109	109	98	86	77	75							31	28	24	20	19	14	7								
BROKEN HILL	115	115	104	92	82	80							39	35	31	27	26	22	15	8							
SALISBURY	115	115	104	92	87	85							45	41	37	33	32	31	24	17	9						
BULAWAYO	120	120	109	97	90	88							50	46	42	38	37	35	29	22	14	6					
PIETERSBURG	120	120	109	97	92	90							54	50	46	42	40	37	32	26	18	12	6				
JOHANNESBURG	125	125	112	100	94	92							56	52	48	44	42	39	34	29	21	15	10	4			
KIMBERLEY	125	125	112	100	96	94							59	56	52	46	44	41	36	31	23	15	11	7	5		
VICTORIA WEST	130	130	115	103	99	97							62	58	54	50	47	44	39	34	26	17	12	10	8	4	
CAPETOWN	130	130	121	109	102	100	97	94	85	78	76	69	63	59	55	51	50	47	42	38	30	21	17	14	13	9	6

* This fare applies to Kampala when the call is made at this port.

COMPARATIVE INTERNATIONAL TIMES

ALL TIMES GIVEN IN THE TABLES ARE LOCAL TIMES

Simultaneous Time

| West Europe Time (Greenwich Mean Time) | Amsterdam Time (used in Holland) Twenty minutes in advance of Greenwich Mean Time | Central Europe Time One hour in advance of Greenwich Mean Time | East Europe Time Two hours in advance of Greenwich Mean Time |

WEST EUROPE TIME is applicable to Great Britain, Belgium, France, Algeria, Spain and Portugal.

CENTRAL EUROPE TIME is applicable to Germany, Austria, Hungary, Switzerland, Italy, Czechoslovakia, Yugoslavia, Lithuania, Poland, Denmark, Norway, Sweden, Tunis and Morocco.

EAST EUROPE TIME is applicable to Bulgaria, Estonia, Finland, Greece, Latvia, Rumania, Russia and Turkey.

DIFFERENCES IN LOCAL TIME AND LONDON (i.e., GREENWICH)

Fast on Greenwich Time

New Zealand	$11\frac{1}{2}$ hours
Victoria, New South Wales, Queensland	10 ,,
South Australia	$9\frac{1}{2}$,,
Sarawak	$7\frac{1}{2}$,,
French Indo-China, Siam, Malaya	7 ,,
Burma	$6\frac{1}{2}$,,
India (except Calcutta)	$5\frac{1}{2}$,,
Iraq, Tanganyika, Kenya	3 ,,
Uganda	$2\frac{1}{2}$,,
Sudan, Rhodesia, South Africa	2 ,,

Slow on Greenwich Time

Madeira, Canary Islands	1 hour
Azores, Cape Verde Islands	2 hours
Eastern Brazil	3 ,,
Uruguay	$3\frac{1}{2}$,,
Central Brazil, Argentina	4 ,,

Miles	Airports of				Airports of			
0	LONDON... ... ...dep	Sat.	12 30		SINGAPORE ... ...dep	Sun.	6 0	
205	PARIS (Gare de Lyon)				ALOR STAR § ... ...dep	§		
	‡ ... ... dep	,,	17 15		BANGKOK ... arr	Sun.	Even.	
1352	BRINDISI ‡ ... arr	Mon.	Morn.		,, ...dep	Mon.	6 30	
	... ...dep	,,	6 0		RANGOON ... ...dep	,,	10 5	
1721	ATHENS ... ...dep	,,	11 40		AKYAB § ... ...dep	§		
2308	ALEXANDRIA ...dep	,,	19 0		CALCUTTA ... arr	Mon.	Aftn.	
2426	CAIRO ... arr	,,	Even.		,, ...dep	Tues.	5 30	
	... ...dep	Tues.	5 30		ALLAHABAD ... ...dep	,,	10 20	
2638	GAZA ... ...dep	,,	8 50		CAWNPORE ... ...dep	,,	11 40	
3241	BAGHDAD ... arr	,,	Even.		DELHI ... ...dep	,,	15 0	
	... ...dep	Wed.	6 0		JODHPUR... arr	,,	Even.	
3519	BASRA ... ...dep	,,	9 50		... ...dep	Wed.	4 30	
3594	KOWEIT § ... ...dep	§			KARACHI ... ...dep	,,	9 0	
3859	BAHREIN § ... ...dep	§			GWADAR § ... ...dep	§		
4194	SHARJAH... arr	Wed.	Even.		SHARJAH ... arr	Wed.	Even.	
	... ...dep	Thurs.	5 0		... ...dep	Thurs.	6 0	
4634	GWADAR § ... ...dep	§			BAHREIN § ... ...dep	§		
4934	KARACHI ... ...dep	Thurs.	16 30		KOWEIT § ... ...dep	§		
5318	JODHPUR arr	,,	Even.		BASRA... ... ...dep	Thurs.	15 0	
	... ...dep	Fri.	5 0		BAGHDAD ... arr	,,	Even.	
5620	DELHI ... ...dep	,,	8 5		... ...dep	Fri.	6 0	
5865	CAWNPORE ... ...dep	,,	10 20		GAZA ... ...dep	,,	14 0	
5973	ALLAHABAD ... ...dep	,,	12 0		CAIRO... ... arr	,,	Even.	
6445	CALCUTTA arr	,,	Even.		... ...dep	Sat.	4 0	
	... ...dep	Sat.	5 0		ALEXANDRIA ...dep	,,	6 0	
6778	AKYAB § ... ...dep	§			ATHENS ... ...dep	,,	14 30	
7091	RANGOON ... ...dep	Sat.	12 45		BRINDISI ... arr	,,	Even.	
7465	BANGKOK arr	,,	Even.		... ...dep	,,	20 27	
	... ...dep	Sun.	7 0		PARIS (Gare de Lyon)‡ arr	Mon.	6 40	
	ALOR STAR § ... ...dep	§			... ...dep	,,	9 30	
8458	SINGAPORE arr	Sun.	Even.		LONDON... ... arr	,,	11 45	

‡ By rail between Paris and Brindisi.   § An intermediate call may be made at this Airport.
A passenger spends the night at this port or in the train.

Distance and Time allowance for conveyance between Airport and Town Terminus

TOWN	AIRPORT	TOWN TERMINUS	Miles	Minutes
LONDON	Croydon	Airway Terminus, Victoria Station, S.W. 1 ...	12	45
PARIS	Le Bourget	Airway Terminus, Rue des Italiens	8	45
BRINDISI	Marine	Hotel Internationale	1	5
ATHENS	Phaleron Bay	Hotel Grande Bretagne	4	15
ALEXANDRIA	Ras-el-Tin (Marine)	Hotel Cecil	1¾	10
CAIRO	Heliopolis	Shepheards Hotel	6	20
GAZA	Gaza	Gaza Railway Station	5	20
BAGHDAD	Bagdad	Maude Hotel	1½	25
BASRA	Shaibah	Railway Rest House; Margil	16	50
KOWEIT	Koweit	No Transport	—	—
BAHREIN	Bahrein	Mesopotamia Persia Corporation Office	2	90
SHARJAH	Sharjah	No Transport	—	—
GWADAR	Gwadar	No Transport	—	—
KARACHI	Karachi	Hotels: Killarney, Bristol, Carlton, Central ...	11	30
JODHPUR	Jodhpur	State Hotel	½	2
DELHI	Delhi	Maiden's Hotel	9	20
CAWNPORE	Cawnpore	Berkeley House	4	15
ALLAHABAD	Allahabad	Allahabad Club	9	30
CALCUTTA	Dum-Dum	Great Eastern Hotel	12	40
AKYAB	Akyab	Government Rest House	2	7
RANGOON	Rangoon	Minto Mansions; Strand Hotel	11	30
BANGKOK	Don Nuang	Aerial Transport Co.'s Office	15	60
ALOR STAR	Alor Star	Government Rest House	7	20
SINGAPORE	Singapore	Raffles Hotel	13	35

Through fares are quoted in English £ and are inclusive of all accommodation, meals, surface transport, and tips en route. As these fares include a proportion of expenditure in foreign currency they are liable to fluctuation without notice in accordance with the prevailing exchange rates.

CANCELLATIONS.—The fare less 10% will be refunded if not less than 14 days notice is given cancelling a reservation. Telegrams or other expenses incurred may be charged for.

RETURN TICKETS

A reduction equivalent to 20% (twenty per cent) of the single fare for the homeward journey is allowed on return tickets taken in advance

SINGLE FARES

	LONDON	PARIS	BRINDISI	ATHENS	ALEXANDRIA	CAIRO	GAZA	BAGHDAD	BASRA	KOWEIT	BAHREIN	SHARGAH	GWADAR
ATHENS	32	30	12										
ALEXANDRIA	40	38	23	14									
CAIRO	42	40	25	16	5								
GAZA	47	45	30	21									
BAGHDAD	82	62	47	38			29						
BASRA	67	67	52	43				6					
KOWEIT	71	71	58	47				10	4				
BAHREIN	78	78	63	54				17	11	7			
SHARGAH	84	84	69	60				23	17	13	6		
GWADAR	90	90	75	66			49	29	23	19	12	6	
KARACHI	96	95	80	71			53	34	28	24	17	11	6
JODHPUR	104	104	89	80			62	43	37	33	26	20	15
DELHI	106	106	91	82			64	45	39	35	29	22	18
CAWNPORE	110	110	95	86			68	50	44	40	33	27	23
ALLAHABAD	114	114	99	87			72	54	48	44	37	31	27
CALCUTTA	122	122	107	93			80	62	56	52	45	39	35
AKYAB	128	128	113	104			86	69	62	58	51	45	42
RANGOON	135	135	120	111			93	76	69	65	59	53	50
BANGKOK	155	155	140	131			113	95	89	85	79	73	70
PENANG													
KUALA LUMPUR													
SINGAPORE	180	190	165	187	146	144	140	123	118	114	108	109	100

LOCAL FARES *

	KARACHI	JODHPUR	DELHI	CAWNPORE	ALLAHABAD	CALCUTTA	AKYAB	RANGOON	BANGKOK	PENANG	KUALA LUMPUR
KARACHI											
JODHPUR	120										
DELHI	220	120									
CAWNPORE	280	190	70								
ALLAHABAD	340	240	120	60							
CALCUTTA	440	350	230	160	120						
AKYAB	550	470	360	300	270	150					
RANGOON	650	580	460	400	380	270	120				
BANGKOK	69	63	54	50	48	40	29	20			
PENANG											
KUALA LUMPUR											
SINGAPORE	100	95	86	82	80	73	62	53	34		

The fares given are based on the transport of a weight of 100 kgs. (227 lb.) The average passenger weighs 75 kgs. (166 lb.) and, therefore, normally 25 kgs. (55 lb.) of baggage may be carried free of additional charge. If the personal weight of a passenger be more than 85 kgs. (187 lb.) an allowance of 10 kgs. (22 lb.) of baggage free of charge is made irrespective of the weight of the passenger. Excess baggage at the rate of 1% of single fare per kg. (2.2 lbs.) Fractions of a kilogramme are charged to the nearest kilogramme with a minimum of one kilogramme.

* Passengers who wish to break their journey must pay the fares quoted for each section. Break of journey cannot be made on through tickets.
* Local fares in India and Burma are quoted in rupees, but in English £ in Siam and in Malaya. In both instances fares are inclusive of all accommodation, meals, surface transport and tips.

239

LONDON—INDIA AND FAR EAST
(Weekly Service)
AIR FRANCE

Route 486

Miles	Airports of		
	LONDON	dep	Wednesday
	PARIS		,,
690	MARSEILLES	🛏 arr	,,
	,,	dep	Thursday
1225	NAPLES	🛏 arr	,,
	,,	dep	Friday
1650	CORFU		,,
1925	ATHENS	🛏 arr	,,
	,,	dep	Saturday
2310	CASTELROSSO		,,
2725	BEYROUTH	arr	,,
	,, §	dep	,,
	DAMASCUS §	🛏 arr	,,
	,,	dep	Sunday
3250	BAGHDAD	arr	,,
	,,	dep	,,
3825	BUSHIRE	🛏 arr	,,
	,,	dep	Monday
4310	JASK (Djask)	🛏 arr	,,
	,,	dep	Tuesday
5040	KARACHI		,,
5475	JODHPUR	🛏 arr	,,
	,,	dep	Wednesday
6070	ALLAHABAD		,,
6540	CALCUTTA	🛏 arr	,,
	,,	dep	Thursday
6900	AKYAB		,,
7385	RANGOON	🛏 arr	,,
	,,	dep	Friday
7850	BANGKOK		,,
8080	ANGKOR		,,
8370	SAIGON	arr	,,

Airports of		
SAIGON	dep	Sunday
ANGKOR		,,
BANGKOK		,,
RANGOON	🛏 arr	,,
,,	dep	Monday
AKYAB		,,
CALCUTTA	🛏 arr	,,
,,	dep	Tuesday
ALLAHABAD		,,
JODHPUR	🛏 arr	,,
,,	dep	Wednesday
KARACHI		,,
JASK	🛏 arr	,,
,,	dep	Thursday
BUSHIRE	arr	,,
,,	dep	,,
BAGHDAD	🛏 arr	,,
,,	dep	Friday
DAMASCUS §	dep	,,
BEYROUTH §	🛏 arr	,,
,,	dep	Saturday
CASTELROSSO		,,
ATHENS	🛏 arr	,,
,,	dep	Sunday
CORFU		,,
NAPLES	🛏 arr	,,
,,	dep	Monday
MARSEILLES	🛏 arr	,,
,,	dep	Tuesday
PARIS		,,
LONDON	arr	,,

§ By Car between Beyrouth and Damascus

🛏 The passenger stays overnight at this port

Distance and Time allowance for conveyance between Airport and Town Terminus or Town Centre

TOWN	AIRPORT	TOWN TERMINUS	Miles	Minutes
LONDON	Croydon	Air France, 52, Haymarket, S.W.1	13	50
PARIS	Le Bourget	Air France, Place Lafayette	6¾	35
MARSEILLES	Marignane	Air France, 1 Rue Papère	18	60
NAPLES	Molo Beverello	Hotel Excelsior	¼	—
CORFU	Phalakon	M. Galatis, 138, Rue Nikiphorou Theodokis	6¼	—
ATHENS	Megalo Pevko	Hotel Grande Bretagne	22¼	—
CASTELROSSO	Castelrosso	No Special Conveyance	—	—
BEYROUTH	Beyrouth	Hotel St. Georges	⅝	—
DAMASCUS	Mezzé	Hotel Omayad	5	—
BAGHDAD	Bagdad	Maude Hotel; Tigris Palace	½	—
BUSHIRE	Bushire	Rest House, Kazerooni	2	—
JASK	Jask	Rest House, Dr. Durning	1	—
KARACHI	Drigh Road	No Special Conveyance	13¾	—
JODHPUR	Jodhpur	State Hotel	4¼	15
ALLAHABAD	Allahabad	No Special Conveyance	7	—
CALCUTTA	Dum-Dum	Great Eastern Hotel	4	30
AKYAB	Akyab	No Special Conveyance	4¼	—
RANGOON	Rangoon	Strand Hotel	1	—
BANGKOK	Don Nuang	No Special Conveyance	13¾	—
ANGKOR	Angkor	No Special Conveyance	1¼	—
SAIGON	Tan-Son-Nhut	No Special Conveyance	3	—

All times given in the Tables are local times, see page 22

Conveyance between an Airport and the Town Terminus is free unless otherwise indicated in the Table

The full names and addresses, etc., of the Companies will be found on pages 30 and 31

Hotels and Meals.—At the end of the day and and on arrival at the station the passenger is accommodated in one of the best hotels available. This is included in the fare which also covers meals and gratuities during the journey. Wines and alcoholic drinks when ordered are charged to passengers, but the Company does not guarantee their supply.

SINGLE FARES IN ENGLISH POUNDS	LONDON	PARIS	MARSEILLES	NAPLES	CORFU	ATHENS	CASTELROSSO	BEYROUTH OR DAMASCUS	BAGHDAD	BUSHIRE	JASK	KARACHI	JODHPUR	ALLAHABAD	CALCUTTA	AKYAB	RANGOON	BANGKOK	ANGKOR
NAPLES	20	18	11																
CORFU	29	27	20	9															
ATHENS	32	30	23	12	4														
CASTELROSSO	38	38	33	22	14	12													
BEYROUTH OR DAMASCUS	47	47	43	32	24	23	12												
BAGHDAD	62	62	58	47	39	38	27	15											
BUSHIRE	72	72	68	57	49	48	37	25	10										
JASK	83	83	79	68	60	59	48	36	21	12									
KARACHI	95	95	91	80	72	71	63	51	34	27	15								
JODHPUR	104	104	100	89	81	80	72	60	43	36	24	§							
ALLAHABAD	114	114	110	99	91	90	82	70	54	47	33	§	§						
CALCUTTA	122	122	118	107	99	98	90	78	62	55	43	§	§	§					
AKYAB	128	128	124	113	105	104	96	84	68	61	49	§	§	§	§				
RANGOON	135	135	131	120	112	111	103	91	75	68	56	§	§	§	§	§			
BANGKOK	155	155	151	140	132	131	123	111	95	88	76	69	63	48	40	29	20		
ANGKOR	159	159	155	144	137	136	128	116	100	93	81	74	68	53	45	34	25	6	
SAIGON	164	164	160	149	142	141	133	121	105	98	86	79	73	58	50	39	30	11	6

Baggage.—20 kilos (45 lbs.) free.—next 20 kilos at rate of ¼ per cent of single fare per kg. (2.2 lbs.). Balance carried by arrangement at rate of ¼ per cent. Charges are made to nearest kilo.—One kilo—approximately 2.2 pounds.

Return Tickets.—Reduction of 20% on the cost of the return portion—validity twelve months—counting from date of outward departure.

Return Half of Ticket.—Passengers, on giving up the cover of their ticket (full fare) and justification of their identity, may benefit—during twelve months dating from the outward departure—by a reduction of 10% on the return portion for the same route.

Cancellations.—The Fare (less 10% and expenses) will be refunded if notice of cancellation is given within 14 days of departure.

§ Inland traffic in India not allowed.

MARSEILLES

HOTEL DE NOAILLES

LA CANEBIERE.

Miles via Budapest	Miles via Rome	Airports of			Airports of	
0	0	AMSTERDAM ... ...dep	Thursday		BANDOENG ...dep	Wednesday
	612	MARSEILLES	,,	§ {	BATAVIA	,,
	1000	ROME ... ... [arr]	,,	{	PALEMBANG	,,
		,, ...dep	Friday		SINGAPORE [arr]	,,
340		HALLE,LEIPZIG ...dep			SINGAPORE ... dep	Thursday
755		BUDAPEST ... ...dep	}¶		MEDAN	,,
955		BELGRADE ... ...dep			ALOR STAR	,,
1450	1705	ATHENS ... ... [arr]	Friday		BANGKOK ... [arr]	,,
		,, ...dep	Saturday		,, ... dep	Friday
1960	2213	MERZA MATRUH ‡ ...	,,		RANGOON	,,
2245	2474	CAIRO ... ... [arr]	,,		CALCUTTA ... [arr]	,,
		,, ...dep	Sunday		,, ...dep	Saturday
2465	2690	GAZA	,,		ALLAHABAD	,,
3055	3283	BAGHDAD ... [arr]	,,		JODHPUR	,,
		,, ...dep	Monday		KARACHI ... [arr]	,,
3545	3771	BUSHIRE	,,		,, ...dep	Sunday
4045	4271	JASK	,,		JASK	,,
4640	4863	KARACHI	,,		BUSHIRE	,,
5025	5245	JODHPUR ... [arr]	,,		BAGHDAD ... [arr]	,,
		,, ...dep	Tuesday		,, ...dep	Monday
5570	5787	ALLAHABAD ... dep	,,		GAZA	,,
6035	6253	CALCUTTA ... [arr]	,,		CAIRO ... [arr]	,,
		,, ...dep	Wednesday		,, ...dep	Tuesday
6705	6923	RANGOON	,,		MERZA MATRUH ‡... ...	,,
7065	7283	BANGKOK ... [arr]	,,		ATHENS ... [arr]	,,
		,, ... dep	Thursday		,, ...dep	Wednesday
7625	7842	ALOR STAR	,,		BELGRADE	
7855	8070	MEDAN ... [arr]	,,		BUDAPEST	}¶
		MEDAN ... ...dep	Friday		HALLE,LEIPZIG	
8240	8455	SINGAPORE ...	,,		ROME ... [arr]	Wednesday
8543	8758	§ PALEMBANG	,,		MARSEILLES ... [arr]	,,
8820	9035	BATAVIA	,,		,, ...dep	Thursday
8886	9101	BANDOENG	,,		AMSTERDAM ... ... arr	,,

‡ Optional stop.   § Combined services of the K.L.M. and K.N.I.L.M.
¶ Summer Route   [icon] The passenger stays overnight at this port.

Distance and Time allowance for conveyance between Airport and Town Terminus

TOWN	AIRPORT	TOWN TERMINUS	Miles	Minutes
AMSTERDAM	Schiphol	K.L.M. Office, Leidscheplein	8	40
MARSEILLES	Marignane	De Noailles Hotel	18¾	60
ROME	Littorio	Palace—Ambassadeurs Hotel	5	15
ATHENS	Tatol	Hotel Grande Bretagne, 64 Rue de Strade ...	10½	30
CAIRO	Almaza	Heliopolis House§ at Heliopolis...	8	10
KARACHI	Drigh Road	Bristol Hotel	8	30
JODHPUR	Jodhpur	State Hotel	3	15
CALCUTTA	Dum Dum	Great Eastern Hotel	4½	30
BANGKOK	Don Muang	Oriental Hotel	14½	45
MEDAN	Medan	De Boer Hotel	1½	10
SINGAPORE	Saletar	Sea View Hotel	10¾	30

§ Heliopolis Palace during the Season

Distance between Airport and Town

TOWN	AIRPORT	Miles	TOWN	AIRPORT	Miles
HALLE/LEIPZIG	Schkeuditz	8¾	JASK	Jask	2
BUDAPEST	Matyasfold	7	ALLAHABAD	Allahabad	5
BELGRADE	Beograd	2½	RANGOON	Rangoon	11½
MERZA MATRUH	Merza Matruh	2	ALOR STAR	Alor Star	6½
GAZA	Gaza	1½	PALEMBANG	Palembang	8¾
BAGHDAD	Baghdad	1½	BATAVIA	Batav's	9½
BUSHIRE	Bushire	1¾	BANDOENG	Bandoeng	

FARES FOR TABLE 240

Childrens' Fares.—Children up to 3 years of age, if not occupying a seat, are charged 10% of the fare (50% if a seat is reserved). Children up to 7 years of age are charged 50% of the fare.

Return Fares.—A reduction of 26⅔% of the single fare for the homeward journey is allowed on return tickets (valid for one year) if taken in advance. A reduction of 10% is allowed for a section of the route over which the passenger flys for a second time if the second flight is made within one year. Conveyance from the Airport to the town for an overnight stay is included in the fare. These conditions do not apply to the sections operated by the K.N.I.L.M. line.

Meals on board and hotel accommodation (except extras) and tips are also included in the fare.

Cancellations.—Passengers should apply to the K.L.M. Office for conditions.

Single Fares in English £

	LONDON	AMSTERDAM	MARSEILLES	ROME	ATHENS	MERZA MATRUH	CAIRO	GAZA	RUTBAH	BAGHDAD	BUSHIRE	JASK	KARACHI	JODHPUR	ALLAHABAD	CALCUTTA	AKYAB	RANGOON	BANGKOK	ALOR STAR	MEDAN	SINGAPORE	PALEMBANG	BATAVIA
ATHENS	32	32	23	..																				
MERZA MATRUH	..	..	..	..	..																			
CAIRO	42	42	38	25	16	..																		
GAZA	47	47	41	30	21	..	5																	
RUTBAH	..	..	..	..	..	..	..	..																
BAGHDAD	62	62	58	47	38	..	25	30	..															
BUSHIRE	72	72	68	57	48	..	35	30	..	19														
JASK	83	83	79	68	59	..	46	41	..	21	12													
KARACHI	95	95	91	80	71	..	58	53	..	34	27	15												
JODHPUR	104	104	100	89	80	..	67	62	..	43	36	21	..											
ALLAHABAD	114	114	110	99	90	..	77	72	..	54	47	33	..	..										
CALCUTTA	122	122	118	107	98	..	85	80	..	62	55	43	..	..	..									
AKYAB	128	128	124	113	104	..	91	86	..	68	61	49	..	..	..	..								
RANGOON	135	135	131	123	111	..	98	93	..	75	68	56	..	..	..	..	..							
BANGKOK	155	155	151	140	131	..	118	113	..	95	88	76	69	63	48	40	23	20						
ALOR STAR	164	164	160	149	141	..	128	124	..	107	101	90	84	79	64	57	46	37	18					
MEDAN	170	170	166	155	147	..	134	130	..	118	107	96	90	85	70	63	52	43	24	6				
SINGAPORE	180	180	176	165	157	..	144	140	..	123	117	106	100	95	80	73	62	53	34	17	13			
PALEMBANG	188	188	185	174	167	..	154	150	..	133	127	116	110	105	90	83	72	63	44	27	21	11		
BATAVIA	195	195	192	181	174	..	161	157	..	140	134	123	117	112	97	90	79	70	51	34	29	19	12	
BANDOENG	197	197	194	183	176	..	163	159	..	142	136	125	119	114	99	92	81	72	53	36	31	21	14	2

Baggage.—Each passenger (children under 7 years excepted) is allowed 20 Kgs. (45 lbs.) of baggage free. Excess up to 40 Kgs. is charged at the rate of ½% of single fare per kg., over 40 kgs. at the rate of 1% per kg.

GERMANY—SOUTH AMERICA
(Service Suspended during Winter)
D.L.H.; L. ZEPPELIN; S. CONDOR LTDA

Route 191

Miles	Airports of						Airports of			
0	BERLIN ... ...dep						Arica § ... ...dep			
333	STUTTGART ... ... arr						Santiago ... ... arr			
	" ... ...dep						" ... ...dep			
407	FRIEDRICHSHAFEN.. arr						Buenos Aires ... ... arr			
	" ...dep						BUENOS AIRES ¶ ...dep			
	NATAL ... ... arr						MONTEVIDEO ... ... arr			
	" ... ...dep						" ... ...dep			
5379	RECIFE { arr						RIO DE JANEIRO ... arr			
	PERNAMBUCO { dep						" ...dep			
6684	RIO DE JANEIRO ... arr						RECIFE { arr			
	" ...dep						PERNAMBUCO { dep			
	MONTEVIDEO ... ... arr						NATAL ... ... arr			
	" ...dep						" ... ...dep			
	BUENOS AIRES ¶ ... arr						FRIEDRICHSHAFEN... arr			
	Buenos Aires ... ...dep						" ...dep			
	Santiago ... ... arr						STUTTGART ... ... arr			
	" ... ...dep						" ...dep			
	Arica §... ... ... arr						BERLIN ... ... arr			

¶—Connection for Asuncion   §—Connection for La Paz

Distance and Time allowance for conveyance between Airport and Town Terminus

TOWN	AIRPORT	TOWN TERMINUS	Miles	Minutes
BERLIN.................	Tempelhof	Linden/Friedrichstrasse. No Special Conveyance	3	—
STUTTGART	Böblingen	Luftreisebüro Würtemberg A.G., Fürstenstrasse I	13¾	55
FRIEDRICHSHAFEN	Friedrichshafen ...	Kurgarten Hotel	—	4
NATAL	Natal			
RECIFE/PERNAMBUCO	Recife Pernambuco	Central Hotel	—	20
RIO DE JANEIRO ...	Rio.....................		—	25
MONTEVIDEO	Montevideo			
BUENOS AIRES ...	Buenos Aires			

D.L.H. Section.—Conveyance between Airport and Town is included in the fare.

A day may be saved on the journey to Montevideo and Buenos Aires by changing at Recife from the Airship to the Express Aeroplane of the Condor Line, instead of changing at Rio (see Fares on next page). The Airports between Recife, Rio and Buenos Aires are served by the regular services of the Condor Line. Departure from Recife on Thursday and from Rio on Friday.

All times given in the Tables are local times, see page 22
Conveyance between an Airport and the Town Terminus is free unless otherwise indicated in the Table
The full names and addresses, etc., of the Companies will be found on pages 30 and 31
152

FARES

	Single	Excess Baggage 20-40 Kgs	Excess Baggage over 40 Kgs per Kg
BERLIN—FRIEDRICHSHAFEN			
STUTTGART—FRIEDRICHSHAFEN...			
FRIEDRICHSHAFEN—RECIFE/P.			
FRIEDRICHSHAFEN—RIO DE JANEIRO ...			
RECIFE/P.—RIO DE JANEIRO			
RECIFE/P.—MONTEVIDEO			
RECIFE/P.—BUENOS AIRES			
RIO DE JANEIRO—MONTEVIDEO			
RIO DE JANEIRO—BUENOS AIRES			

During the High Season a Supplement of RM. 150 is charged. On the Zeppelin Section meals (except wines, etc.) are included in the fare. Single Berth Cabins are obtainable for 50% Supplement.

Children's Fares

D.L.H. Section.—Children up to 3 years are charged 10% of the fare and from 3 to 7 years 50%.

Zeppelin Section.—Children up to 6 years are charged 25% of the fare and from 6 to 12 years 50%.

Condor Section.—Children up to 3 years are charged 10% of the fare and from 3 to 12 years 50%.

Family Reductions

On the Zeppelin Section 15% is allowed on each ticket for 4 or more full fares or for parties of 10 or more people (except during High Season).

Return Tickets

Reductions on advanced bookings for:—

D.L.H. Section (Validity 6 months).—30% of Single Fare allowed on the return journey.

Zeppelin Section (No limit to validity).—10% of return fare allowed. Combined return tickets for travel by German boat or airship are available.

Condor Section.—20% of single fare allowed on the return journey.

Cancellation of Tickets

At least 14 days' notice must be given and a sum of 10% is charged for cancellation fee, otherwise 50% or in some instances full fare is charged.

Baggage Allowance

D.L.H. and Condor Sections.—20 Kgs is allowed free. Excess up to 40 Kgs is charged at the rate of $\frac{1}{2}$% of single fare per Kg, over 40 Kgs at rate of 1%.

Zeppelin Section.—Baggage must contain personal effects only. 20 Kgs is allowed free. See Fares Table for excess rates. Baggage over 50 Kgs or $\frac{1}{4}$ cbm may be refused. A further 100 Kgs (children under 12 years half the amount) may be sent free by German boats sailing between the East Coast of South America and Hamburg, Bremen, Boulogne or Vigo. For baggage over 100 Kgs sent by boat, a charge is made at the rate of 10 RM per 100 Kgs.

SUPPLEMENTARY LIST OF FARES

Towns	Single	Ret'n 15 days	Ret'n 60 days	Ex. Bg. perKg, 2·2 lbs.
ALCUDIA	Ptas	Ptas	Ptas	Ptas
To Algiers	250	...	425	2.50
ALGIERS	Frs.	Frs.	Frs.	Frs.
To Alcudia	500	...	850	5
ALICANTE	Ptas	Ptas	Ptas	Ptas
To Casablanca	335	...	570	3.35
Marseilles	335	...	570	3·35
Rabat	310	...	527	3·10
Tangier	260	...	442	2·60
Toulouse	335	...	570	3·35
AMSTERDAM	Fl.	Fl.	Fl.	Fl.
To Berlin	42	...	71·40	0·42
Hanover	24	...	40·80	0·24
London	42	...	71·40	0·42
ANTWERP	B.Frs.	B.Frs.	B.Frs.	B.Frs.
To Cologne	215	344	366	2.15
BARCELONA	Ptas	Ptas	Ptas	Ptas
To Casablanca	510	...	867	5·10
Marseilles	130	...	221	1·30
Rabat	485	...	824·50	4·85
Tangier	435	...	739·50	4·35
Toulouse	165	...	280·50	1·65
BELGRADE	Dinar	Dinar	Dinar	Dinar
To Bucharest	1,050	...	1,785	10·50
Budapest	780	...	1,326	7·80
Istanbul	3,290	...	5,590	32·90
Nürnberg	3,160	...	5,370	31·60
Paris	5,060	...	8,600	50·60
Prague	1,850	...	3,150	18·50
Sofia	810	...	1,377	8·10
Strasbourg	3,900	...	6,630	39
Vienna	1,230	...	2,100	12·30
BRUSSELS	B.Frs.	B.Frs.	B.Frs.	B.Frs.
To Amsterdam	215	...	365	2·15
Berlin	730	...	1,241	7·30
Cologne	215	344	366	2·15
Dortmund	250	...	425	2·50
Düsseldorf	215	344	366	2·15
Essen	235	...	400	2·35
London	480	768	816	4·80
Paris	250	...	425	2·50
Rotterdam	170	...	289	1·70
BUCHAREST	Lei	Lei	Lei	Lei
To Belgrade	3,150	...	5,350	31
Budapest	5,330	...	9,060	53
Istanbul	3,440	...	5,850	34
Nürnberg	10,520	...	17,880	105
Paris	14,940	...	25,400	149
Prague	7,500	...	12,750	75
Sofia	5,350	...	9,100	53
Strasbourg	12,250	...	20,820	122
Vienna	6,850	...	11,640	68
Warsaw	12,240	...	20,800	122

Towns	Single	Ret'n 15 days	Ret'n 60 days	Ex. Bg. perKg, 2·2 lbs.
BUDAPEST	Pen.	Pen.	Pen.	Pen.
To Belgrade	62	...	105·40	0·60
Bucharest	180	...	306	1·80
Istanbul	296	...	503	3
Nürnberg	175	...	297·50	1·75
Paris	276	...	469	2·75
Prague	105	...	178·50	1·05
Sofia	126	...	214·20	1·25
Strasbourg	233	...	396	2·35
Vienna	40	...	68	0·40
Warsaw	233	...	396	2·35
CANNES	Frs.	Frs.	Frs.	Frs.
To London	1,330	...	2262·5	11 75
Paris	925	...	1572·5	9·25
CASABLANCA	Frs.	Frs.	Frs.	Frs.
To Alicante	675	...	1147·5	6·75
Barcelona	1,020	...	1,734	10·20
Rabat	60	...	102	1
Tangier	200	...	340	2
COLOGNE	RM.	RM.	RM.	RM.
To Antwerp	25	40	42.50	0.25
Düsseldorf	10	...	17	0·15
Frankfort	23	...	39·10	0·23
Karlsruhe	39	...	66·30	0·39
Mannheim	32	...	54·40	0·32
Paris	55	...	93·55	0·55
COPENHAGEN	D.Kr.	D.Kr.	D.Kr.	D.Kr.
To Amsterdam	155	...	294·50	0·75
Berlin	90	...	153	0·90
Hamburg	85	...	144·50	0·85
Malmö	10	...	17	0·10
Paris	240	...	456	2·40
DANZIG	RM.	RM.	RM.	RM.
To Kaunas	28	...	47·60	0·28*
Königsberg	20	...	34	0·20*
Moscow	130	...	221	1·30*
Welikije Luki	80	...	136	0·80
	* Half this rate per Kg for more than 15 Kgs.			
DORTMUND	RM.	RM.	RM.	RM.
To Brussels	30	...	51	0·30
DRESDEN	RM.	RM. (60 days)		RM.
To Prague	20	17+ Kc. 136		0·20
Vienna	60	51+ Sch. 102		0·60

154

SUPPLEMENTARY LIST OF FARES—Continued

Towns	Single	Ret'n 15 days	Ret'n 60 days	Ex. Bg. perKg. 2·2 lbs.
DÜSSELDORF	RM.	RM.	RM.	RM.
To Cologne	10	...	17	0·10
Dortmund	10	...	17	0·10
Essen	10	...	17	0·10
Frankfort	24	...	40·80	0·24
Karlsruhe	40	...	68	0·40
Mannheim	33	...	56·10	0·33
ERFURT	RM.	RM.	RM.	RM.
To Frankfort/M.	27	...	45·90	0·27
Saarbrücken	42	...	71·40	0·42
ESSEN	RM.	RM.	RM.	RM.
To Dortmund	10	...	17	0·10
FRANKFORT-on-M.	RM.	RM.	RM.	RM.
To Cologne	23	...	39·10	0·25
Düsseldorf	24	...	40·80	0·25
Karlsruhe	16	...	27·20	0·16
Mannheim	12	...	20·40	0·12
Saarbrücken	20	...	34	0·20
GENEVA	S.Frs.	S.Frs.	S.Frs.	S.Frs.
To Barcelona	113	...	192·10	1·13
Marseilles	56	...	95·20	0·56
Stuttgart	56	...	95·20	0·56
HAAMSTEDE	Fl.	Fl.	Fl.	Fl.
To Flushing	4	...	6·80	0·05
HALLE/L.	RM.	RM.	RM.	RM.
Erfurt	13	...	22·10	0·13
Frankfort	35	...	59·50	0·35
Saarbrücken	50	...	85	0·50
Stuttgart	50	...	85	0·50
Zürich	75	...	127·50	0·75
HAMBURG	RM	RM.	RM.	RM.
To Copenhagen	50	...	95	0·50
Malmö	57	...	96·90	0·55
HANOVER	RM.	RM.	RM.	RM.
To Amsterdam	40	...	68	0·40
London	110	...	187	1·10

Towns	Single	Ret'n 15 days	Ret'n 60 days	Ex. Bg. perKg. 2·2 lbs.
ISTANBUL	Turk£	Turk£	Turk£	Turk£
To Belgrade	82·20	...	140	0·80
Budapest	109·50	...	186	1·10
Nürnberg	174·20	...	295	1·75
Prague	151·60	...	256	1·50
Strasbourg	195·85	...	330	1·95
Vienna	128·35	...	218	1·30
Warsaw	195·65	...	330	1·95
KAUNAS	Lit.	Lit.	Lit.	Lit.
To Berlin	188	...	319·60	1·88*
Danzig	67	...	113·90	0·67*
Königsberg	43	...	73·10	0·43*
Moscow	245	...	416·50	2·45*
Welikije Luki	125	...	212·50	1·25*
* Half this rate per Kg for over 15 Kgs.				
KÖNIGSBERG/PR.	RM.	RM.	RM.	RM.
To Kaunas	18	...	31·60	0·18*
Moscow	120	...	204	·60§
Welikije Luki	70	...	119	0·35§
* Half this rate per Kg for more than 15 Kgs § 30 Kgs allowed free.				
LYONS	Frs.	Frs	Frs.	Frs.
To Geneva	100	...	170	1
London	755	...	1,285	6
Paris	350	...	595	3·50
MALTA	£.s.d.	£.s.d.	£.s.d.	s. d.
To Naples	6 16 0	...	§	2 6
Rome	8 16 0	...	§	1 4
Syracuse	2 6 0	...	§	1 9
Tripoli	3 18 0	...	§	0 6
§ 30% reduction on homeward Journey				
MANNHEIM/L/H.	RM.	RM.	RM.	RM.
To Karlsruhe	10	...	17	0·10
Saarbrücken	25	...	42·50	0·25
MARSEILLES	Frs.	Frs.	Frs.	Frs.
To Barcelona	330	...	519	3·30
Cannes	225	...	382·50	2·25
Geneva	270	...	459	2·70
London	1,105	...	1,880	9·50
Paris	700	...	1,190	7
Stuttgart	540	...	918	5·40

Towns	Single	Ret'n 15 days	Ret'n 60 days	Ex. Bg. per Kg. 2·2 lbs.	Towns	Single	Ret'n 15 days	Ret'n 60 days	Ex. Bg. per Kg. 2·2 lbs.
MUNICH	RM.	R.M	RM.	RM.	**RABAT**	Frs.	Frs.	Frs.	Frs.
To Rome	90	...	153	0·90	To Alicante	625	...	1,062·5	6·25
Venice	55	...	93·50	0·55	Barcelona	970	...	1,650	9·70
					Casablanca	60	...	102	1
Vienna	55	RM. (60 days) 46·75+ Sch. 85		0·55	Tangier	150	...	255	1·50
Zürich	40	34+ S. Frs.		0·40					
			42·50						
					ROTTERDAM	Fl.	Fl.	Fl.	Fl.
					To Brussels	12	...	20·40	0·10
		15 days	60 days		Flushing	8	...	13·60	0·10
NÜRNBERG	RM.	RM.	RM.	RM.	Haamstede	6·75	...	11·50	0·05
To Belgrade	185	...	314·50	1·85	Paris	30	...	51	0·30
Bucharest	263	...	447	2·65					
Budapest	130	...	221	1·30					
Istanbul	346	...	588	3·45	**SOFIA**	Leva	Leva	Leva	Leva
Paris	103	...	175	1·05	To Belgrade	1,590	...	2,700	15
Prague	45	...	76·50	0·45	Bucharest	4,456	...	7,575	44
Sofia	240	...	408	2·40	Budapest	3,120	...	5,300	31
Strasbourg	43	...	73	0·45	Nürnberg	7,980	...	13,565	80
Vienna	92	...	156	0·90	Paris	11,665	...	19,830	116
Warsaw	134	...	228	1·35	Prague	6,465	...	10,990	64
					Strasbourg	9,415	...	16,000	94
					Vienna	4,070	...	6,920	41
					Warsaw	9,415	...	16,000	94
PARIS	Frs.	Frs.	Frs.	Frs.					
To Cannes	925	...	1,572·5	9·25					
Geneva	450	...	765	4·50	**STETTIN**	RM.	RM.	RM.	RM.
Lyons	350	...	595	3·50	To Danzig	35	...	59·50	0·35
Marseilles	700	...	1,190	7	Königsberg	45	...	76·50	0·45
					STRASBOURG	Frs.	Frs.	Frs.	Frs.
POSEN	Zl.	Zl.	Zl.	Zl.	To Belgrade	1,305	...	2320·5	13·65
To Berlin	59	...	100·30	0·59	Bucharest	1,840	...	3,125	18·40
					Budapest	1,040	...	1,765	10·40
					Istanbul	2,430	...	4,130	24·30
					Nürnberg	260	...	440	2·60
					Prague	530	...	904	5·30
					Sofia	1,695	...	2881·5	16·95
PRAGUE	Kc.	Kc. (60 days)		Kc.	Vienna	810	...	1,377	8·10
To Belgrade	1,112	1,890	...	11·10	Warsaw	835	...	1,420	8·35
Berlin	336	285·60+ R M.		3·36					
		35·70			**STUTTGART**	RM.	RM.	RM.	RM.
Bucharest	1,200	2,040		12	To Mannheim	12	...	20·40	0·12
Budapest	560	952		5·60	Saarbrücken	25	...	42·50	0·25
Dresden	160	136+ RM. 17		1·60	Zürich	25	...	42·50	0·25
Istanbul	2,430	4,130		24·30					
Nürnberg	363	617		3·65					
Paris	1,247	2,120		12·50	**TANGIER**	Frs.	Frs.	Frs.	Frs.
Sofia	1,552	2,638		15·50	To Alicante	525	...	892·50	5·25
Strasbourg	710	1,207		7·10	Barcelona	870	...	1,479	8·70
Vienna	320	272+ Sch. 68		3·20	Casablanca	200	...	340	2
Warsaw	350	595		3·50	Rabat	150	...	255	1·50

Towns	Single	Ret'n 15 days	Ret'n 60 days	Ex. Bg. perKg, 2·2 lbs.	Towns	Single	Ret'n 15 days	Ret'n 60 days	Ex. Bg. perKg, 2·2 lbs.
VENICE	Lire	Lire	Lire	Lire	WARSAW	Zl.	Zl.	Zl.	Zl.
To Berlin	470	...	799	4·70	To Belgrade	395	...	671	3·95
Munich	250	...	425	2·50	Bucharest	588	...	1,000	5·90
					Budapest	248	...	421	2·50
					Istanbul	820	...	1,394	8·20
					Nürnberg	281	...	477·50	2·80
VIENNA	Sch.	Sch. (60 days)		Sch.	Paris	350	...	595	3·50
To Belgrade	185	314·50		1·85	Prague	92	...	156·50	1
Bucharest	345	586·50		3·45	Sofia	510	...	867	5·10
Budapest	50	85		0·50	Strasbourg	312	...	530	3·15
Istanbul	515	875		5·15	Vienna	112	...	190·40	1·15
Nürnberg	185	314·50		1·85	WELIKIJE LUKI	Rbls.	Rbls.	Rbls.	Rbls.
Paris	350	595		3·50	To Berlin	60	...	102	0·30§
Prague	80	68+ Kc. 272		0·80	Danzig	37	...	62·90	0·37*
Sofia	295	501·50		2·95	Kaunas	25	...	42·50	0·25*
Strasbourg	270	458		2·70	Königsberg	33	...	56·10	0·33§
Warsaw	112	190·40		1·15					

§ 30 Kgs. allowed free.
* Half this rate over 15 Kgs.

HENRY BLACKLOCK & CO. LTD.

(Proprietors of Bradshaw's Guides),

GENERAL PRINTERS, LITHOGRAPHERS,
AND ACCOUNT-BOOK MANUFACTURERS

Bookwork, Invoices, Statements, Memo Forms, Letter Headings, Note Headings, Bill Forms, Cheques, Show Cards, Posters, Pamphlets, Brochures, and Time Tables for Air Services specially designed and printed.   Estimates free.

BRADSHAW HOUSE, SURREY STREET, STRAND, LONDON, W.C.2.
Telephone—TEMPLE BAR, **2676.**   — and —   _Telegrams_—BRADSHAW, LONDON.
ALBERT SQUARE, MANCHESTER.
Telephone—BLACKFRIARS **4218** (2 lines).   _Telegrams_—GUIDE, MANCHESTER.

GENERAL CONDITIONS OF CARRIAGE OF PASSENGERS AND BAGGAGE

CHAPTER I.

Scope—Definitions.

Article 1: Undertakings and carriage to which these Conditions are applicable.

§ 1: These Conditions are applicable to all carriage (internal and international) of persons (passengers) and baggage performed by an air transport undertaking (carrier) which is a member of the International Air Traffic Association. Nevertheless the special provisions referred to in paragraph 2 sub-paragraph 1 of this Article are only applicable to the special categories of international carriage defined in paragraph 2 sub-paragraph 2 of this Article.

(2) The expression " days " when used in these Conditions means current days, not working days.

§ 2: (1) The provisions of Article 2 paragraph 3 sub-paragraphs 2 and 3 and paragraph 6 (second sentence), Article 9 paragraph 2 sub-paragraph 2 and paragraph 3 (second sentence, Article 12 paragraph 4 sub-paragraph 1 (third sentence), Article 19 paragraph 1 sub-paragraph 2, Article 22 paragraph 4 sub-paragraph 2 and Article 23 paragraph 1 sub-paragraph 1 are applicable only: o the special categories of international carriage defined in sub-paragraph 2 of this paragraph.

(2) The special categories of international carriage referred to in sub-paragraph 1 of this paragraph include all carriage by air in which, according to the contract made by the parties, the place of departure and the place of destination, whether or not there be a break in the carriage or a trans-shipment, are situated either within the territories of two High Contracting Parties to the Convention of Warsaw for the unification of certain rules relating to International Air Transport of the 12th October, 1929, upon which these Conditions are based, or within the territory of a single High Contracting Party if there is an agreed stopping place within a territory subject to the sovereignty, suzerainty, mandate or authority of another Power, even though that Power is a non-contracting Power.

(3) A carriage to be performed by several successive air carriers is deemed, for the purpose of sub-paragraph 2 above, to be one undivided carriage, if it has been regarded by the parties as a single operation, whether it has been agreed upon under the form of a single contract or of a series of contracts, and it does not lose its international character within the meaning of sub-paragraph 2 above merely because one contract or a series of contracts is to be performed entirely within a territory subject to the sovereignty, suzerainty, mandate or authority of the same High Contracting Party.

§ 3: In the case of combined carriage performed partly by air and partly by any other mode of carriage (combined transport) these Conditions apply only to the carriage by air, unless other terms have been agreed and provided such other terms comply with the provisions of paragraphs 1 or 2 above.

§ 4: The Carriers reserve the right to make additional Conditions for special lines or for carriage privately arranged.

CHAPTER II.

Carriage of Passengers.

Article 2: Passenger tickets.

§ 1: Before he begins his journey the passenger must be provided with a passenger ticket.

§ 2: The passenger is bound to retain his ticket throughout the journey. He must when required produce it to any official in charge and surrender it at the end of the journey.

§ 3: (1) The passenger ticket shall contain the following particulars:
  (a) the place and date of issue;
  (b) the places of departure and destination;
  (c) the name and address of the carrier or carriers.

The passenger ticket shall contain also the name of the passenger and the amount of the fare.

(2) So far as concerns international carriage, as defined by Article 1 paragraph 2, the passenger ticket shall contain in addition the following particulars:
  (d) the agreed stopping places, for which summarized descriptions published by the carrier may be used;
  (e) a statement that the carriage is subject to the rules relating to liability set out in the Convention of Warsaw of 12th October, 1929, upon which these Conditions are based.

(3) The carrier has the right to alter the agreed stopping places in case of necessity without any such alteration having the effect of depriving international carriage, as defined by Article 1 paragraph 2, of its international character within the meaning of this provision.

§ 4: (1) The passenger ticket is valid only for the date and service specified thereon and for the party named. A special aircraft can only be provided by special agreement.

(2) The passenger ticket is not transferable.

§ 5: Return tickets are valid only for the period specified thereon. If no period is specified they are valid for a maximum period of three months from the date of issue. They are subject to the same regulations as single tickets.

§ 6: The absence, irregularity or loss of the ticket does not affect the existence or the validity of the contract of carriage, which shall none the less be subject to these Conditions. If the carrier accepts a passenger for international carriage, as defined by Article I paragraph 2, without a ticket having been delivered the carrier shall not be entitled to avail himself of those provisions of Article 19 paragraph I sub-paragraph 3 and paragraph 2 sub-paragraph I which exclude or limit his liability.

Article 3: Carriage of minors.

§ 1: Up to 3 years of age children, when accompanied by an adult and when no separate seat is required for them, are carried at a charge equivalent to 10% of the normal rate for passengers.

§ 2: Children aged more than 3 years and less than 7 years, and younger children for whom a separate seat is required, are carried at a reduced price representing one-half of the normal rate.

Article 4: Allocation and distribution of seats.

Subject to the provisions of Article I paragraphs 3 and 4 the allocation and distribution of seats is governed by the regulations in force with the individual carriers, which apply both to single and return tickets.

Article 5: Persons excluded from flights or accepted conditionally.

§ 1: In every case the following are excluded from carriage:
> (a) persons under the influence of drink or drugs or other narcotics, and those who conduct themselves in an improper manner or who do not observe the instructions of any authorised official;
> (b) persons of unsound mind and those afflicted with a contagious disease or who, because of illness or for any other reason, might inconvenience other passengers.

§ 2: The persons referred to in paragraph I above are not entitled to repayment of the fare paid.

Article 6: Articles which passengers are forbidden to take with them into an aircraft.

§ 1: Passengers are forbidden to take with into an aircraft:
> (a) Articles which according to the regulations of the carrier must be carried in the baggage compartment;
> (b) dangerous articles, especially arms, munitions, explosives, corrosives and articles which are easily ignited; things which are offensive or evil-smelling and other articles of a character likely to inconvenience passengers or which are dangerous to aircraft, passengers or goods;
> (c) photographic apparatus, carrier pigeons, wireless apparatus and other articles the carriage of which by aircraft is prohibited by law or other authority.

§ 2: Passengers are permitted, unless prohibited by law or other authority, to take with them arms and ammunition forming part of hunting or sporting equipment on condition that the arms and ammunition are packed in such a manner as to cause no danger to persons or things. Firearms must be unloaded and dismantled as much as possible or at any rate carried in a case.

§ 3: The carriers' employees are authorised to verify, in the presence of the passenger, the nature of articles introduced into an aircraft.

§ 4: Any person contravening the provisions of paragraphs I and 2 of this Article is liable for all damage resulting from such contravention, and is also subject to the penalties, if any, imposed by the regulations of the carrier.

§ 5: The passenger is entirely responsible for the supervision of articles which he takes charge of himself. The carrier accepts no responsibility for the supervision of such articles even if his employees assist in loading, unloading or transshipping them.

Article 7.

§ 1: (1) Passengers must observe the instructions of the officials of the carriers concerning all matters connected with the air service.

> (2) Furthermore they must obey instructions posted in the offices and aircraft of the carrier.

§ 2: (1) The presence of passengers upon the area of departure or near aircraft is forbidden without the express permission of the officials of the carrier.

> (2) Passengers must only enter or leave aircraft at the request of such officials.
> Passengers are forbidden to open exterior doors during flight; when the aircraft is on the ground passengers are only permitted to open these doors in case of danger. It is also forbidden to throw articles from aircraft.

§ 3: Smoking and lighting matches in aircraft is prohibited unless and except as provided by regulations to the contrary posted therein.

§ 4: Any person contravening these regulations is responsible for all damage resulting from such contravention. He may be excluded from carriage, and in this event he shall not be entitled to repayment of the fare paid.

GENERAL CONDITIONS OF CARRIAGE OF PASSENGERS AND BAGGAGE—*Continued*

CHAPTER III.
Carriage of Baggage.
Article 8: Articles excluded from carriage.

§ 1: The following are excluded from carriage as baggage:

    (a) the articles enumerated in Article 6 paragraph 1 (b) and (c) in so far as exceptions are not permitted under the provisions of paragraph 3 of this Article;

    (b) articles which, owing to their dimensions, their weight or their character, are in the opinion of the carrier unsuitable for carriage in the aircraft of any of the carriers concerned;

    (c) goods (merchandise).

§ 2: Live animals can only be carried by special arrangement.

§ 3: Arms can only be carried as baggage in exceptional cases. In such cases they must be packed in such a manner as to cause no danger to anyone; firearms must be unloaded and dismantled as much as possible. In so far as photographic apparatus, carrier pigeons and wireless apparatus are accepted as baggage, they must be packed in such a way as to prevent their being used during flight.

§ 4: Baggage will be carried when possible in the same aircraft as the passenger, if the load of the aircraft permits, without the carrier being under any obligation in this respect.

Article 9: Registration. Baggage check.

§ 1: (1) When baggage is registered the carrier will furnish a baggage check.

    (2) One copy of this check will be delivered to the passenger and another will be retained by the carrier.

§ 2: (1) The baggage check shall contain the following particulars:

    (a) the number of the passenger ticket (or the number of the ticket folder when this contains more than a single passenger ticket);

    (b) the number and weight of the packages;

    (c) the name and address of the carrier or carriers;

    (d) the places of departure and of destination;

    (e) where required, the amount of the sum representing the declared value at delivery in conformity with Article 19 paragraph 2 sub-paragraph 2;

    (f) where required, the amount of the value specially declared for insurance by the carrier in conformity with Article 14 paragraph 2;

    (g) the place and date of issue;

    (h) a statement that delivery of the baggage will be made to the bearer of the baggage check.

    (2) So far as concerns international carriage, as defined by Article 1 paragraph 2, the baggage check shall contain in addition:—

    (i) a statement that the carriage is subject to the rules relating to liability set out in the Convention of Warsaw of 12th October, 1929, upon which these Conditions are based.

§ 3: The absence, irregularity or loss of the baggage check does not affect the existence or the validity of the contract of carriage which shall none the less be subject to these Conditions. If the carrier accepts baggage for international carriage, as defined by Article 1 paragraph 2, without a baggage check having been delivered, or if, under similar circumstances, this does not contain all the particulars set out in paragraph 2 (a), (b) and (i), the carrier shall not be entitled to avail himself of those provisions of Article 19 paragraph 1 sub-paragraph 3 and paragraph 2 sub-paragraph 2 which exclude or limit his liability.

Article 10: Liability of the passenger concerning his baggage.

§ 1: The bearer of the baggage check must observe the provisions of Article 8. He is responsible for all the consequences of non-observance of these provisions.

§ 2: If any contravention is suspected, the carrier has the right to verify if the contents of packages comply with the regulations. The bearer of the baggage check will be called to assist at such verification. If he does not attend or if he cannot be found, verification can be effected by officials of the carrier alone. If a contravention is proved, the cost of verification must be paid by the bearer of the baggage check.

§ 3: In the case of a breach of the conditions of Article 8, the bearer of the baggage check shall pay an extra charge (surtaxe) without prejudice to the supplementary charge (supplément de taxe) and compensation for damage; also penalties, if required.

Article 11: Packing and condition of baggage.

§ 1: Baggage unsatisfactorily packed or defective in condition may be refused, but if it is accepted the carrier shall have the right to specify its condition on the baggage check.

§ 2: The carrier may require that packages shall bear in Latin characters on durable labels the name and address of the passenger and the airport of destination.

§ 3: The carrier may require that old labels, addresses or other particulars concerning former journeys shall be removed by the passenger. The carrier has the right to remove them himself.

Article 12: Delivery.

§ 1: Delivery of baggage will be made to the bearer of the baggage check against delivery of the baggage check. The carrier is not bound to verify if the bearer of the check is entitled to take delivery.

§ 2: Failing presentation of the baggage check, the carrier is only bound to deliver the baggage if the claimant establishes his right ; if such right appears to be insufficiently established the carrier may require security.

§ 3: Baggage will be delivered at the place of destination to which it is registered. Nevertheless, at the request of the bearer of the baggage check, if made in sufficient time and if circumstances permit, baggage can be delivered at the place of departure or at a stopping place against delivery of the baggage check (without any liability to refund the cost of carriage paid) provided this is not precluded be regulations of the Customs, Revenue (octroi), Fiscal, Police or other administrative authorities.

§ 4: (1) The receipt without complaint of baggage by the bearer of the baggage check or other party entitled is prima facie evidence that the baggage has been delivered in good condition and in accordance with the contract of carriage. In case of damage the passenger must complain to the carrier forthwith after discovery of the damage, and at the latest within three days from the date of receipt of the baggage. So far as concerns international carriage within the meaning of Article 1 paragraph 2, in case o fdelay the complaint must be made at the latest within fourteen days from the date on which the baggage has been placed at his disposal. Every complaint must be made in writing upon the baggage check or by separate notice in writing despatched within the times aforesaid. Failing complaint within the times aforesaid no action shall lie against the carrier save in the case of fraud on his part.

(2) The expression " days " when used in these Conditions means current days, not working days.

CHAPTER IV.

Provisions applicable to the Carriage of both Passengers and Baggage.

Article 13: Conclusion of the contract of carriage.

§ 1: Except as provided by Article 2 paragraph 6 and Article 9 paragraph 3, the contract of carriage is made effective immediately on acceptance by the passenger of the passenger ticket, and, so far as concerns the carriage of baggage, the baggage check.

§ 2: The carrier reserves the right to refuse to enter into a contract of carriage without giving any reason.

§ 3: If there is any question of an aircraft being overloaded the parties authorised by the carrier to supervise the loading of aircraft shall decide which persons or articles shall be carried.

§ 4: In the event of a passenger or any baggage being excluded from a flight under the provisions of paragraph 3 above the passenger has the right only to repayment of the total sum paid by him for the carriage.

Article 14: Basis of calculation of charges for carriage. Tariffs. Insurance.

§ 1: The charges for carriage are calculated according to the published tariffs.

§ 2: The carriers offer facilities to passengers for the insurance of themselves against accident under special conditions and at special rates; they also offer facilities for the insurance of their baggage under special conditions and at special rates.

Article 15: Formalities required by Customs, Revenue (octroi), Fiscal,
Police and other administrative authorities.

§ 1: The passenger must observe the regulations prescribed by the Customs, Revenue (octroi), Fiscal, Police and other administrative authorities concerning himself, his registered baggage and his hand luggage. He must attend the inspection of his registered baggage and of his hand luggage if required. The carrier accepts no responsibility towards the passenger in the event of the latter failing to observe these regulations. In the event of a passenger causing damage to a carrier by non-observance of these regulations the passenger must compensate the carrier.

§ 2: The passenger must attend at the airport or elsewhere as prescribed by the carrier sufficiently in advance of the time of departure to enable the formalities mentioned in paragraph 1 above to be complied with before departure. If the carrier has specified a certain time for this purpose the passenger must arrive at or before such time.

Article 16: Refunds.

§ 1: No claim for refund of the fare paid for carriage can be entertained when a traveller does not arrive or arrives late for a journey for which a reservation has been made.

§ 2: If a flight is cancelled owing to meteorological conditions or for any other reason, or if the aircraft returns to the airport of departure with the passenger, the latter shall be entitled to the return of the fare paid for the carriage of himself and his baggage.

§ 3: In the event of a flight being interrupted the passenger is entitled to the return of a proportion of the fare paid for himself and his baggage corresponding with the non-flown mileage, unless the carrier completes the carriage by other means or makes himself responsible for the cost of forwarding by another means of transport. In such event he shall only be liable to refund the difference in fare, if any.

§ 4: All rights to refund are extinguished unless a claim is made within a period of 3 weeks from the date fixed for the journey.

Article 17: Disputes.

Disputes between passengers and carriers' employees are provisionally settled at airports by the official in charge, and in the course of flight by the commander of the aircraft or by the person specially designated by the carrier.

CHAPTER V.

Liability of Carriers. Actions.

Article 18: General provisions. Periods of liability.

§ 1: In the case of carriage to be performed by various successive carriers, each carrier who accepts passengers or baggage is deemed to be one of the contracting parties to the contract of carriage in so far as the contract deals with that part of the carriage which is performed under his supervision.

§ 2: The liability of carriers under the provisions of Article 19 paragraph 1 sub-paragraph 1 (a) applies to accidents occurring on board the aircraft or in the course of any of the operations of embarking or disembarking.

§ 3: The liability of carriers under the provisions of Article 19 paragraph 1 sub-paragraph 1 (b) covers the period during which the baggage is in charge of the carrier, whether in an airport or on board an aircraft or, in the case of a landing outside an airport, in any place whatsoever. It does not extend to any carriage by land, by sea or by river performed outside an airport. Nevertheless, if such a carriage as last aforesaid takes place in the performance of a contract for carriage by air, for the purpose of loading, delivery or trans-shipment, any damage is presumed, subject to proof to the contrary, to have been the result of an occurrence which took place during the carriage by air.

§ 4: The liability of carriers under the provisions of Article 19 paragraph 1 sub-paragraph 2 covers the period of carriage by air.

§ 5: Passengers and baggage are accepted for carriage only upon condition that, except in so far as liability is expressly provided for in these Conditions of Carriage, no liability whatsoever is accepted by the carriers, or their employees, or parties or undertakings employed by them in connection with their obligations, or their authorised agents, and upon condition that (except in so far as liability is expressly provided for in these Conditions) the passenger renounces for himself and his representatives all claims for compensation for damage in connection with the carriage, caused directly or indirectly to passengers or their belongings, or to persons who, except for this provision, might have been entitled to make a claim, and especially in connection with surface transport at departure and destination, whatever may be the legal grounds upon which any claim concerning any such liability may be based.

Article 19: Extent of liability.

§ 1: (1) Within the limits prescribed by Article 18 carriers are liable for damage sustained during the period of the carriage as defined in Article 18 paragraphs 2 and 3;

    (a) in the event of the death or wounding of a passenger or any other bodily injury suffered by a passenger;

    (b) in the event of destruction or loss of or damage to registered baggage.

(2) So far as concerns international carriage, as defined by Article 1 paragraph 2, the carriers are likewise liable, within the same limits, for damage sustained during the period of the carriage as defined by Article 18 paragraph 4, in case of delay of passengers and baggage.

The time-tables of carriers furnish indications of average times without these being in any way guaranteed. The carrier reserves the right to decide if the meteorological and other conditions for the normal performance of a flight are suitable, if especially the times of departure and arrival should be modified and if a departure or landing should not be made at all at any particular time or place. In addition the carrier reserves the right to arrange at landing places such periods of stoppage as may be necessary to ensure connections, the maximum duration of which periods of stoppage will be mentioned in the time-tables; no responsibility concerning the making of connections can be accepted.

(3) Carriers are not liable if they prove that they and their agents have taken all necessary measures to avoid the damage, or that it was impossible for them to take such measures. In the carriage of baggage the carriers are not liable if they prove that the damage was occasioned by negligent pilotage or negligence in the handling of the aircraft or in navigation, and that, in all other respects, they and their agents have taken all necessary measures to avoid the damage.

(4) If the carrier proves that the damage was caused by or contributed to by the negligence of the injured person, the Court may, in accordance with the provisions of its own law, exonerate the carrier wholly or partly from his liability.

§ 2: (1) In the carriage of passengers the liability of carriers for each passenger is limited to the sum of 125.000 francs unless a larger sum has been agreed upon. Where, in accordance with the law of the Court seized of the case, damages may be awarded in the form of periodical payments, the equivalent capital value of the said payments shall not exceed 125.000 francs.

(2) In the carriage of registered baggage the liability of carriers is limited to the sum of 250 francs per kilogram, unless the passenger has made a special declaration of the value at delivery and has paid such supplementary charge as is required. In that case the carrier will be liable to pay a sum not exceeding the declared sum, unless he proves that that sum is greater than the actual value to the passenger at delivery.

(3) As regards articles of which the passenger takes charge himself, the liability of the carrier is limited to 5.000 francs per passenger.

(4) The sums mentioned above shall be taken to refer to the French franc consisting of sixty five and a half milligrams gold of millesimal fineness.

Article 20: Claims.

§ 1: Claims must be addressed in writing to the carriers referred to in Article 22.

§ 2: The right to make a claim belongs to the parties who have the right to bring an action against the carriers under the provisions of Article 21.

§ 3: (1) The originals or duly authenticated copies of tickets, baggage checks and other documents which the party entitled deems it advisable to attach to his claim must be produced.

(2) When a claim is settled the carrier can require the return to him of the tickets and baggage checks.

Article 21: Persons who are entitled to bring actions.

Only the party who produces the ticket or baggage check as the case may be, or who in default of production establishes his right, is entitled to bring an action arising out of the contract of carriage against the carrier.

Article 22: Undertakings against which action can be taken. Jurisdiction.

§ 1: An action for the return of a sum paid under the provisions of a contract of carriage can only be brought against the undertaking which received the sum.

§ 2: In the case of the carriage of passengers, the passenger or his representatives can take action only against the carrier who performed the carriage during which the event giving rise to the action occurred, save in the case where, by express agreement in writing, the first carrier has assumed liability for the whole journey.

§ 3: In the case of the carriage of baggage, except so far as concerns actions under the provisions of paragraph 1 above, the party entitled will have a right of action against the first or the last carrier, and in addition, so far as concerns actions arising under Article 19, against the carrier who performed the carriage during which the event giving rise to the action took place. For actions arising under the provisions of Article 19 these carriers will be jointly and severally responsible to the party entitled

§ 4: (1) Actions must be brought before the Court of the carrier's principal place of business. The national law of the Court seized of the case shall apply.

(2) Nevertheless actions arising under the provisions of Article 19, in connection with Article 1 paragraph 2, must be brought, at the option of the plaintiff, in the territory of a State which is a contracting party to the Convention of Warsaw, either

(a) before the Court having jurisdiction where the carrier is ordinarily resident, or has his principal place of business, or has an establishment by which the contract has been made, or

(b) before the Court having jurisdiction at the place of destination.

(3) Questions of procedure shall be governed by the law of the Court seized of the case.

Article 23: Limitations of actions.

§ 1: (1) The right to damages arising under the provisions of Article 19, in connection with Article 1 paragraph 2, shall be extinguished if an action is not brought within two years, which may be reckoned either from the date of arrival at the destination, or from the date on which the aircraft ought to have arrived, or from the date on which the carriage stopped.

(2) All other rights to damages arising out of the contract of carriage shall be extinguished if an action is not brought within a period of six months.

§ 2: The method of calculating the period of limitation, as well as the grounds for suspension or interruption of the period of limitation, shall be determined by the Law of the Court seized of the case.

Article 24: Legislative provisions.

Where in any country legislative provisions conflict with these Conditions of Carriage, the latter shall be applicable only in so far as they do not conflict with such legislative provisions.

The GRANVILLE HOTEL *Ramsgate*

Telephones : Ramsgate 12 and 13
Telegrams : "Granville, Ramsgate."

The BUSHEY HALL HOTEL *Bushey* HERTS.

Telephone : Watford 4221
Telegrams : "Welcome, Watford."

VALLEY *of* ROCKS HOTEL *Lynton*

OPEN EASTER TO OCTOBER
Tel. : Lynton 49 Telegrams : "Valrocks, Lynton."

The GRAND HOTEL *Scarborough*

Telephone : Scarborough 1053
Telegrams : "Grand, Scarborough."

HOTEL METROPOLE *Blackpool*

Telephone : Blackpool 1040
Telegrams : "Metropole, Blackpool."

The EMPIRE HOTEL *Bath*

Telephones : Bath 4207-8-9
Telegrams : "Empire, Bath."

The SOUTH WESTERN HOTEL *Southampton*

Telephone : Southampton 5031
Telegrams : "Welcome, Southampton."

London BAILEY'S HOTEL

Gloucester Road, Kensington, S.W.7
Telephone : Frobisher 8131
Telegrams : "Bailey's Hotel, London."

SOUTH KENSINGTON HOTEL

Queen's Gate Terrace, S.W.7
Telephone : Western 7181
Telegrams : "Skenotel, South Kens., London."

LONDON

Sisters of the world-famed
Basil Cocker Spaniel Kennels

o o o

Telegrams : SPOTLESS, LONDON.
Telephone : SLOANE 3411 (12 lines).

BASIL STREET • HOTEL

KNIGHTSBRIDGE

The English Country Home in
London's best position, with
every modern improvement,
and convenience.

150 Rooms - - 150 Rooms

HOTEL BELGRAVIA

GROSVENOR GARDENS, LONDON, S.W. 1.

MOST CONVENIENT FOR

VICTORIA AIR STATION

250 Rooms with Hot and Cold Running Water, Telephone, Heating, etc.

RESTAURANT

(OPEN TO THE PUBLIC)

Renowned for Cuisine, Service and Cellars.

'PHONE: VICTORIA 9640.   CABLES: "HOTEL BELGRAVIA," LONDON

Three West-End Family Hotels

HOTEL SOMERSET, Orchard Street, London, W.I.
(200 Rooms)   'Phone: Welbeck 8311.

HOTEL QUEBEC, Old Quebec Street, Marble Arch, W.I.
(150 Rooms)   'Phone: Welbeck 9141.

HOTEL SEYMOUR, 15, Seymour Street, W.I.
(100 Rooms)   'Phone: Welbeck 7464.

CADOGAN HOTEL

Situated centrally in the West End, overlooking Gardens and within a few minutes of Victoria Station, Hyde Park and Piccadilly. All rooms with telephone and running hot and cold water. Excellent restaurant renowned for Cuisine & Service.

SLOANE STREET, LONDON, S.W.1.

Telephone - Sloane 7141.

Wedding Receptions.

FULLY LICENSED.

Single Bedroom per day, from 8/6
Single Bedroom (with private Bath Room) per day, from 14/6
Double Bedroom per day from 18/6
Double Bedroom (with private Bath Room) per day, from 25/-
Private Suites per day, from 35/-
Inclusive En Pension Terms per week - - - from 6 Gns

ALMOND'S HOTEL

CLIFFORD STREET, BOND STREET, W.1

Old Established High-Class Family Hotel.

Centrally situated in the best part of London, near Hyde Park, Rotten Row, Regent Street, Bond Street and Piccadilly, the Clubs, and Theatres. Entirely redecorated. Thoroughly modernised. Telephone and Central Heating in all Rooms. Private Bath Rooms. Moderate Charges. Special Terms for lengthened stay.

Telegrams—"ALMOND'S HOTEL, LONDON."
Telephone—0535 REGENT (3 lines).

G. BRANCHINI, Proprietor.

ARUNDEL HOTEL

ARUNDEL STREET, - - - STRAND, W.C.2

"The Riverside Home of London Visitors."

Established in the XVII Century. Original site, Town Mansion Earls of Arundel. Many beautiful examples of antique painted glass windows illustrating heraldry of Howard family. Overlooking the Thames and Temple Gardens. **100 Bedrooms.** MODERN EQUIPMENT.

BEDROOM, BATH AND TABLE D'HOTE BREAKFAST 10/6.

Opposite Temple Station, Underground Rly.

Telegrams :
Arundelian London.

LONDON.

J. C. BISSET.
Manager.

JULES HOTEL & RESTAURANT,

Jermyn Street, Piccadilly, London.

NICE QUIET HOTEL IN THE CENTRE OF LONDON. HOT AND COLD RUNNING WATER AND TELEPHONE IN ALL BEDROOMS.

Single Rooms, including Breakfast, from 12/6
Double Rooms   „   „   „   25/-
Restaurant noted for its French Cuisine Luncheons 5/-
or Plat du Jour Garni 2/6   Dinners 5/6 and 7/6

Telegrams—"JULAISON PICCY LONDON."   Phone—WHITEHALL 1471

THE ROMANTIC TRADITIONS OF A BYGONE DAY

—*Combined with Modern Luxury*

● *Your visit to England can be made all the more enjoyable by the luxurious comfort of one of these Country Hotels—both within half-an-hour of London.*

Every room with Hot and Cold running water and phone. Rooms and Suites with private bathrooms.

AT SELSDON PARK you may enjoy free golf on a private 18-hole golf course (6,361 yds.) in our own park of 230 acres, over 500 feet up on the Surrey Hills. Dancing, tennis, squash—with a magnificent solarium and electric gymnasium—all free.

WICKHAM COURT where Henry VIII courted Anne Boleyn, a wonderful Tudor Manor House (3 miles from Selsdon Park) has been restored and modernised and, with all the sports facilities of Selsdon Park, provides the perfect location for a restful holiday.

Write Resident Proprietor, Mr. A. D. SANDERSON, for Illustrated Brochure.

REDUCED WINTER TERMS.
— **NO ALTERATION IN STANDARD.** —

The SELSDON PARK
SANDERSTEAD, SURREY.

AND

WICKHAM COURT
WEST WICKHAM, KENT.

HOTELS

BATH—See pages 15 and 164

BELFAST—(Ireland)

The Leading Hotels in Northern Ireland.
Owned and managed by L M S Railway, Northern Counties Committee.

MIDLAND STATION HOTEL,
BELFAST.

Hot and cold running water in all Bedrooms.
Bedrooms with private Bathrooms attached.

GARAGE ON THE PREMISES.   Telegrams : "Midotel, Belfast."

NORTHERN COUNTIES HOTEL,
PORTRUSH.
OPEN THROUGHOUT THE YEAR.

HOT and cold running water in all bedrooms. Bedrooms with private bathrooms attached. Close to Royal Portrush Golf Club. Portrush is the nearest station to the famous Giant's Causeway. Cheap combined 1st Class Rail and Hotel Tickets issued from Belfast.

Telegrams : "Midotel, Portrush."

*Illustrated tariff
on application to Resident Managers.*

GRAND CENTRAL HOTEL,
BELFAST. Officially approved by : R.I.A.C., R.A.C., and A.A.

For Airways Bookings.

THE Grand Central Hotel, Belfast, has been selected as a Booking Office for Air Services available from Belfast. The Grand Central provides every modern comfort for its guests. 200 Bedrooms (a number with Bathrooms). Telephone ; bedside switch ; bell and hot and cold water in every room.   Single from 7/6d.   Double from 14/–. 21 Stockrooms with Telephone.   Orchestral music.

Breakfast from - - - 2/-	Table d'Hote Dinner 5/-
Table d'Hote Luncheon 3/-	Table d'Hote Tea- - 3/-

Also a la Carte.

GRILL ROOM OPEN TILL 11-45 P.M.

Phone : Belfast 7090 (6 lines).   Grams : "Grancent Belfast."

BERLIN

Berlin-Charlottenburg

Fasanenstr. 9

Tel. Steinplatz 8161

Hotel SAVOY

in the centre
of Berlin-W.

Best selected first-class family hotel.
All rooms with private bath.

MOMMSEN - COMMODORE — HOTEL PENSION

A refined Private Hotel situated in a quiet and select district near the Zoological Garden Station.

Single Room RM. 4-5, with Bath 5-50 to 7-50.
Double Room with Bath 9-13.
70 Rooms.   50 Private Baths.
Excellent cooking and service.

Berlin-Charlottenburg 2, Mommsenstr 71
(Kurfurstendamm, off Knesebeck Strasse).

Telegrams.   Telephone:
"Commodore," Berlin.   J. I. Bismarck 7126-29.

E. ROESSLER, Manager for many years at the HOTEL ESPLANADE, BERLIN

BOURNEMOUTH (England)

CENTRAL HOTEL

THE SQUARE, BOURNEMOUTH.

Hot and Cold Water in all Bedrooms. Bona fide Licensed Hotel.
Officially appointed A.A. and R.A.C. Hotel.
Inclusive Terms or à la Carte.   Write for Illustrated Tariff.

Tel: No. 71   -   -   -   *Grams:* Central, Bournemouth.

Close to all places of Amusement,
Principal Shops, Sea Front and
New Pavilion.
Modernised.   Electric Lift.
Heated throughout. Electric Light.

Special Inclusive Week-end Terms,
Friday to Monday from **42/-,**
Saturday (Dinner) to
Monday (Breakfast) from **30/-**
Resident Proprietors.

OVERLOOKING THE SQUARE AND CENTRAL GARDENS.

COLOGNE (Germany)

EXCELSIOR
HOTEL
ERNST

The
LEADING HOTEL
IN
COLOGNE
Facing the
Famous Cathedral

CROYDON—See Purley

DOUGLAS (Isle-of-Man)

DUCKER'S
TREVELYAN
Residential Hotel,
QUEEN'S PROMENADE.
(Established 1901.)
ACCOMMODATION FOR **160** GUESTS.

Central for three Golf Links. Handsome Entertaining Rooms, including Lounge, etc. Garage. Hot and cold running water in all Bedrooms. Electric Passenger Lift to all Floors.

Four Guarantees.—Good Cooking. Good Food. Perfect Sanitation. Moderate Tariff. "But don't take my word.— Come and try it yourself."

DINNER 6-30 p.m.   **Tariff on application.**
Appointed R.A.C. and A.C.U. Hotel.
J. DUCKER, Proprietor.
Telegrams—"Ducker, Douglas."

DUBLIN—See page 8

EXMOUTH—See page 174

HAMBURG (Germany)

HAMBURG
The
Leading
Hotels

HOTEL ATLANTIC
HOTEL ESPLANADE
PALAST HOTEL
STREITS HOTEL
HOTEL
VIER JAHRESZEITEN

HASTINGS—See page 11

JERSEY (Channel Islands)

GRAND HOTEL

● *Jersey's Premier Hotel.*
NEAREST HOTEL TO AIRLINE LANDING STATION.

RIGHT ON SEA FRONT. IN OWN GROUNDS. ALL PUBLIC AND MOST BEDROOMS FACE THE SEA. LIFT. SUN VERANDAH. GARDEN LOUNGE. FIRST CLASS EN PENSION FROM £4 4 0. NO EXTRAS. *Illustrated Booklet Free.*

MONTREUX (Switzerland)

MONTREUX PALACE HOTEL

(Montreux—Lake of Geneva). The Very Best at Reasonable Rates.
NEAREST AIRPORT—LAUSANNE.

HOTEL LORIUS - - HOTEL NATIONAL

Two First-class Family Hotels. | *Preferred by British.*

18-hole Golf. Own Tennis.
All Sports. Large Gardens on the Lake side. Own Garage.

OTTERBURN (England)

ON THE AIR ROUTE TO THE NORTH

25 MILES W.N.W. OF NEWCASTLE **STANDS** 14 MILES FROM THE SCOTTISH BORDER

OTTERBURN HALL HOTEL

FISHING — RIDING — 18-HOLE GOLF COURSE — 5 TENNIS COURTS — SQUASH — OPEN AIR SWIMMING POOL — DANCING

WRITE FOR BROCHURE AND TARIFF TO:

TELEGRAMS : } OTTERBURN 26
TELEPHONE : }

THE MANAGER
OTTERBURN HALL HOTEL
OTTERBURN, NORTHUMBERLAND

PARIS

STAY AT THE

HOTEL SCRIBE

14 Boulevard des Capucines

THE VERY CENTRE OF PARIS

OR AT THE

HOTEL ASTORIA

Avenue des Champs Elysées

NEAR ARC DE TRIOMPHE

THE GREATEST COMFORT
MODERATE PRICES
FAMOUS RESTAURANTS AND BARS

—

UNDER THE SAME MANAGEMENT

CARLTON HOTEL
CANNES

FACING THE SEA

PARIS—See also page 44

PAIGNTON (England)

PAIGNTON   SOUTH DEVON   EXMOUTH.

REDCLIFFE || MAER BAY

HOTEL   A.A.   R.A.C.   HOTEL

BOTH HOTELS HAVE DIRECT ACCESS TO THE SEA AND
STAND IN THEIR OWN EXTENSIVE GROUNDS. :: :: ::
HERE YOU WILL FIND EVERY MODERN AMENITY.
A GOOD CUISINE AND SERVICE.   ::   ::   ::   ::

Phone : PAIGNTON 82533.   **FULLY LICENSED.**   Phone : EXMOUTH 588.

PORTRUSH—See page 169

PURLEY (England)

NEAR CROYDON AERODROME

KNIGHTON HOTEL
PURLEY.

Half-hour London. Extensive Grounds. Garages. Saloon Car Kept.
Own produce.   Spacious Reception Rooms.   Billiards and Library.
Near Golf and Ice Rink.   Moderate inclusive Terms.

R.A.C.   *ILLUSTRATED TARIFF FREE.*
Telephone — Purley 4522 and 1730.

RESIDENT PROPRIETORS:—MR. & MRS. OLIVER L. BOYSE.

RAMSGATE—See page 164

ST. ANNES-ON-THE-SEA (England)

HOTEL
MAJESTIC
(Centre of Promenade.)

180 Bedrooms, Hot & Cold Water in each.
The rendezvous of the West Lancashire Coast.
Tennis, Swimming Pool, Golf, etc. Dancing and
Cabarets.   Jack Martin and his Majestic
Orchestra (Broadcast.) Telephone 620 (3 lines.)

Garage.   Week-End Terms.
Apply for Tariff to Manager.

SANDERSTEAD—See page 168 | SHREWSBURY—See page 5
SCARBOROUGH—See page 164 | SOUTHAMPTON—See page 164

TORQUAY (England)

PATRONISED
BY ROYALTY
GRAND HOTEL
TORQUAY'S
LEADING HOTEL.

FINEST POSITION ON THE SEA FRONT
200 ROOMS 70 WITH PRIVATE BATHS.

Hot and Cold Running Water and Radiators in every
Bedroom.   Luxuriously Equipped.   Perfect Cuisine.
New Squash Court.   Hard Tennis Court.   Ballroom.
FREE GOLF. (Stover Golf Links) 18 Holes. Direct Air Service from Croydon Daily.

PERMANENT ORCHESTRA & DANCE BAND.

Officially appointed by R.A.C. & A.A. (5 Star).   Garage for 100 Cars on
Premises, with excellent Chauffeur's accommodation.   Phone—2234.

ALSO —
HEADLAND HOTEL
(Unlicensed)
TORQUAY.
(Formerly SAVOY HOTEL).

A First Class Private Hotel.   Situated on the Famous
Livermead Cliff.   A sea view from every window.   Hot
and cold water and radiators in all bedrooms, palatial
appointments, finest cuisine.   Tennis.   Croquet.   Garage.
FREE GOLF. (Stover Golf Links) 18 Holes. Direct Air Service from Croydon Daily.

MODERATE TERMS.   **PHONE—2161.**

WENGEN (Switzerland)

AIRPORT—BELPMOOS BERN.

WENGEN—BERNESE OBERLAND. 4,500 feet above sea level.
Ideal Summer and Winter Sports Centre.

THE REGINA

THE MOST RECENT AND UP-TO-DATE HOTEL IN FINEST POSITION.

The real English Home abroad.   ::   ::   ::
All the Latest Comforts.   Orchestra.   Bar.   **NEAR THE WENGEN
SWIMMING POOL.** ::

Inclusive terms : Summer from Frs. 15.00. Winter from Frs. 17.00.

WEST WICKHAM—See page 168

WEYMOUTH—See page 5

HENRY BLACKLOCK & CO. LTD.

——(Proprietors of Bradshaw's Guides),——

**GENERAL PRINTERS, LITHOGRAPHERS,
AND ACCOUNT-BOOK MANUFACTURERS**

Bookwork, Invoices, Statements, Memo Forms, Letter
Headings, Note Headings, Bill Forms, Cheques, Show Cards,
Posters, Pamphlets, Brochures, and Time Tables for Air
Services specially designed and printed.   Estimates free.

BRADSHAW HOUSE, SURREY STREET, STRAND, LONDON, W.C.2.
Telephone—TEMPLE BAR, 2676.   — and —   Telegrams—BRADSHAW, LONDON.
ALBERT SQUARE, MANCHESTER.
Telephone—BLACKFRIARS 4218 (2 lines).   Telegrams—GUIDE, MANCHESTER.